RUSSELL'S INDEX

- Percentage of persons in the U.S. who have an impairment: 20

- Percentage of the population who will experience a disabling condition in the course of their lives: 80

- Number of Americans said to be disabled: 43 million in 1989, 49 million in 1995, 54 million in 1997

- Number of "voluntary" euthanasia deaths in Holland that are involuntary: an estimated 25,000 have been killed by their physicians when they did not request it

- Percentage of U.S. insurance applicants genetically screened for "defects" who were denied health insurance: 47.

- Percentage of the national poverty guideline represented by the federal SSI benefit: 74 for an individual, 82 for a couple

- Number of days SSA takes to process a disability claim: 348

- Percentage of first time applicants turned down by SSA: 69

- Percentage of those who appeal that win their benefits: 62

- "Waiting period," in years, that an American deemed disabled by SSA must endure before becoming eligible for Medicare: 2

- Amount of cash per year that flows through the nursing home industry: $70 billion

- Percentage of nursing homes certified by the Health Care Financing Administration that have repeatedly violated federal standards, including critical aspects of patient care standards: 40

- Percentage of California nursing homes cited for violations in 1993: 58

    Number of citations issued: 1,515

    Amount of fines levied for violating state and federal regulations: $3.8 million

    Number of deficiency notices issued: 32,720

Percentage of fines waived, reduced or dismissed: 44

- National average annual cost to house one aging and/or disabled American in a nursing home: $40,784

  Average cost to provide Medicaid Personal Assistant Services: $9,692

- Percentage of working-age disabled who were unemployed around the world in 1996: 65-70

  Percentage of working-age severely disabled not working: 73.9

- Percentage of working-age disabled persons who say they would like to have a job: 66

- Percentage of working-age disabled persons who say they have encountered job discrimination because of their disability: 25

- True or false? The Americans with Disabilities Act was followed up with affirmative action like other minorities' civil rights bills: False

- Average amount a severely disabled person makes per month: $1,562

  Average a non-severely disabled person makes: $2,006

  Average a nondisabled person makes: $2,446

- Number of disabled people purged from disability rolls in 1981 under President Ronald Reagan: 490,000

- Amount Social Security Administration received to remove people from the disability rolls in 1996: $320 million—pushing up the total budget to $720 million

- Number of disability reviews SSA expects to conduct over the next two years: 1.4 million; over the next five years: the remaining 5 million

- Percentage of children applying for SSI disability benefits who are turned down: 2 out of 3

- Number of disabled children estimated to be terminated from SSI due to welfare "reform": between 300,000 and 715,000

Beyond Ramps

Disability at the End of the Social Contract

Marta Russell

A Warning from an Uppity Crip

COMMON COURAGE PRESS   MONROE, MAINE

Library of Congress Cataloging-in-Publication Data

Russell, Marta.

Beyond Ramps: Disability at the End of the Social Contract/ Marta Russell

p.   cm.

Includes Index

1. Discrimination against the handicapped—United States. 2. Sociology of
disability—United States. 3. Handicapped—Civil rights—United States.
4. Social darwinism—United States. 5. United States—Social policy.

I.Title.

HV1553.R87 1997   97-16590
362.4'0973—dc21   CIP

1567511074 (cl.) -- #36739674 (lc)
LET

Common Courage Press
P.O. Box 702, Monroe, Maine 04951
email: comcour@agate.net
207-525-0900   fax: 207-525-3068

First Printing

ABOUT THE AUTHOR

Marta Russell has been a producer and photographer whose investigative reporting earned her a Golden Mike Award for best documentary from the Radio and Television News Association of Southern California in 1994.

Disabled from birth, Russell began writing when her disability progressed and she had to navigate the disability policy netherworld to survive. Russell has been published in the *Los Angeles Times*, the *San Diego Union Tribune*, *New Mobility Magazine*, *Ragged Edge*, *Mouth: the voice of disability rights*, *Mainstream Magazine* and *Z Magazine*, among others. "Disabled and the Cost of Saying I Do" was nominated for a MAGGIE in 1995. Her articles have been reprinted in two anthologies, *The Ragged Edge* and *The Disabled*. She has a seventeen-year-old daughter and lives in Los Angeles.

She can be reached at ap888@lafn.org.

CONTENTS

Part III
Ending the Social Contract

In Germany, they came first for the communists and I didn't speak up because I wasn't a communist.* Then they came for the Jews, and I didn't speak up because I wasn't a Jew. Then they came for the trade unionists, and I didn't speak up because I wasn't a trade unionist. Then they came for the Catholics and I didn't speak up because I was a Protestant. Then they came for me, and by that time no one was left to speak up.

—Martin Niemoeller

*As eloquent as Niemoeller is, to be historically correct he needed to include, "Then they came for the disabled, and I didn't speak up because I wasn't disabled." This book is dedicated to the hundreds of thousands of disabled people left out of history.

—Marta Russell

INTRODUCTION

Wisdom comes by disillusionment.

—George Santayana

In one of his better moments, Thomas Jefferson wrote, "The care of human life and happiness, and not destruction, is the first and only legitimate object of good government." That is the social contract a government has with its people...in a democracy, with *all* the people. Yet anti-government forces attacking "big bad government" would have us believe that government is unworkable when it *is* vital, as the Constitution calls for, to "promote the general welfare." Hypocritically, those same forces tolerate a "big" government that perpetuates an ostentatious military-industrial complex and a deep-pocket corporate welfare system of subsidies and tax loopholes, but would have us believe that social programs that support "the care of human life and happiness" are no longer "sustainable."

The social contract encompasses a wide arena. It includes hard-won popular entitlements serving the entire citizenry like Social Security, Medicare, and Medicaid, and it includes the promise of freedom from discrimination as directed by our civil rights laws. It includes democratic gains made at the voting booth and the right for labor to bargain with capital. But the social contract, which has never been fully fleshed out (for example, we lack universal health care in America), has only somewhat curbed the power of capital.

The immediate environs in which I find myself writing this book is one of extreme corporate domination, where "the people" are conformed into corporate identities: consumers, clients, target populations, or potential consumers. Any significant difference between Republicans and Democrats is certainly elusive. Former President Bush's New World Order is revealed to be a McNew-World-Order while President Clinton proudly eats Big Macs in public—a walking advertisement for it.

The spoken word rarely means what it says, so we live in a world in need of constant decoding. Deciphering "kindler, gentler nation," one finds that in practice "kinder, gentler" means leaner, meaner "tough love," where Social Security offices in the Midwest beef up security forces in anticipation of hostile reaction to welfare cuts, and lethal weapons are unabashedly our number one profit-making export. "Devolution" translates into undoing our national standards on welfare and health care; welfare "reform" means undoing entitlements; "balancing the budget" means redistributing wealth upwards, more corporate welfare, and tax cuts for the rich; "downsizing" means massive firings, increased job insecurity, and record corporate profits; and HMO "managed care" means managed-for-profit, lucky-if-you-survive-it care.

Not even the planet is free of the ill effects of current trends. No-vision short-term business profiteers are stripping the earth of its finite resources. The idea that we can have infinite growth on this finite planet is preposterous, yet corporate plunder is still viewed as the right to live the American dream; no one is immune from the consequences.

Most people are in deep economic pain in this country regardless of what the business pages and Washington politicians say. That is the nonpolitical truth. At the heart of the ills of our times is an economic oppression that is not only pervasive, but planned. The austerity forces, intent on undoing the social contract, are globalized; people are experiencing similar pain all over the world. The power of global capital via the corporate state is busily rolling back the rights of workers, and the right of citizens to access the benefits of common government, and in the process threatens democracy itself. Many more than those who recognize the faceless enemy are affected.

Americans seem to have lost sight of the fact that policies are social decisions and that these decisions can result in the de-valuation and even loss of human life. I am often asked why I write so much about disability. Other topics are far more "sellable"(that is certainly true). But the past years have made it insidiously apparent that the plight of disabled people, like canaries released into the coal mines to detect whether there was enough oxygen in the air to survive, is a barometer for the "progress" or lack of it in our over-capitalized civilization. Disability and disability policy—past, present and future—is a tool for all to rate our present socio/economic order.

Part One, The Nature of Oppression, explores how concepts of "normalcy" can be used for social control, to demean and de-value. It covers the extermination of "lives not worth living" in Nazi Germany, underscoring the connection between capitalism and social Darwinism. In our brave-new-world genetic future that maps "defects" and marks those carrying "bad" genes, asks Chapter 4, who won't be tainted as "disabled"? Who is "safe" from discrimination... or worse?

Part Two, The Mechanics of Oppression, details how social policies, which are social decisions, underlie economic oppression. It exposes the vested interests that have shaped social policy and the resulting institutional bias. Since work, the ability to do it or not, is central to the capitalist/labor paradigm, this section questions the wisdom of using work as the measure of human worth. It analyzes the Americans with Disabilities Act (ADA) in the age of public relations politics: what the movement hoped the ADA to do, what it may or may not be able to achieve in an era of corporate downsizing, shrinking wages, and growing inequalities. In a broad context, this section poses whether civil rights, alone, can create the economic equality we seek.

Part Three, Ending the Social Contract, outlines the immediate threat where whole categories of people are being severed from entitlements. It explores the relationship between deficit reduction and paring disabled people from the rolls ($720 million to Social Security designated for such purposes). Chapter 12—the tie-it-all-together chapter—explains what Mother Teresa and corporate America have in common. It unmasks the GOP "revolutionaries' " real intent behind the "efficiency" rhetoric, by detailing the dangers of devolving federal public programs to the states, busts the myth that charity is a realistic substitute for entitlements, and proposes that military and corporate welfare be cut instead of social services.

The last two chapters ask, what does excessive "free market" ideology bring into our lives? What are the consequences when corporations control government policies—not the people—and the economy is raised to highest esteem?

The danger is that all may fall victim to the austerity forces if we do not recognize their existence and take direct action to stop them, as people in France, Canada, Spain, Italy, and Belgium have organized in protest over attempts to roll back the social contract in their countries. Collective action is vital to obtaining individual security. I outline some guides for social reorganization, but as we all know, any road map for change must be backed up by solid support from people with whom we share the democracy. The greatest challenge is organizing beyond our separate identities to achieve worthy universal goals like full employment, universal health care, and livable incomes.

During the French resistance to Hitler, Camus recognized the importance of becoming neither victim nor executioner, and this is unequivocally the challenge of our times, witnessed by genocide in Bosnia, the Middle East, East Timor, to name a few—that we all may survive without becoming oppressors or killers, that we may find the solutions that will arrest the callous and inequitable current path. We the people, including people with disabilities, must change the economic paradigms which greatly benefit the few, marginally benefit some, but leave others to some twisted, capitalist, social Darwinist end.

PART I

THE NATURE
OF OUR OPPRESSION

Most of the greatest evils that man has inflicted upon man have come through people feeling quite certain about something which, in fact, was false.

—Bertrand Russell

CHAPTER 1

WHY BE "NORMAL"?

"NORMALCY" AS A MECHANISM FOR SOCIAL CONTROL

Too many of us don't go near others who aren't like us.
— Colman McCarthy on C-SPAN

The framers of the U.S. Constitution began the Preamble with the simple words, "We the People." What they really meant was, "We the normal, the homogeneous white propertied males." What was "normal" in 1788 was defined by class, race, and gender. The framers omitted women, males without property (the poor), and people of color from access to the "equality" they professed to hold sacred.

Decades later citizen movements successfully challenged the limitations on just who "the People" were. "All men are created equal" was taken literally by abolitionists, suffragists, populists, socialists, the unions, and, later, disabled people. Importantly, these social movements challenged what was politically "normal," and in so doing broadened the democratic power base, extended the vote, and enlarged the group of Americans who participate in common government. Popular unrest shaped a social contract which provides a measure of collective security from birth through old age: Social Security, Medicare, Medicaid, disability benefits, and a minimum wage are the most well-known results of those struggles. Today that contract is threatened by forces which would have entitlements cut back, wages and benefits leveled to the lowest common global denominator.

We the people are the ultimate defenders and interpreters of the Constitution. It is a labor of love, of hope, and of self-interest that requires a clear understanding of the subtleties and history of oppression and a recognition that the exclusion of one will lead to the exclusion of more. Implicit in the word "normal" is a threat to each of us, individually and collectively.

THE NAME GAME

FREAK...all boogered up, gimp, goon, spastic, spaz, cripple, creep, cretin, handicapper, handi-capable, handicapped, monster, mongoloid, invalid, idiot, retard, defective, deaf, dumb, mute, devil, blind, blind as a bat, people with differing abilities, physically challenged, differently abled, disabled.

Obviously these labels are not value-free, rather they mark physical or sensory differences and are charged with meaning. Some say labels aren't so important. Wrong! In our hierarchical society it is the social meaning of words that have power. Why do we choose "disabled?" It has negative connotations; the dictionary definition is "unfit" or "useless." But being disabled/impaired is not a negative, not something to be ashamed of, rather it is a shared identity amongst those who have the common experience of being disabled in a world dominated by nondisabled people.

"Physically challenged" sounds so politically correct, but it is loaded with the faulty notion that it is the individual who is challenged to "overcome" his or her disability, rather than society's responsibility to overcome its prejudice against disabled individuals. If a "physically challenged" wheelchair user cannot access the grocery due to a barrier of steps, is it her fault for not "overcoming" the steps by popping supercrip wheelies, or is it society's responsibility to put in a ramp?

Discrimination is absent in the "challenged" scenario; no wonder it has caught on like wildfire! Disabled people—at least those I listen to—have determined that we prefer "disabled," plain and simple—because it underlines the social oppression. Forget the euphemisms!

The social tendency is to negatively link impairment with "uselessness" and to view disability as a personal tragedy, a matter for medicine to "correct."

Disability historian Paul Longmore wisely concludes that the medical model is most harmful because it presents disabled people with "an impossible dilemma":

> ...being made over after the model of nondisabled people is exactly by definition what people with disabilities can never do, can never achieve... [1]

The dominant Caucasian race has cast women as inferior, has relegated people of color to second- and third-class citizenship, and has also "ism-ed" disabled people. Oppressive views of women and of people of color are termed sex-ism and rac-ism; oppression of disabled people is called *able-ism or physical-ism*.

Physicalism is rating an individual's social value solely on his or her muscular, sensory, and/or mental prowess. When people do not run and jump, are blind or deaf, and do not exhibit able-bodied standards of physical or mental competence, nondisabled and some disabled people themselves perceive this as a "less than" situation. These differences are interpreted as negatives, as "not normal" and therefore, not desirable. These attitudes are so pervasive most people don't notice them. For instance, the saying "you must be blind not to see that..." is a raw example of how blindness is equated with being dense, yet how many would realize that they insult blind people when they allude to blindness in this manner?

Amplifying these phenomena is what is called "the spread effect of prejudice." If one "deviates" from the norm by having a disability, then one can also expect that people will make assumptions about one's overall capacities. For example, I gave a talk called "Disability, Civil Rights, and Dignity" at a high school where afterwards a young woman (who was blind) and a friend approached me, very excited to make contact with a disabled adult. The young woman happened to be friends with the daughter of world-renowned physicist Stephen Hawking. She relayed an instance when she, Hawking, and Hawking's daughter went to a restaurant together. The waitress took the girls' orders and then turned to the able-bodied child and asked, "What does he want?" referring to Hawking without looking at him. Quick to see the slight, the young woman exclaimed to me, "Can you imagine the smartest man in the world not knowing what he wanted to eat?" Often, if one has a disability, as in Hawking's case, uses a wheelchair, and is not able to walk, one is perceived to be emotionally immature and mentally incapable as well. Hawking, the adult, was perceived incompetent to order his own lunch, so the child was asked to do it for him.

The physicalist mindset establishes a hierarchical way of thinking about people's worth that is challenged by disability rights activists.

Dangerously, when people interpret impairment as solely a matter for medicine to "cure," the social discrimination we experience is put aside as though it has no validity. All money and effort is then directed to cure rather than on *removing barriers which make it possible to participate in the dominant culture with an impairment.* Activist Liz Crow accurately points out that:

> Dominant perceptions of impairment as a personal tragedy are regularly used to undermine the work of the disabled people's movement and they rarely coincide with disabled people's understandings of their circumstances.[2]

Disabled people have begun the work to *put the disability first*, to say that disability is exactly what we need to accept about ourselves and what nondisabled people need to accept about us. We are the "unexpected" minority having undeniable similar socio/political experiences that make disability our primary identity. The fact that we often *do* require accommodation because of our disabilities must be at the very heart of that identity and of our resistance. Only then can we achieve liberation and equality.

OVERRATED "NORMALS"

The issue is not what causes disability but the reaction to it.

Disability is often treated as though it were a deviation from the rule. In fact, it is not an anomaly. One out of five persons in the U.S. has an impairment, yet disability is perceived as an "oddity" rather than as a natural occurrence. The concept of "normal" gained much scientific credibility around the turn of the century as the anthropological and genetic sciences developed in Europe and the U.S. These sciences were not economically value-free (science has always been controlled by those who pay the bills; for instance, the corporate development of expensive toxic chemicals like DDT has polluted our farmlands and water in the name of scientific "progress"), nor were they independent of political currents, as in the development of the nuclear bomb. As these sciences developed they gave power to emerging eugenic and racial hygienic ideologies, which were to have particularly severe political consequences for their "inferior" targets: disabled people, the deaf, nonwhites, Jews, Gypsies, gays, and others.

Dr. Carol Gill, a psychologist who has written much about disability pride, has coined the term "ablecentric thinking." She writes:

> It really rocks people when we so clearly reject the superiority of nondisability. We're attacking the old yardstick of human validity— the reassuring bottom line: At least I have my health (independence; all fingers and toes; ability to walk; vision; mind).[3]

The disability liberation movement has a bumper sticker that confronts physicalism by asking, "Why Be Normal?" That's like asking "Why Be White?" "Why Be Male?" or "Why Be Straight?"

If "normal" has been created as a construct, then there must be a benefit. As Alex Cockburn noted in a talk at the Midnight Special bookstore in Santa Monica, "What is normal and abnormal is imposed on us at all levels. We must resist this. We must be on the alert as to how we are made objects to be disposed of." We must also ask, who does "normal" serve?

Cockburn's warning rings literally true for our minority, because disabled people have in great numbers been "disposed of" via lethal injections, gas chambers, and starvation, as will be covered in the next chapter. Cockburn too would rate as "abnormal" because of his politics; "normal" demands political conformity as well as physical conformity, and as such can be used as a tool for social control.

The danger of the "normal" construct is that it serves to make disabled people seem *less than human*. When disabled people are not seen as fully human, it is easy to justify continuing inhumane policy towards us, to cut us out of the social contract, even to eliminate us at political will. We become too easily disposable.

CHAPTER 2

NAZI AND AMERICAN EUGENICS, EUTHANASIA AND ECONOMICS

Wisdom comes by disillusionment.

—George Santayana

Most people, excluding the neo-Nazis, accept that there was a holocaust in Germany, but how many know that disabled people were the first to be systematically exterminated by physicians?

Disabled people know that quality-of-life judgments made about us by nondisabled people can prove not only inaccurate but deadly. To combat oppression, we must understand its historical roots, particularly the institutional support that makes it possible.

"LIVES NOT WORTH LIVING" AND "USELESS EATERS"

The phrase "lives not worth living" came from the title of a book published in 1920, *Release and Destruction of Lives Not Worth Living*, by two German social Darwinists Alfred Hoche, a professor of medicine, and Rudolf Binding, a professor of law. The book defended the right to suicide, and called for the killing of not only incurably sick people but also the mentally ill, the feeble-minded, the retarded, and deformed children. Arguing that such people led "ballast lives" and were only "empty human husks," these professors medicalized the concept of killing disabled people by making it seem therapeutic; they upheld that it would be "healing work" and humane to destroy such lives which, in their view, were "not worthy of life."[1] These were not uniquely German ideas; support for eugenics also existed in the United States and in England, where euthanasia was viewed as a way to "economize" into a more "efficient" society.

Not long after the publication of this book, hundreds of thousands of disabled people were systematically killed in German gas chambers set up in the very institutions where people went for treatment. How can a society be maneuvered into a regimen of murder? The answer is found in the ideas that led to a "science" of eugenics, the economics that made the practice attractive, and the history of the agents applying euthanasia.

THE ROOTS: RACISM, PHYSICALISM, AND CLASSISM

With the publication of *Origin of the Species*, Charles Darwin introduced his theory that man evolved by way of a gradual adaptation of varied life forms to the environment by the process of "natural selection, or the preservation of *favoured races* in the struggle for life" (italics mine). "Favoured races" translated meant his race, the Caucasians.

The English philosopher Herbert Spencer substituted the phrase "survival of the fittest" for "natural selection" and is credited with the development of social Darwinism, the application of Darwin's ideas to sociology.[2]

In 1871, with *The Descent of Man*, Darwin clarified his thoughts on artificial selection:

> We civilized men, on the other hand, do our utmost to check the process of elimination; we build asylums for the imbecile, the maimed, and the sick; we institute poor-laws; and our medical men exert their utmost to save the life of everyone to the last moment...Thus the weak members of society propagate their kind. No one who has attended to the breeding of domestic animals will doubt that this must be highly injurious to the race of man.[3]

If this undesired situation were to be "corrected," then selective breeding of humans would follow as the next logical step, to rid civilization of disabled, sick, and poor people and to limit the propagation of unfavoured races.

In 1883 a cousin of Darwin's, biologist/geneticist Francis Galton, coined the term "eugenics," furthering the march towards selective breeding. Drawn from Darwin's ideas, eugenics upheld that biological groups could be strengthened (cleansed) by eliminating the "unfit" through genetic and hereditary screening. Sickness, indigence, dependence, immorality, and race were factors in the determination of fitness.[4] Darwin himself suggested that people ought to refrain from marriage if they "are in any marked degree inferior in body and mind."[5] Galton's solution was widely accepted in scientific circles all over the world.

Spencer, a staunch supporter of the eugenics movement, became a guru in the U.S. on the subject, presenting seminars and lectures on the benefits of eliminating the "unfit," largely those in need of public services.

The pre-Nazi "scientific" theory of Racial Hygiene (originally coined in 1903), in keeping with the work of Darwin, Spencer, and Galton, held that the German race could and must be kept pure and not allowed to "degenerate." Social Darwinists such as Alfred Ploetz feared that the misfits and the poor were multiplying at a faster rate than the fit (bourgeoisie) and that elimination was necessary to preserve the German plasm. They professed that those "weak" who were surviving with the assistance of medicine were interfering with the natural selection process and should die in order to keep the German gene strain strong. Racism, physicalism, and classism formed a cultural triad that permitted eugenic theory to turn into a full-blown societal frenzy of murder.

THE NAZI/AMERICAN PHYSICIAN CONNECTION

The Nazi Party relied on scientists and physicians to give eugenics and racial hygiene scientific credibility and to win the support of the German people.

In 1933 the Nazi government passed the Law for the Prevention of Genetically Diseased Offspring, or the Sterilization Law, as it came to be known. It designated people for sterilization who "suffered" from "genetic illness," including feeble-mindedness, schizophrenia, manic-depressive insanity, genetic epilepsy, Huntington's chorea, genetic blindness or deafness, or severe alcoholism. Physicians became the genetic police, with genetic courts to back up their findings.

> An influential manual of Rudolf Ramm of the medical faculty of the University of Berlin proposed that each doctor was to be no longer merely a caretaker of the sick but was to become a "cultivator of the genes," a "physician to the Volk," and a "biological soldier"...To carry

out these programs properly, the individual physician must become a "genetics doctor" (Erbarzt). He could then become a "caretaker of the race" and a "politician of population."[8]

The eugenic purge was widespread. Targeted for sterilization were 200,000 congenitally feebleminded (mentally retarded); 80,000 schizophrenics; 20,000 manic-depressives; 60,000 epileptics; 600 people with Huntington's chorea; 4,000 blind; 16,000 deaf; 20,000 gravely bodily deformed; and 10,000 alcoholics. Reich Interior minister Wilhelm Frick, forming the Expert Committee on Questions of Population and Racial Policy, estimated the number of genetic "defectives" in Germany to be 500,000, noting that "some experts consider the true figure to be as high as 20 percent of the German population."[9]

Sterilization practices eventually expanded to encompass race, especially to control what became known as the "black scourge" and were widely and cruelly practiced on Jewish people in the death camps.

In the U.S., eugenics policy focused on the incarcerated population, developing into an entire "science" of criminal anthropology. Physical characteristics were linked to criminal behavior and disabled people were said to be predisposed to commit crimes. A 1911 textbook on treating disabled people stated, "A failure in the moral training of a cripple means the evolution of an individual detestable in character, a menace and burden to the community, who is only too apt to graduate into the mendicant and criminal classes." American physicians were performing vasectomies on the penal population as early as the turn of the century. By 1920, sterilization was compulsory for criminals considered genetically inferior in twenty-five states. And by 1950, according to the Human Betterment Foundation, 50,707 Americans had been sterilized, many against their will.[10]

Eugenic propaganda institutions existed in England and the U.S. such as the one at Cold Spring Harbor in New York led by Charles B. Davenport and funded by the Carnegie Institution and Mary Harriman. The Rockefeller Foundation funded the Kaiser Wilhelm Insititute for Anthropology, Eugenics and Human Heredity, which was headed by Ernst Rudin, who also headed the Racial Hygiene Society under the Nazis. Fritz Lenz, the physician-geneticist and propagator of racial hygiene theory in Germany, complained that the Germans were being held back, in comparison to their U.S. counterparts, by the socialist Weimar Constitution (which prohibited alterations of a person's body).[11]

German sterilization did not stop until the end of the war. Even so, the physicians performing sterilization were immune from prosecution because "allied authorities were unable to classify the sterilizations as war crimes, because similar laws had only recently been upheld in the United States."[12]

Due to mounting evidence that not enough was known about heredity to draw the conclusion that sterilization did in fact eliminate the "defectives" from the gene pool, eugenic practices were eventually quelled. In the U.S. and England, continual legal pressure was applied to halt sterilization, under the banner of individual rights (interestingly now an argument for physician-assisted suicide). "Rational" science proved not to be immune from physicalist and racist tendencies that resulted in the unnecessary destruction of the reproductive rights of thousands of innocent people.

USELESS EATERS AND ECONOMICS

What happened to disabled people in Germany must be understood in the context of the broader socio/economic issues. German philosopher Friedrich Nietzsche had proclaimed that "the sick person is a parasite of society."[13] The phrase "useless eaters" became popular descriptive speech during the deep recession after World War I. Such ideas served to turn the German people into supporters of the euthanasia program, by branding disabled people as deplorable consumers of state funds at a time when the German people were experiencing economic hardships. It became openly shameful to be disabled. No longer just an "aberration" of nature, the "disabled parasite" was a social cost not to be tolerated.

But the social funds "saved" by eliminating the useless eaters were to be devoted to beefing up the Reich's military for an attempt at Aryan world domination. Since "defectives" were unproductive to the war effort (not soldier material), even seen as taking away from it by consuming social funds, we became highly disposable.

In 1930s Germany, biomedical scientists combined eugenics with social Darwinism to produce a biological ideology that not only called for man-made selection but began the mechanisms to *socially engineer* it. The German state took these actions:

In 1933, the first year of Nazi government, expenditures for the handicapped and invalid were drastically cut. In 1933 German medical insurance companies paid 41.5 million RM for invalids—10 million less than in 1932, in the depths of the recession. . . . For the Nazi medical philosopher, support for the mentally ill was simply not worth the cost.[14]

Reich propagandists took every opportunity to inculcate resentment toward "defective" Germans. Schoolchildren were a primary propaganda target. Adolf Dorner's 1935-36 high school mathematics textbook included the following problems:

Problem 94

In one region of the German Reich there are 4,400 mentally ill in state institutions, 4,500 receiving state support, 1,600 in local hospitals, 200 in homes for the epileptic, and 1,500 in welfare homes. The state pays a minimum of 10 million RM/year for these institutions.

I. What is the average cost to the state per inhabitant per year?

II. Using the result calculated from I, how much does it cost the state if:

    A. 868 patients stay longer than 10 years?

    B. 260 patients stay longer than 20 years?

    C. 112 patients stay longer than 25 years?

Problem 95

The construction of an insane asylum requires 6 million RM. How many housing units @ 15,000RM could be built for the amount spent on insane asylums?[15]

So it is not surprising that 1939 was designated by Hitler as the year of "the duty to be healthy." The state shifted the public focus away from social welfare onto the "culprits" using all the public resources. Those who could not be "cured" must be killed.

THE NEEDLE BELONGS IN THE HANDS OF THE DOCTOR

Physicians were the among the most numerous and strongest supporters of state-sanctioned killing. When Hitler ascended to power he congealed Racial Hygiene into a political biology which became the mold for Nazi social policy. Large numbers of German physicians joined the Nazi Party. Robert Proctor, author of *Racial Hygiene: Medicine Under the Nazis* writes:

> In 1937 doctors were represented in the SS seven times more often than was the average for the employed male population. Membership records for the Nazi Physicians' League indicate that nearly 40,000 physicians joined the league in 1942; Georg Lilienthal has discovered archival evidence that by the beginning of 1943, some 46,000 physicians had joined. If 90,000 physicians were active from 1931 to 1945, then roughly half of all physicians joined the Nazi Party.[16]

The German physicians were charged with the duty to determine who was worth health care costs and who was not. They became the gatekeepers marshaling the "health" of the state. There were four categories for extermination:

> 1. Patients suffering from specified diseases who are not employable or schizophrenia, epilepsy, senile diseases, therapy-resistant paralysis and other syphilitic sequelae, feeblemindedness from any cause, encephalitis, Huntington's chorea and other neurological conditions of a terminal nature.
> 2. Patients who have been continually institutionalized for at least five years.
> 3. Patients who are in custody as criminally insane.
> 4. Patients who are not German citizens, or are not of German or kindred blood, giving race and nationality.[17]

Disability was the primary qualifier for death in the eyes of the physician and the state. It is most important to understand that disability persecution was all-encompassing. If one was of pure Aryan blood and disabled, one was slated for extermination for contaminating the race. If one had a job but was disabled, one could still be determined as genetically "unfit" based on the disability and murdered. And euthanasia was not limited to "sick" people, it was imposed upon mentally retarded people even though they were "healthy." Without question, *all* disabled people were considered to be not worthy of life and all were given the unsubstantiated diagnosis of "terminal" illness with one exception: Nazi Germany did not euthanize its disabled veterans.

Disabled children became the first victims of the euthanasia program. Baby Knauer was the first official victim. Born blind, without part of one arm and a leg, Baby Knauer, according to Dr. Karl Brandt, a leading physician in the euthanasia program, "*seemed* to be an idiot" (italics mine). Her father, a full-blooded German, asked Hitler to grant a "mercy" death. Hitler granted the request for death; from this point on physicians were guaranteed immunity from prosecution for infanticide by proclamation. The results were monstrous.

Soon thereafter, the Committee for the Scientific Treatment of Severe Genetically Determined Illness required that all children born with congenital deformities be registered with the health authorities. These included "idiocy or Mongolism (especially if associated with blindness of deafness); microcephaly or hydrocephaly of a severe or progressive nature; deformities of any kind, especially missing limbs, malformation of the head, or spina bifida; or crippling deformities such as spastics[Littleschen Erkrankung]."[18] The list was expanded to include epilepsy, paralysis, and any disfigurement of the body.

Officials estimated that by 1945 some five thousand children of all ages had been systematically killed by their physicians. The physicians' choice of methods included lethal injection, starvation, withholding of treatment, exposure to the elements, and the use of cyanide gas or other chemical warfare weapons. Some twenty-eight institutions were fitted with extermination facilities, "including some of Germany's oldest and most highly respected hospitals (Eglfing-Haar; Brandenburg-Gorden; Hamburg Rotherburg and Uchtspringe; Meseria-Obrawalde, among others)."[19]

The adult phase began in 1939, with a plan to exterminate all of Germany's mental patients. The operation was given the code name T-4, shortened from Tiergartenstrasse 4, the address of the nonprofit Patient Transport Corporation which rounded up the economically unfeasible culprits slated for disposal and took them to the nursing homes, mental institutions, and hospitals which housed the killing chambers. In fact, the prototype for the gas chambers that exterminated the Jews in Poland was created in a hospital in Brandenburg to kill the disabled. It was a shower-like room with benches around the walls, equipped with small holes from which the carbon monoxide gas would be piped into the chamber:

> The first gassing was administered personally by Dr. Widmann. He operated the controls and regulated the flow of gas. He also instructed the hospital physicians Dr. Eberl and Dr. Baumhardt, who later took over the exterminations in Grafeneck and Hadamar...At this first gassing, approximately 18-20 people were led into the "showers" by the nursing staff. These people were required to undress in another room until they were completely naked. The doors were closed behind them. They entered the room quietly and showed no signs of anxiety. Dr. Widmann operated the gassing apparatus; I could observe through the peephole that, after a minute, the people either fell down or lay on the benches. There was no great disturbance or commotion. After another five minutes, the room was cleared of gas. SS men specially designated for this purpose placed the dead on stretchers and brought them to the ovens...At the end of the experiment Viktor Brack, who was of course also present(and whom I'd previously forgotten), addressed those in attendance. He appeared satisfied by the results of the experiment, and repeated once again that this operation should be carried out only by physicians, according to the motto: "The needle belongs in the hand of the doctor." Karl Brandt spoke after Brack, and stressed again that gassings should only be done by physicians. That is how things began in Brandenburg.[20]

The word got out that killing was taking place, so disabled people often had to be dragged onto the T-4 buses forcefully. Those who resisted were beaten into submission. Entire wards of epileptics were killed and the families told that they died of flu, inflammation of the lungs, or apoplexy. Some living in institutions knew beforehand that they were scheduled for disposal and would write their parents that their death was imminent. Elderly people feared they were next and refused to go into institutions for the aged.[21]

It is estimated that 275,000 (one estimate puts it at over one million) disabled people were exterminated before the church, which had the power to stop it all along, belatedly brought an end to the official euthanasia program in 1942. A small group of pastors and some incensed citizens motivated Bishop Von Galen of the

Roman Catholic Church to stand up to Hitler and these physicians in a sermon, in which he said:

> Broadly speaking, there is near certainty that none of the unexpected deaths of these mental cases have been due to natural causes, but were artificially induced, in accordance with the "unworthy lives" and, consequently, the killing of innocent people, if their existence is no longer held to be productive for the nation or for the state. It is a frightful concept that seeks to justify the murder of innocents and allows the killing of invalids incapable of work or the infirm, or incurable, and of old men and women afflicted by senility. Confronted with this doctrine the German bishops declare: No man has the right to kill an innocent person, no matter what the reason, except in case of war or in legitimate self-defense.[22]

Hitler called off the T-4 euthanasia program in August 1941. He recognized that killing the Bishop would be political suicide and he was deeply involved in the Russian front fighting, which was not going well. The gas chambers were dismantled and moved to Poland, where extermination was horrifically escalated.

But the official end to the euthanasia program did not stop the killing of disabled people. Physicians were encouraged to continue with methods of killing that were less noticeable and that fit better into normal hospital routine. They switched from "active" to "passive" killing of disabled children by simply withholding treatment or food. The children died slowly and in agonizing pain. The killing of "defective" adults continued, too, but it was contrived in a less visible manner, performed quietly by doctors who gave their "patients" lethal injections or doses of medication, withheld treatment, or starved them within their own tightly controlled institutions.

OFF THE HOOK AT NUREMBERG

At the Nuremberg trial Dr. Brandt defended his actions, saying that euthanasia was "out of pity for the victim and out of a desire to free the family and loved ones from a lifetime of needless sacrifice." He emphasized that Hitler's proclamation was not an "order to kill" children but gave physicians the right to do so if the patient was "incurably sick."[23]

Baby Knauer was not "incurably sick." She had multiple disabilities; with prosthetic devices and training in braille, her ability to function in the world would only have been limited by what the world would allow. Disabled people who were employed and thus no "burden" to their families were also indiscriminately slaughtered.

The Nuremberg court avoided the euthanasia of the disabled by shifting the debate. The court said, "The evidence is conclusive that almost at the outset of the program *non-German nationals* were selected for euthanasia and extermination . . . We find that Karl Brandt was responsible for, aided and abetted, took a consenting part in, and was connected with plans and enterprises . . . in the course of which murders, brutalities, cruelties, tortures and other inhumane acts were committed [against non-German nationals]. To the extent that these criminal acts did not constitute war crimes they constituted crimes against humanity"[24] (italics mine).

The original victims of Nazi cleansing were not non-German individuals but the German disabled. Some interpret the killings of disabled people as the beginning of the Jewish holocaust, but the murders of thousands of disabled people represented a holocaust of its own. The logic for killing disabled people was distinct from the rationale for killing other identity groups.

The Nuremberg court did not view disabled people as equal citizens against whom it would be illegal to commit a crime. The treatment of disabled people by the court was discriminatory; no reparations were ever made to the families of those killed, no one was punished for their murders.

Social Darwinism marked the beginning of the need for the disabled to justify our very existence. If medicine could be viewed as an inhibitor to biological cleansing, even seen as reversing some "natural selection" process where the disabled and sick should die, then who would be safe? Disabled people's struggle for survival took on a new dimension. It was not Darwin's "natural" world that we would be pitted against; it was man's "civilized" world of dominant physicalist notions and the growing culture of wealth accumulation that would become our biggest adversary.

CHAPTER 3

BACKHANDED SOCIAL DARWINISM

THE "RIGHT TO DIE" AND DISABILITY

Those who forget the past are condemned to repeat it.

—George Santayana

Shoppers looking for "peace of mind in a changing world" at the Preparedness Expo '96 in Denver, a trade show designed to prepare Americans for economic instability, natural disasters, political unrest, and nuclear war, could buy a t-shirt that said, "Some People Are Alive Simply Because It's Illegal to Kill Them."[1] As former Aryan Nation member Floyd Cockran discovered, the unwanted "some people" would include his disabled son, because euthanasia for handicapped people is strongly supported by the White Supremacist movement. Ingo Hasselbach, another defector from the Nazi movement, tells the story of his skinhead friend Frank Lutz beating up a "deaf-mute" because, Lutz said, in keeping with the Third Reich, handicapped people "cost money only to exist." In 1992 German papers reported that a disabled man committed suicide after ongoing harassment from youths who taunted him with remarks like "Under Hitler, people like you would have been gassed long ago." In a suicide note, the man said he would "destroy the cripple" that others thought should not live.[2]

Support for euthanasia is not limited to neo-Nazi extremists; it has moved to the middle of the road. In 1996 former Colorado governor Richard Lamm drew national attention when he proclaimed that terminally ill and disabled people had a "duty to die" and "get out of the way."[3] His sentiment, shared by many others, is that the state has no business prolonging or enhancing the lives of the elderly or disabled who in an efficient economy would naturally be dead. Hospital staff often take matters into their own hands. Jack Kevorkian, chief assisted suicide practitioner in the U.S., made the statement, "The voluntary self-elimination of individuals and mortally diseased or crippled lives can only *enhance* preservation of public health and welfare."[4] Two courts, the 9th Circuit Court (San Francisco) and the 2nd Circuit Court (New York), have challenged the current ban by ruling that individuals have a constitutional right to physician-assisted suicide; the 9th Court specifically named disabled people as "beneficiaries" of legalizing the practice and defended the practice of using assisted suicide to keep medical costs down.[5]

In order to reach clarity about "Death with Dignity," the social services system must be exposed for what it is: the by-product of "survival of the fittest" capitalism with a touch of government intervention—but not enough to remove the inequities or solve human need. Our "support" system tends to covertly accomplish what Herbert Spencer advocated overtly—to bring death to the economically "weak" by making public support systems so disastrous an experience that death appears preferable to life. Social prejudice and inadequate public policy that offers no alternative to institutionalization *can* make life so unbearable, impoverished, and devoid of quality that disabled people, after years of struggle, may feel they have no recourse but to ask for "peace of mind" in the form of the "right" to kill themselves. Society, by calling these requests to die courageous, rather than viewing them as the outcome of inhumane social policy, practices a cruel backhanded social Darwinism, disposing of the "unproductive" population without recognizing its own complicity in the "chosen" deaths.

LARRY MCAFEE AND THE SWITCH

Larry McAfee is your average guy, an engineer who became a quadriplegic in the state of Georgia in 1985. McAfee broke his neck when he lost control of his motorcycle and spun into a crash. It could happen to anyone who drives anything. McAfee's subsequent treatment by all the players in his story, the social services bureaucracy, the insurance company, the court, and the medical professionals, could also happen to anyone, anytime.

McAfee had insurance through his employer, so his post-accident rehabilitation and home care came from a lump sum insurance settlement which, at the time McAfee agreed to it, seemed plentiful. For a while McAfee contentedly lived in his home, intent on switching his career from engineering to computer consultancy which, he believed, would better accommodate his disability. But in eighteen months, unnecessary but physician-recommended "round the clock" medical supervision in the form of nursing care consumed all of his settlement. McAfee, like most newly disabled, didn't know about personal assistance services (PAS), nonmedical (and less costly) assistance to help with dressing, toiletry, bathing, and transferring. He soon ran out of cash.

When McAfee could no longer pay the nurses, he faced institutionalization in a nursing home because the state of Georgia did not have an adequate PAS program. Georgia's in-home program offered two attendant hours a day for a limited number of people and it did not allow control over those services, making independent living unfeasible for significantly disabled individuals.

In California, Ed Roberts, another ventilator-dependent quad, became director of the California Department of Rehabilitation under Governor Jerry Brown and headed up the World Institute on Disability in Oakland largely because, as a California resident, he had a PAS attendant for enough hours and could direct the hours of service. But in Georgia, McAfee faced imprisonment in an institution at the age of 32.

McAfee's descent into the contradictions and confines of disability policy had just begun. No Georgia nursing home would take him because he used a ventilator. Since Georgia Medicaid paid the same rate for ventilator users as it paid for patients who did not use one, quads like McAfee were "extra" work (and therefore not maximally profitable for the Georgia nursing home industry). In 1987 the state shipped him away from his family and friends to a "skilled" nursing home in Ohio, which would get compensated at a higher rate. McAfee spent two lonely years in Ohio; then in January 1989 the Ohio nursing home shipped him back to Atlanta, where he was placed in the intensive care unit at Grady Memorial Hospital with terminally ill patients.

McAfee "lived" for seven months at Grady Hospital before Medicare, which got the bills for McAfee's hospital stay, recognized that he did not need to be hospitalized and refused to pay the $175,300 bill, offering only $3,000 to $8,000 for his stay.[6] By failing to provide McAfee with PAS, which would cost $1,500 per month, the state ended up with a hospital bill *roughly $22,350 more per month than it would have cost to allow McAfee to live at home*.[7] McAfee could have lived happily in his own home with attendants for more than nine and a half years with the money spent on Grady Hospital for seven months. Two days before the bureaucracy was to ship him away from his family again to a nursing home in Alabama, McAfee petitioned the Georgia court for the "right" to die.

McAfee told Joseph Shapiro of *U.S. News & World Report* that he hated losing control of his body but that losing control of his life was worse.[8] McAfee had hoped to remain a valued participant in society, but found his way blocked at every turn by catch-22's. The lack of PAS in Georgia meant that McAfee had to be institutionalized; institutionalization meant that McAfee could not respond to want ads or take computer courses; no job retraining meant no chance for employment; and employment itself could mean that work disincentives built into disability policy would risk the very support he needed to survive. Wouldn't any motivated person become despondent over such overwhelming obstacles?

Eleanor Smith and other disability rights activists, outraged that society was willing to step in and help a disabled person die rather than provide the means to live, held demonstrations during the court hearings.[9] The attorney, the physician, and the judge all participated in moving the suicide agenda forward.

The attorney who pleaded his case said McAfee was "depressed" but did not insist (as he surely would have if a nondisabled client made a suicide request) that McAfee immediately receive crisis intervention therapy. Rather he directly filed the petition with the court, bypassing any depression therapy.[10] During the court proceedings, McAfee explained to the judge that the seven months spent in Grady hospital were a low point for him and said, "Every day when I wake up there is nothing to look forward to."[11] The judge did not hear McAfee's plea to bring quality into his life. Judge Johnson ruled that McAfee had no "emotional or psychological disabilities" and granted his request to disconnect his ventilator. No psychological evaluation or intervention was ordered. The court assumed that a quadraplegic life would not be worth living, and that death was a rational choice. The judge called him "heroic" and "courageous."[12]

Dr. Russ Fine, who had become a friend to Larry, assisted with the construction of a mechanism that would shut off Larry's oxygen supply with the flip of a switch. Didn't Dr. Fine's validation of suicide go against all practices of psychological intervention for a nondisabled depressed person?

McAfee's case offers an opportunity to contribute some clarity to the muddled thinking that so often accompanies these emotional right-to-die court decisions. The court's rationale for granting McAfee the right to die was that switching off the respirator would not be suicide, but rather would "allow the injury process to take its natural course."[13] The judge viewed the respirator as an *unnatural obstacle* placed between McAfee and death. Following this logic, a diabetic who stopped taking insulin wouldn't be committing suicide because the insulin "unnaturally" prevented death.

The court said that removing the unnatural obstacle, the oxygen, gave McAfee the right to refuse medical treatment. The precedent was established by the 1986 ACLU/Elizabeth Bouvia court case in southern California, which gave the patient, regardless of age, condition, or motive, the right to refuse treatment. Disability activists thought McAfee's situation went far beyond refusal of medical treatment. Dr. Paul Longmore, historian and professor at San Francisco State, wrote in the *Atlanta Constitution*:

> The non-handicapped people connected with this case call Mr. McAfee's ending of his life "a refusal of medical treatment." That is just playing with words to avoid the real issue. Giving him a sedative and setting up a timer to shut off his ventilator makes this a case of assisted suicide.[14]

Muddled and emotional thinking also clouded the definition of "terminal" illness. The plot of the docudrama "The Switch," which was based on McAfee's ordeal and focused on assisted suicide, offers an illustration of how disability and terminal illness become dangerously combined in right-to-die rhetoric. In "The Switch," the Fine character explains that his father, also a doctor, had a terminally ill cancer patient who was in a lot of pain. The elder doctor, wanting to ease his patient's suffering, found himself in a moral life/death quandary. The younger Dr. Fine character emotionally justifies constructing the switch to McAfee's ventilator as a situation analagous to his father's dilemma. But quadriplegia is not a terminal illness (nor are cerebral palsy, spina bifida, etc).[15] The McAfees of the world, unlike dying cancer patients, have a lifetime ahead of them.

Activists pointed out that "the state creates an unbearable quality of life and then steps in and says disabled people should be assisted to die because their quality of life is so poor."[16] None of the officials supported the attendant services that McAfee, the disabled citizen, requested. None seriously addressed the fact that PAS is a more cost-effective means of solving care needs, or the simple fact that disabled people prefer a self-determined lifestyle. Most importantly, none of the experts addressed the fact that McAfee had been robbed of his self-esteem, demeaned, intruded upon, and humiliated by Georgia's social services bureaucracy. Instead, they gave him the "right" to die.

In McAfee's story the physician ignored his Hippocratic oath, the state conveniently disposed of its mandate to preserve life in the face of death, and the court chose not to address the systemic problems within Georgia's social service delivery system that brought McAfee to its doorstep. It could happen to anyone at anytime.

As it turned out, McAfee did not flip the switch, and resides in a group home in Georgia, still short of living independently in his own home with an attendant. Others like Kenneth Bergstedt, a 31-year-old quadriplegic in Nevada who petitioned the state for the right to assisted suicide in fear that his aging father would die and leave him without care (Nevada did not provide attendant services), have killed themselves. In Michigan, David Rivlin clearly requested the right to die because the state was forcing him into an institution when what he wanted was to stay in his own apartment with an attendant. When the state would not budge, he ended his life. Said Ed Roberts, then director of the World Institute on Disability, about these two people's deaths, "The only difference between me and them is money."[17]

THE MONIED INTERESTS REAP PROFITS
WHILE THE CITIZEN SUFFERS

The McAfee case raises questions for all of society. Why would the government allow McAfee's insurance company to settle his claim for less than what it actually takes to get on with his life? Why is the insurance company allowed to shift its responsibility onto the state taxpayers? Why was the state so eager to assist this man to his death? What is the state's interest in supporting assisted suicide?

Some answers can be found by following the money trail. The private insurance company, by settling McAfee's case, ultimately shifted the cost onto the public and kept its profits. The Georgia Attorney General, the Georgia Medical Association, and the Roman Catholic Archdiocese of Atlanta all submitted briefs to the court in support of McAfee's right to die. The superior court, backed up by the Georgia Supreme Court, followed all the monied parties' interests. The medical community protected the status quo nursing homes' interests (what if grannies also decide that they would rather have attendants than be placed in nursing homes?) by not promoting the concept of independent living and in-home personal assistance. The state, which was obligated to pay McAfee's bills, endorsed cost-saving physician-assisted suicide and set the precedent for other disabled to follow in McAfee's steps. For the Catholic church to follow suit is hypocritical, professing to value an individual's life as it does.

Social Darwinists claim that capitalism is a part of God's design to "naturally" weed out the "unfit" at the bottom by leaving the unproductive in poverty to die. McAfee's story illustrates that it is not God but the monied interests who, by determining where our social resources go, hold power over the lives of the economically disadvantaged. Those complicit in this state of affairs—judges, policy-makers, bureaucrats, physicians, and even the people—only appear to have their hands washed clean when disabled people are the ones "choosing" to die.

BEHIND CLOSED DOORS: TRIMMING THE HERD

The danger of legalizing physician-assisted death is that the process of determining who makes the choice of death for whom is a much more slippery slope than the well-intentioned might envision. Brain death as a measure for pulling the plug has already been superseded; now family members request and expect to obtain the right to remove food and fluids from their disabled or sick relatives even though they may be *conscious, interactive, and in some cases, express a distinct desire to live.*

Dr. Carol Gill, psychologist and president of the Chicago Institute of Disability Research, documented the death of one young woman, Christine Busalacchi, whose father simply wanted his daughter to die after she became brain-injured in a car accident.[18]

Pete Busalacchi claimed, "My daughter is damn full gone," but according to Dr. Gill's research, hospital workers said Christine interacted with them, said "hi," giggled when they joked with her, made funny faces, watched soaps on TV, used simple communication switches to request food, and even mouthed the words to "Rudolph the Red-nosed Reindeer" at Christmas. Staff felt that with proper rehabilitation, Christine could regain more function. However, Christine's father could not accept his cognitively disabled daughter , and wanted to move her to a place where her food and water could be taken away.

Dr. Gill explains the grief dynamics involved:

When a child is born imperfect or when a family member acquires a significant disability, the family experiences a profound sense of loss. Shock, denial, anger, despair and all the other concomitants of mourning may occur. With proper emotional support, medical guidance, information, and the passage of time, most families seem to weather the loss. They deal with the fact that the disability won't go away. They learn to recognize the ways their loved one is still the same person she/he was before the disability while coming to terms with the ways she/he is different.

Occasionally, however, family members get stuck in grief, particularly some parents of children and adults who become disabled. Like Pete Busalacchi, they seem unable to let go of their picture of their loved ones as non-disabled so they can accept them following injury or illness. Initially, they hope and pray for recovery. But when all options for cure are exhausted and they are confronted with the irreversibility of a severe disability, they begin to accept the idea of death as a resolution. Death may seem more finite and manageable a loss than the never-ending pain of having a loved one altered by severe disability. . . . [The family member sees] the person as an imposter. They resent those who argue for the continued support of the imposter's life.

In such instances, says Dr. Gill, the family may project that the disabled person is the one suffering and use that to legitimize a decision to terminate his or her life. But Dr. Gill points out that it is often the family that is suffering, and it is the family in this frame of mind who is making the life or death decisions for their disabled relative.

Since Christine was only 17, her father had the power to make her medical decisions. One choice he made was to have a feeding tube inserted into her abdomen, although according to staff, Christine was taking food by mouth. The feeding tube is critical to Christine's outcome because it represented the legal "artificial nutrition" that would be used in court to uphold that Christine was on "extraordinary" life support. Since the 1986 Bouvia court decision gave the individual the right to determine her or his medical care and remove feeding tubes, Christine's father, now the arbiter of her care, could have the "artificial" nutrition removed and allow her to die *even though Christine could eat on her own.*

Despite hospital staff's testimony to Christine's abilities and their insistence that rehabilitation would further improve her condition, despite the existence of a video that showed Christine to be interactive and communicative (which her father wanted suppressed, threatening legal action against persons who circulated the tape), the Missouri Attorney General granted the father's wish. The medical professionals then moved Christine to a facility where they withheld all food and water and *starved her to death.*

Wesley Smith, a consumer advocate from Oakland, California, who follows right-to-die cases across the country, is worried that increasingly euthanasia decisions are being made silently, quickly, and routinely in institutions behind closed doors.

> All over the country, in hospitals, nursing homes and other facilities, conscious but cognitively disabled and aged people are being denied adequate care and/or are being starved and dehydrated to death in the name of patient autonomy, "quality of life" and "best interests of the patient" determinations. But what is really going on is the creation of a disposable caste of people whom we the healthy find too emotionally painful, too expensive or too inconvenient to care for, and whose intentional killing we increasingly find all too easy to rationalize.[19]

Even in cases where the adult patient expresses a distinct desire to live, the institutional momentum seems to be towards death, not life. Take Marjorie Nighbert, a woman who had an advanced directive to stop treatment if she became incapacitated, had a stroke, and was hospitalized. Because Marjorie had written the advanced directive, her brother demanded that the feeding tube which saved her life be withdrawn. But a fully conscious Marjorie changed her mind upon disablement and decided that she wanted to live after all. She specifically begged the nurses for food. Smith wrote, "This was so upsetting to one nurse that she blew the whistle. Enter the court, where, after a hurried investigation, it was determined that Marjorie was not medically competent to retract her advanced directive (in other words, to ask for the "treatment" of food). Thus even though she had asked to be fed, the starvation was allowed to continue."

Dr. William J. Burke, Professor of Neurology at St. Louis University, calls what is going on in our institutions "stealth euthanasia." He says, "The deaths of these patients are a dire warning about the increasingly perilous state of our medical ethics."[20]

Disability activist Lucy Gwin warns that:

> When they speak of the burden that life must be for people like us, let us beware. When they talk about our right to death with dignity, what they're really after is cutting us out of the herd.[21]

The descent down that slippery slope from voluntary to involuntary euthanasia has begun *without* the legalization of full blown physician-assisted suicide. How slippery will that social Darwinist slope become when there is no fear of reprisal? Will we see another socially engineered holocaust where many more players—the state, the family, the physician, the hospital, the nursing home—become agents for death?

If physician-assisted suicide becomes the law of the land, will disabled people be targeted and pressured into dying to permit others "more worthy" to live? New York State Attorney General Dennis Vacco thinks so. Commenting on the Second Circuit Court's decision to support physician-assisted suicide, he says, "Inevitably, the lifting of the prohibition will lead to pressure on people to elect suicide."[22]

Take this statement appearing in a 1990 Detroit paper:

> Applications are being accepted. Oppressed by a fatal disease, a severe handicap, a crippling deformity? . . . Dr. Jack Kevorkian will help you kill yourself, free of charge.[23]

The view that a "crippling deformity" is the oppressor, rather than society's reaction to disability, drives much of the "better off dead" thinking that leads people to pick up the phone and call Jack the Death Counselor. It lead 43-year-old Sherry Miller, who had been diagnosed with multiple sclerosis, to make the call. Sherry could have lived for years, but felt she was "becoming a burden on other people." Her husband, like many partners of a spouse who becomes disabled, had left her and taken the children. Kevorkian has stated that his goal is to establish a "new specialty" of obitiatry, that is, medical killing, and to carry out human experimentation in death centers he plans to set up all over the country.[24] Harvesting organs for lucrative transplantation works into this scheme.[25] Depressed and alone, Sherry became one more experiment in his plan.

Dr. Jack Kevorkian already succeeds without reprisal. A fast slide down the slippery slope, he does not limit "voluntary" assisted suicide to those on their deathbeds or to "terminal" illnesses. Published reports and court records indicate that the majority of Kevorkian's twenty-five "patients" did not fall within the generally described category of "terminally ill" (life expectancy of six months or less). Judith Curren had chronic fatigue, was depressed, and had filed domestic abuse charges against her husband two weeks before her killing. Janet Adkins, who had recently been diagnosed with Alzheimers, was reported to have played tennis the week before her appointment with death. Yet another who called Dr. Kevorkian was a depressed battered wife who did not have multiple sclerosis (not a terminal illness) as he claimed. Kevorkian defines terminal illness as "any disease that curtails life even for a day."[26]

The desire to rid the world of those perceived to have no quality of life is not the entire picture. The 9th Circuit Court's decision in support of physician-assisted suicide specifically targeted the handicapped as "beneficiaries." The court stated that it may be acceptable for "competent, terminally ill adults to take the economic welfare of their families and loved ones into consideration" when deciding whether to live or die, and defended the use of assisted suicide to control medical costs. The economics of euthanasia are in the background of this picture and need to be brought into focus.

MAKING THE CONNECTION: BOTTOM-LINE$ EUTHANASIA

A survey published in the February 1996 *New England Journal of Medicine* found that doctors are increasingly in favor of helping "terminally" ill patients end their lives. Oregon, home of the nation's first "quality-of-life" health care rationing plan, birthplace of the Hemlock Society, and the first state to pass a Death With Dignity Act, in 1994, was the state of choice for the survey.

60 percent of the physicians surveyed supported assisted suicide. Seven percent of the respondents said they prescribed lethal doses to patients who asked to die and that these patients "had taken their medication."[27] But what is most disturbing is that *more than 80 percent of the Oregon physicians said that finances might motivate some patient or hospital decisions*, raising the specter of physicians helping poor or uninsured people kill themselves to cut costs, while continuing to care for those who can afford it.

Some assisted suicide advocates, such as Margaret Pabst Battin, think that financial degradation is a good argument for physician-assisted suicide. She says "[assisted suicide] might be warranted for elderly people worried about the prospects of extreme old age and the possibility of being without money, food, shelter, and medication. Many elderly people are enormously afraid of being totally dependent in their final years."[28]

Battin doesn't question the cultural ethics or inhumane social policy that is responsible for this lowly state of affairs. Patients *are* driven into poverty under the current health care system. Many who have private insurance reach their maximum benefit cap and *are* forced to spend down in order to qualify for public health care programs like Medicaid. Pressure *is* brought to bear on family members when expensive care over-reaches the family's means. But are patients who face destitution really choosing death? Or are they victims of social Darwinist euthanasia policy under which the rich can buy all the care they need while the poor must do without?

Finances *already* motivate institutional decisions. Under the Omnibus Budget Reconciliation Act of 1990, service providers *must* inform Medicaid/Medicare patients of their right to die and ask them to sign a Do Not Resuscitate(DNR) order before rendering treatment. This means that in the event one stops breathing, CPR will not be performed, and no costly life-saving measures will be taken that could result in expensive prolonging of life. Those who cannot be "cured" enter dangerous waters when they get admitted to a hospital. Take "Slow Code," reported in *Mouth, the voice of disability rights*:

Slow Code is medical slang for an unofficial policy where medical staff—even student nurses and nursing aides—take death into their own hands. Slow Code goes into effect when an elderly or disabled person has not signed a DNR order. Some health care professionals believe it's wiser to withhold CPR from someone "reaching their maximum age," or who "has no quality of life." What happens is this: Staff members put on a masquerade of CPR. They walk, not run, to the patient, do fake chest compressions, then watch the patient die. Slow Code is rationalized as follows: "His sufferings (and the expense) are over."[29]

Medicaid/Medicare mental patients are sometimes given the red circle treatment, called a CTD or "circle the drain," which is hospital code for leave them alone and wait for them to die. One survey found that 20 percent of the nurses in intensive care units had hastened the death of "critically ill" patients at least once in their careers, in some cases without explicit permission from patients, doctors, or family members.[30]

The Weekly Standard, the voice of the new congressional majority, went so far as to state, "Sick people are expensive. The dead are a burden on no one. Fifty years ago there was whooping cough and diphtheria. The child either lived or died and cheaply. Now that child will grow up to be a very expensive old man or woman. *The only answer is some kind of rationing, Gingrich knows that.*"[31]

Five days after this appeared in print, the House passed a "Medigrant" law that would allow the states to ration health care by ending the federal entitlement to Medicaid. Under the guise of "flexibility," the states would be given one third less funding with few strings attached. The states could choose not to spend money on treatment, and eliminate coverage for hundreds of thousands on Medicaid, which amounts to the authority to passively kill by negligence. Although Clinton vetoed this bill, the campaign to block grant Medicaid is not dead. The cutback forces did succeed in removing the Congressional ban on Medicaid assisted suicide, which would allow these vulnerable patients to opt for assisted suicide once their health care was terminated, foreshadowing the inevitable growth of bottom-line$ euthanasia and widespread insititutional killing.

Consider the advent of managed care. In the name of "containing" health care costs, managed care corporations have come to dominate hospital and physician practices. As a consequence, there has been a payment paradigm shift; hospitals and doctors no longer get paid for individual services rendered, they get paid a flat fee as they would if medicine were socialized. However, unlike a socialization scenario, there are financial incentives for physicians and hospitals to keep costs low, resulting in a form of corporate "natural selection." When gatekeeper physicians become the guardians of HMO profits and business managers determine what is "medically necessary," it is inevitable that less will be spent on patients.

Those who have complained that patients are being kept alive despite their wishes won't have that concern with managed care. Physician-assisted suicide is much cheaper than long-term care. Even if "Dr. Death" Kevorkian were to charge $3,000 per assisted suicide, that would be minimal in comparison to what hospitals charge for a two-day stay or what nursing homes charge by the month.

Fee-for-service insurance companies may also come to view euthanasia for their elderly and disabled policy holders as a lucrative option to making payments for lengthy hospital stays, providing home care, or paying for medications over extended periods of time.

And what about the state's interests? People who rely on the public purse for health care are in jeopardy because state officials are instructed to make "cost-effective" decisions as to how they spend public money. Public health care is being taken over by managed care corporations contracting for Medicaid dollars. Once physician- assisted suicide is made legal, what bearing will that have on life or death decisions being made in hospitals about impoverished, vulnerable, and powerless Medicare/Medicaid patients?

How can society equate "efficiency" with life and death issues? That seems to be easier and easier, especially when euthanasia can be presented as "voluntary" and decisions are bureaucratized, made by insulated institutions removed from the actual people "choosing" to die.

In our entreprenuerial nation, where every aspect of life becomes part of the investment, banking, and business culture, legalizing physician-assisted death is sure to result in a commerce of killing. Entreprenuers will find the means to profit from a new industry of death; electronic brokers on Wall Street will value death corporations based on how much business and profits they are making; the more killing, the higher the dividends, the happier the investors.

Government-proposed cuts to both Medicaid and Legal Services Corp. (often the only resource for poor disabled individuals to combat social injustices) have alarmed advocates for developmentally disabled people. James Ellis, a professor at the University of New Mexico, stated, "The way in which we are going to save people with mental retardation is to pass laws that say you cannot kill them." Eleven states have passed such laws.[32]

NETHERLANDS SAFEGUARDS?

Can we put safeguards into assisted suicide law that keep the extremists like Kevorkian from taking matters into their own hands?

The Netherlands is one country where health care policy is oriented towards "cost containment," assisted suicide is prevalent, and safeguards are on the books. Although voluntary euthanasia is not legalized in Holland, it is court sanctioned. However, according to the 1991 Remmelink Report, the majority of all Dutch euthanasia deaths are *involuntary*.[33] This study concluded that in 1990, 1,040 (on average three per day) died from involuntary euthanasia, meaning doctors made the decisions to kill patients without the patient's knowledge or consent.[34] Of these, 14 percent were fully competent, 72 percent had never given any indication that they would want their lives terminated, and in 8 percent of the cases, doctors performed involuntary euthanasia despite the fact that they believed alternative options were possible. In 45 percent of the involuntary euthanasias performed in hospitals, families had *no* knowledge that the physicians were deliberately terminating their relatives. The report figures do not include thousands of other cases in which life-sustaining treatment was withheld or withdrawn without the patient's consent. Nor do the figures include cases of involuntary euthanasia performed on disabled newborns, children with life-threatening conditions, or psychiatric patients.

Estimates are that Dutch doctors have murdered over 25,000 people who did not ask for it. In spite of the fact that medical care is provided to everyone in Holland, palliative care (comfort care) programs are poorly developed.[35] Clearly, factors well beyond a patient's "right" to die come into play when euthanasia is sanctioned by society. Safeguard words like "terminally ill" and patient "choice" intended to contain and control the course of assisted suicide can be rendered meaningless.

DEVELOPING PALLIATIVE CARE IN THE U.S.

In one of those rare instances where the American Medical Association echoes disabled people's concerns, it has come out against physician-assisted suicide in the United States because, the association says, legalization "poses a serious risk of abuse that is virtually uncontrollable."[36]

New York Attorney General Vacco, who has challenged the Second Circuit Court's decision, said that if society "really wanted to show concern for the needs of the dying, we would not be thinking up ways to kill them."[37] Thinking up ways to help them might include easing their pain, treating their depression, requiring that insurance providers cover hospice stays, and expanding community-based interdependent living goals. In-home personal assistance programs, which allow cognitively compromised and other sick or disabled people to be removed from hospitals, nursing homes, or difficult family situations and placed in a setting where they can live to their optimum potential, should be made available nationally. James Brady, President Reagan's press secretary, was shot and brain injured but continues to live at home and function in the community thanks to a wife who did not want him dead and adequate civil service insurance that provided for necessary services. All should have access to such care.

DEMISE OR FREEDOM?

The events described in this chapter are a dire warning about the dangers inherent in a society that places its focus on economic concerns rather than human ones. Living in a socio-political climate that measures one's worth by economic efficiency demands that we scrutinize the "right" to die beyond a liberalist expansion of individual rights. We must look at the timing of these court decisions. Why now, with the increase of mysterious viruses and incurable illnesses like chronic fatigue, AIDS, and fibromylagia, which require costly drugs and long-term care? Why now with managed care corporations rationing health care, and with public health care under the budget ax? Could liberal court decisions be used for social Darwinist purposes? The issue of physician-assisted suicide must be viewed within the context of an economic order which is eviscerating the social contract by encouraging government to retreat from its responsibilities to the public's welfare.

The Nazis never legalized euthanasia or assisted suicide. Hitler simply guaranteed that physicians would not be prosecuted for killing their patients; that alone was enough to lead to massive deaths in Germany. There are similarities in Holland, and in the U.S. where "cost containment," "efficiency," Slow Codes, CTDs, DNRs, and managed care have infiltrated our health care system. The sanctioning of physician-assisted suicide in this country will clearly lead to the legal and medical de-valuation of all our lives and most likely to a commerce of killing.

Yet the political dynamics are complex. While those on the right profess a right-to-life philosophy by coming out against physician-assisted suicide and euthanasia, they are nonetheless busily slashing public health care programs and they have staunchly opposed universal health care which could *entitle* everyone to equal services. Those on the left often view the right to die as "progressive," not comprehending that physician-assited suicide opens the door to dumping the socially expendable by forcing them to "choose" to die. There is no "Death with Dignity" when people "choose" to die because health care economics and the social services system prevent life with dignity.

Why doesn't the ACLU make the case for the "individual" right to in-home attendant services and decent health care? Isn't it a matter of personal liberty to remain in one's home and not be forced into profiteering institutions like nursing homes? Isn't it an individual right to quality community hospice care rather than assisted suicide chosen out of economic terrorism?

People have been successfully taking their lives since the beginning of time, for a variety of reasons and in countless ways, without the state's legal sanction. The first judge in the ACLU/Elizabeth Bouvia right-to-die case put it succinctly: a person has the right to kill themselves, "but not with the assistance of society." Because society is not educated about disability and retains biases, it is the duty of the state to act in the people's interests and protect them.

There is an organized resistance composed of people with disabilities to counter the elimination of the disposable in this country. Not Dead Yet has camped on the steps of the Supreme Court, holding vigils as the court heard arguments for physician-assisted suicide—but can any identity group alone prevail against an economic system which increasingly sheds all those of no use to generating capital?

CHAPTER 4

THE POLITICS
OF PERFECT BABIES

WITH "BAD" GENES EVERYWHERE, WHO IS "SAFE"?

The more complete the despotism, the more smoothly all things run on the surface.

—Elizabeth Cady Stanton

You might think a resurgence of eugenics impossible. After all, the Pioneer Fund, the New York foundation formed in 1937 (with money from Wickliffe Draper, Nazi sympathizer and textile magnate) which bankrolled much of the pro-eugenics forces in America, is almost defunct.

Emerging evidence makes it clear that eugenics is more deeply rooted in the world than previously thought. From 1935 until 1976, the democratic socialist government in Sweden sterilized 60,000 women to rid society of the "inferior," those with learning difficulties who were from "poor or mixed racial quality," not of Nordic stock. Although the sterilization was called voluntary, victims reported that they were forced to agree or risk losing other children and benefits. The Swedish government's rationale was doublefold, to improve the racial stock and to save the costs of providing welfare.[1]

Following this revelation about eugenic history, the Finns confessed to sterilizing 11,000 people and to performing 4,000 involuntary abortions between 1945 and 1970. The Danes admitted to having eugenic laws in effect before the Nazis, through 1967, and to the sterilization of about 11,000, more than half against their will. The Swiss conceded to compulsory sterilization of the mentally handicapped until the 1970s. While these nations condemned their past actions, Japan, which had eugenics laws on the books until 1996, allowing doctors to sterilize 16,000 physically and mentally disabled women without their consent, offered no apologies for its laws or actions.

Even though genetic determinists admit that genes do not wholly determine many conditions, in that environmental factors are at work and causal networks complex, threads of early eugenic thought still reside in the American conscious.

For instance, Bob Grant, talk show host for WABC radio in New York, advocates openly for eugenics in America. Calling African Americans subhuman, he proposes eugenics to solve social ills like the black crime problem, complaining, "I didn't breed them."[2] While some may dismiss Grant for being on the fringe, he was seen marching alongside Bob Dole on the '96 presidential campaign trail; his views and others like his are not so easily dismissed.

In the same decade that the disability community is insisting that developmentally disabled people are to be valued and given a chance to work regardless of IQ, the authors of the best-selling *The Bell Curve*, called for cutbacks in welfare to discourage people with low IQs from reproducing. They cite low IQ as the cause of poverty and claim that society can eliminate low IQ by birth control and socially engineer poverty out of existence. Their view of poverty may be rationally skewed, but it sells very well. Is it coincidental that this is also the decade in which the U.S. government did "end welfare as we know it" by eliminating the federal guarantee of minimal income to poor women and their children, massively reducing the food stamp program and eliminating financial assistance for over 300,000 disabled children?

The goal of the Human Genome Project is to genetically map the entire three-billion-letter genetic code, and to eventually match genes to disease. What will happen when we can know the intricacies of our genetic legacies? What will happen when insurance companies, schools, medical bureaucracies, and government agencies have access to that information? What does the desire to wipe out disability say about our culture? With neo-Nazism on the rise and with scientists capable of manipulating genes, the primacy of IQ, the production of the perfect baby, and the quest for physical perfection need to be scrutinized.

Bell curves, IQ values, and genetic tests are tools; we must prevent their ill-use and find their best use. We can take responsibility for our families and their futures by demanding equal dignity for all, by repudiating discrimination, by lobbying for strict guidelines for the use of personal information, by requiring that our elected officials uphold their oaths by mending and strengthening government's contract with its citizenry to promote and not destroy human life and happiness.

WHO JUDGES WHAT LIFE IS WORTH?

Prenatal screening now offers prospective parents a glimpse into a wide range of genetic characteristics, detecting many life-threatening conditions such as anencephaly and Tay-Sachs disease. Genetic screening can also inform parents that their child may need additional post-natal care for conditions such as a correctable heart condition, or blue wallpaper in the nursery to signal the eminent arrival of a boy. It can signal parents that they may need education about Down's syndrome, or spina bifida. Any of these genetic facts may influence an abortion decision and we as a society must ensure that parental deliberations are not influenced soley by the fact of a genetic marker but by the whole spectrum of reality which attends that marker. Parents must be apprised of available treatments for their child's condition, probable life-style modifications, emotional and financial support systems, and potential future family impacts. They need access to a variety of experts, including those who have direct knowledge of the disability at hand.

Bree Walker, former KCBS news anchor in Los Angeles, who has a genetic disability, recently elected to have a baby that had a 50 percent chance of inheriting her disability. Walker's disability is not terminal or life-threatening. Her choice to *not* abort was openly criticized on KFI radio by talk show host Jane Norris, who asked her audience, "Is it fair to pass along a genetically *disfiguring* disease to your child?"[3] (italics mine), making it apparent that Norris's objection was based on her own "aesthetic anxiety" about people who look different.[4] She diverted the issue onto "fairness to the child," when what she and other callers who agreed with her really were expressing was their own desire to have a quick solution—abortion—to a "problem."

The real expert, Bree Walker, was not granted any credibility. Since Walker has a visible disability, her decision came as close as you can get to being an informed one and a fair one. Who knows better than a woman who has lived with a disability all her life, yet her right to make the decision to have a baby with a disability was grounds for a public attack.

Bioethicist Adrienne Asch accepts abortion for conditions which would cause death within months or the first year or two, but points to the fact that most disabilities entail a wide range, variety, and unpredictability of what life will be like and cannot be dismissed without interfering with that potential life's possibilities. Asch supports a woman's legal right to choose, but offers moral guideposts as to how to make that choice:

> Selective abortion differs from the decision to end a pregnancy because one's adult life has radically changed in that it is a statement not about the adult but about the value assigned to potential life that has characteristics we dislike. Aborting because of our own lives says something very different than aborting because we don't like what we find out about the potential life we carry. Support for women's equality with men should not be obtained by subverting other people's equality or potentiality—people with disabilities, or people of a certain sex—by the message we give of the rightness of selective abortion.[5]

Some parents will abort at the least sign of a less than "perfect" child, regardless of available support, and some parents will never opt for any genetic screening. For the vast number in the middle, social, medical, and economic pressures will influence the decisions they make.

DAMAGED GOODS ABORTION

The KFI attack exposed the deep fear, anxiety, and misunderstanding of disability in our culture, but it sadly betrayed that some would rather stop the disabled child from entering the world than stop anti-disability bias and enhance the quality of life for disabled children.

If a medical professional neglects to provide the full range of available information parents must have to make decisions regarding the potential birth of a disabled infant, that professional is guilty of practicing a kind of back-door eugenics, of lobbying in silence for the elimination of a whole category of people. If the insurance industry controls an individual's "choices" about abortion by refusing to cover disabled infants, then we as citizens and consumers have allowed corporate interests too much control over our lives. Freedom to have a child, any child, is then restricted by profit margins. The perfect baby becomes a commodity and the disabled child becomes little more than damaged goods.

What kind of society makes parents believe that having a child with a disability is not an option for them? What kind of culture views disability as a burden placed on society, stigmatizing children who happen to have one? One where the individual is harshly expected to do it entirely on their own while collective responsibility diminishes. For instance, mothers still bear most of the responsibility for raising all children, but support structures for families with disabilities are severely lacking; in an era when it takes two paychecks to make ends meet, women often can't afford to sacrifice their careers and return home to care for children with disabilities; when public support is literally being wiped out and health care unaffordable for many, the costs associated with raising a child with a disability appear *larger than life*. The fear that insurance companies might label a prenatal disability a "pre-existent" condition and refuse to cover disabled infants became reality in 1989, when an insurance company refused insurance to a mother because she had been told of her baby's disability prior to birth and did *not* choose to abort.[6]

Why is it that in the richest nation in the world support services aren't readily available? Why is the pressure so squarely placed on the shoulders of the two parents? Why is quality child care for *all* children—disabled or nondisabled—not public policy? Americans must view health care and disability support systems in the same way that we view paved streets and public utilities—as part of the public domain. If we as a government refuse to spend the meager amounts of public monies necessary to support assistance services and medical care for our disabled population, we are guilty of a subtle eugenics policy that forces expectant parents into abortion through the absence of our tax dollars.

WHEN EVERYONE IS "DISABLED"

As selective abortion merges with selective (genetic) breeding, the number of people that will be affected will dramatically rise. Geneticists calculate that when the Human Genome project is complete they will be able to link many more genes to diseases. When that happens, even if it happens only in limited ways, anyone carrying genes linked to diseases like breast cancer, Alzheimer's, maybe even heart attacks will be under microscopic scrutiny. The "healthy" baby of today will no longer be so when detection goes beyond what is now possible to know at birth. "Nondisabled" people with a genetic flaw will join the ranks of the underclass of disabled people who already know that circumstances beyond one's control can be socially and economically limiting.

Robert Cook-Deegan explains in *The Gene Wars* that finding a link to a gene is still a long way from finding cause. For instance, it is known that several genes may cause Alzheimer's and that genes do not wholly determine the disease. Identical twins can differ in age of onset by a decade or more, indicating environmental factors at work. He warns:

> Even if all the "genes for" Alzheimer's disease were to be discovered, there is likely to be a long and highly branched causal network. And this for a relatively well-circumscribed biological phenomenon—a disease running in families as a Mendelian [hereditary] trait. How much more complex are other human characters likely to prove?

> The point is not that genes don't matter for such characters, or that science will never find "genes for" such characters, but rather that the relative power of the genetic explanation should not be projected from the case of Huntington's, where it is high, to the case of alcoholism or schizophrenia or, worse still, to criminal proclivity or intelligence.[7]

But what is known to be true or not true in molecular biology does not necessarily relate to what goes on in the everyday world. Already people subjected to genetic testing are experiencing negative fallout from their insurance carriers and employers, even when genetic testing cannot predict the outcome of having a gene. And in the process, the "nondisabled" are learning what disabled people have experienced all our lives: that insurance companies do not want to take risks on insuring people who they perceive to be costly and employers do not want to hire people who will be perceived costly to their insurance companies, *regardless of the reality of their perceptions.*

Experts estimate that due to sophisticated new genetic tests or a family history of inherited illness, thousands of Americans are being discriminated against:

- A Michigan market research analyst whose two brothers had colon cancer decided to have a colonoscopy—a test to see if she was at risk for the disease—since two genes have been pinpointed as causes. The woman was tested several times and each test came back fine. But when she attempted to purchase health insurance, she was turned down. The fact that she had been tested at all was a red flag.

- An Arizona man was hired for a manufacturing job. During a physical examination, the company doctor asked about blood he spotted in the man's urine. The man said that years before, his family had been tested for Alport's syndrome, a genetic kidney disorder. Although he had been instructed to keep an eye on his blood pressure, he otherwise had no medical problems and was not sure if he had the disease. He lost his job.[8]

It does not seem to matter whether the genetic test is accurate or whether the condition is predictable; insurance companies tend to equate having a gene for a certain disease automatically with onset of that disease. Business has no interest in protecting the rights of individuals; its sole purpose is to generate profits. Insurance company underwriters look at data on an individual and then make a calculation as to whether that person will be profitable to them. When profit incentives intersect with an individual's health care needs, the consequences can be drastic. A 1996 study revealed that 47 percent of those insurance applicants who had been screened for "defects" were *denied* health insurance.[9]

Hillary Clinton noted in a speech during the 1993 health care reform debate, "It is likely [with future genetic testing] that every one of us will have what is called a 'pre-existing' condition and be uninsurable."[10] The more recent passage of the Kennedy-Kassenbaum bill prohibits discrimination based on pre-existing conditions but still allows a six to twelve month waiting period where treatments will not be covered. Since this reform applies only to employer-based group coverage, that leaves the self-employed, the unemployed, and the growing numbers whose employer does not provide health insurance still subject to pre-existing condition exclusions. It does nothing for the 41 million uninsured and does not limit premium charges.

There is little legal protection. The Americans with Disabilities Act does offer some protection in employment under the definition of disability. For instance, the Arizona man noted above, because he was already employed, would have standing to bring a discrimination case before the Equal Employment Opportunity Commission under the third prong of the definition of disability, as someone who is "regarded as having an impairment," and the employer could not legally fire him (as long as he is able to do his job). But a job applicant with a known genetic condition will have a much harder time proving that a prospective employer discriminated.

The insurance industry has made it quite clear that they expect the right to genetic information. The Medical Information Bureau has collected genetic data on more that 15 million people already since medical records are computerized and quite accessible. Corporations have put genetic screening to use for other purposes. The *Journal of Australian Political Economy* reports that businesses have begun screening for genetic susceptibility to certain work-related illnesses in order to avoid the cost of workers' compensation. Chemical industries, for instance, screen workers for sensitivity to some substances, rather than correcting the hazards.[11]

A Maryland banker obtained a list of local cancer patients, cross-referenced it with loan customers at his bank, and then called in their loans.[12] People rightly fear that the uncontrolled use of genetic information may cause them to lose their jobs, lose their health coverage, or see their premiums jacked up beyond affordability. They worry that they might not get bank loans. And they worry about their children's future—that "bad genes" might keep them from obtaining a job or health care.

These are realistic concerns. The outcome of the Human Genome Project may be much broader than linking a gene to a condition. Historian Daniel Kevles cautions that the genome project *grew out of the eugenics movement.* For instance, Dr. Franz Kallman, who was part of the Kaiser Wilhelm Institute for Anthropology, Eugenics and Human Heredity funded by the Rockefellers, directed both the American Eugenics Society and the American Society of Human Genetics which organized the Human Genome Project. (The American Eugenics Society changed it's name to the Society for the Study of Social Biology, its current name.)[13] Kelves warns, "In its ongoing fascination with questions of behavior, human genetics will undoubtedly yield information that may be wrong, or socially volatile, or, if the history of eugenic science is any guide, both."[14]

We need to expand privacy legislation to safeguard our personal information and we must expand health care delivery into univeral single-payer coverage (such as the Canadian system), which will guarantee appropriate medical care regardless of one's medical condition, disability, "bad genes," or employment status. We must conscientiously identify and restructure social policies and legislation that are discriminatory to ensure that society never again turns it attention to eliminating a class of "defects."

"IT'S ALL IN THE GENES" ESSENTIALISM

Perhaps the greatest social danger in the developing gene culture is the ideology that accompanies genetic determinism. Genetic essentialists could argue today, as did the Spencerian survival-of-the-fittest capitalists, that there is no reason to spend social dollars on correcting the social environment because it is nature, via genes, that has brought people to the bottom of the socio-economic hierarchy, not the existence of class-based social policy that rejects egalitarianism and denies quality, disability-sensitive[15] health care to all.

According to the World Institute on Disability, 80 percent of the population will experience a disabling condition in the course of their lives. The road between birth and death is not controllable; accidents happen, people lose limbs, sever their spinal cords, become brain-injured. Even if genetic re-engineering finds a way to cure all genetic conditions before birth, we will still get sick (viruses are clever), and all of us will age and die.

Disabled people are just awakening to our oppression and to resist the physicalism that put us there. Genetic determinism, if improperly used, can widen the opening for corporate, government, and social oppression of almost everyone. Who doesn't have genetic conditions running in their families?

Common ground exists for nondisabled and disabled people who are concerned about retaining enlightenment social contract principles that extend economic justice and social security to all people. Will we submit to the insurance company profiteers, the genetic capitalists, and subhuman corporate-driven social policy, or will we create and insist on social policy which is people-centric and assures all, disabled and temporarily-abled alike, the resources to live to our potential?

PART II

THE MECHANICS OF POVERTY

There are a thousand hacking at the branches of evil to one who is striking at the root.

—Henry David Thoreau

Outside of ideologues, the academy and the press, no one thinks that capitalism is a viable system and nobody has thought that for sixty or seventy years—if ever.

—Noam Chomsky

CHAPTER 5

A MISSING LINK

BODY POLITICS AND THE SOLE ECONOMIC ORDER

There has never existed a truly free and democratic nation in the world...I have entered the fight...against the economic system under which I live.

—Helen Keller, socialist, addressing the
Women's Peace Party and the Labor Forum
in New York City, 1916

The *American Heritage* dictionary defines capitalism as "an economic system characterized by freedom of the market with increasing concentration of private and corporate ownership of production and distribution means, proportionate to increasing accumulation and reinvestment of profits." If democracy is the practice of promoting social equality where more people participate in governance, then capitalism with its economic tendency to concentrate wealth works against that equality, because wealth and ownership reside in fewer and fewer hands. This glaring contradiction is at the heart of modern-day inequities, and this is what Helen Keller meant above when she addressed the Women's Peace Party and the Labor Forum at Carnegie Hall. There can be no democracy without economic democracy .

The godfather of capitalism, Adam Smith, in *An Inquiry into the Nature and Causes of the Wealth of Nations*, recognized that class-based policy was not beneficial to the democratic masses. He pointed out two centuries ago that "the vile maxim of the masters" was "all for ourselves and nothing for other people." In Smith's day the "masters" were the rich mercantile class who manipulated government and public policy to their advantage. In Nazi Germany, the "masters" were the Aryan militarists and entrepreneurial class that dismantled the democratic Weimar Republic health care system, the most respected and comprehensive social services program in the world, to shift public funds to the fascist goal of world domination.

Smith advocated for a capitalism that would advance economic equality—something that has never materialized—and he opposed the concentration of wealth—something the U.S. government defends by protecting the rich against the poor. Since Smith's day, capitalism has worked its will upon the people to produce an enormous gap between rich and poor. Author Michael Parenti explains:

> Income and wealth disparities are greater today than at any time since such information was first collected in 1947. As one economist put it: "If we made an income pyramid out of a child's blocks, with each layer portraying $1,000 of income the peak would be far higher than the Eiffel Tower, but almost all of us would be within a yard of the ground."[1]

Today we have the "masters" of the market—the corporations, speculators, banks, and global capitalists—maintaining the inequality and widening the income disparity.

The social Darwinists were masters at keeping societal recources in the hands of the wealthy by marginalizing lives perceived to be of no use to the economic order, but, as this chapter will explore, capitalism's production dynamics adversely affected disabled people's ability to participate in the sole economic order.

THE SOLE ECONOMIC ORDER

It is an obscure fact that industrialization and entrepreneurialism were prominent in both the U.S. and the Nazi National Socialist government of Germany. Although the Nazis called themselves National Socialists, Nazis were pro-profiteering industrialists like the Rockefellers, duPonts, and Mellons. Hitler made this clear when he wrote, "We stand for the maintenance of private property . . . We shall protect free enterprise as the most expedient, or rather the sole possible economic order."[2]

Walter Russell Mead writes that "major U.S. corporations collaborated with Hitler throughout the '30s and into WWII." For example, Rockefeller's Standard Oil was partnered with the German corporation I.G Farben, which patented and made gasoline from coal with the help of concentration camp slave labor. Mead points out that Hitler had repeatedly offered to send the Jews to the U.S. instead of to death camps, but the U.S. refused to take them. Historian Howard Zinn explains that the U.S. did not get involved in the war over the persecution of the Jews, nor over Hitler's invasion of Poland, Czechoslovakia, or Austria, nor over Italy's attack on Ethiopia, rather it "was the Japanese attack on a link in the American Pacific Empire that did it;" it was the attack on U.S. business interests that determined our "vital" interest in World War II.[3] This is to say that economic interests rose above democratic and humane principles, even delayed our involvement in World War II because businesses in the U.S. and Nazi Germany had a common hatred of egalitarian economic ideals. The U.S. saw fascists like Hitler (and Mussolini) as infinitely preferable to communism because he fostered the sole economic order, capitalism.

BODY POLITICS & CAPITALIST BEGINNINGS

Capitalism is characterized by certain disadvantages. One by-product is that large numbers of people remain unemployed and in poverty (covered in detail in Chapter 10). While capitalism held the promise of expanding the base of people benefiting from it, it is inherently exclusionary.

Some segments would fall harder to the bottom of the market-driven society, like the disabled and the elderly. The effects on disabled people can be explained by tracing how work got shaped by industrial capitalism. As the grinding of human beings into the "satanic mills" changed the manner in which things got made for the competitive market, impediments were erected to disabled people's survival.

Political theorist Michael Harrington explains some characteristics of the transition from feudalism to capitalism:

> In a precapitalist society, and above all in the late feudalism that preceded the capitalist revolution, one encountered workers who owned or controlled their own means of production. There were artisans with their own tools, peasants with the use of their own plots of land. The resulting mode of production was based upon atomized, isolated property, and consequently was characterized by low levels of productivity. Capitalism begins, Marx argues, with the "expropriation . . . of that private property which is based upon the labor of the individual." The peasants are driven from their land, the artisans "deskilled" by the process that leads to the capitalist enterprise.[4]

In precapitalist societies, economic exploitation was made possible by a feudal (political) concentration of ownership of land. While a few owners reaped the surplus, the many living on an estate worked for subsistence. Harrington points out that with the advent of capitalism, "Discipline was now economic, not political. . .The worker was 'free' in the double sense that he or she was no longer tied to a given manor and had the right to choose between work and death."[5] The new economy meant that people were no longer tied to the land but were forced to find work that would pay a wage or starve.

Under the feudal system, disabled people were seen as subhuman but survived by doing what work they could in the fields or kitchen. Some became skilled artisans, exerting control over a trade that, importantly, allowed one to work at one's own pace. If one could not work at all, the fact that one lived on a manor was some assurance that food would be available. With the means of production removed from the worker and seated in the hands of capitalists, people who were capital-less were thrown at the mercy of being hired by others looking to profit from their labor. While one may have previously worked to produce for the landowner's use, capitalism meant that one was expected to produce for another's profit.

This sea change presented disabled people (unless one was a wealthy capitalist and not a laborer) with less than an equal chance to be a productive member of a community, for industrial capitalism set up production dynamics that further de-valued our bodies. To philosopher Descartes, the body was a machine; to the industrialist striving for more profits, people's bodies were valued for their ability to function like machines. The capitalists used labor to generate larger output to accumulate more wealth. Nondisabled workers had value because management could push them to produce at ever increasing rates of speed, which in turn increased profits for the owner class. But as work became more compartmentalized, requiring precise mechanical movements of the body repeated in quicker succession, disabled people were seen as less "fit" to do the tasks then required of the working class.

The emerging market society meant that disabled people who were perceived to be of no use to the competitive profit cycle would be excluded from work. There was no room under market tyranny to accommodate the disability by providing work schedules or adjusting jobs to fit disabled people's needs (a goal of the Americans with

Disabilities Act today); rather the disabled person was expected to conform to the needs of the industrialists, an impossible task for many. The social consequence would be that the disabled were perceived as not capable of working at all. The injured workers, the congenitally disabled would be excluded from the workforce, demeaned socially. Out of a job and not likely to get another, they were made to feel worthless for not having an arm, using a wheelchair or crutches. Indeed, many were forced to become Dickens street beggars to survive, but generally all disabled people came to be viewed as "unfit." In capitalist jargon we became part of that immoral concept, the surplus population, in company with the elderly, the unskilled, those injured on the job, the unemployed who would never get a job (because there were not enough jobs for all).

The phenomenon of "disability" itself came to be defined in relation to a capitalist labor market. For instance, under workers' compensation statutes, a laborer's body is rated according to its functioning parts. One is rated a "10" if one has all one's fingers, arms, legs, but one's value is significantly altered to a 7.5 or less if any parts do not "work" by capitalist production standards. In Social Security law, disabled means unable to "engage in substantial work activity," that is, unable to perform work to a standard required to earn a living in a capitalist economy. This is to say that physicalism is perpetuated through social policy built to serve the market economy instead of all members of the society.

While the accumulation of wealth remained of paramount import, the fact that large segments of the population were excluded from benefiting from the sole economic order did not rate concern. The expendable were squeezed out while the social Darwinists who were profiting from the status quo justified this state of affairs as the "natural" order of things.

Nazi Germany viewed disabled people as a burden on the state and a drag on the economy, and exterminated us. The desire to solve the "defect" problem in America was inextricably mixed with matters of money; masters of efficiency in the U.S. were bean-counting like their Nazi counterparts. Economics factored into the widespread support for eugenics and euthanasia. In 1935 Dr. J.N. Baker, a health officer in Alabama, stated, "With bated breath, the entire civilized world is watching the bold experiment in mass sterilization recently launched by Germany. It is estimated that some 400,000 of the population will come within the scope of this law, the larger portion of whom fall into that group classed as inborn feeblemindedness. . . It is estimated that, after several decades, hundreds of millions of marks will be saved each year as a result of the diminution of expenditures for patients with hereditary diseases." Dr. Baker included as targets for compulsory medical intervention any "sexual pervert . . . or any prisoner who has been twice convicted of rape" or imprisoned three times for any offense, as well as those "habitually and constantly dependent on public relief or support by charity."[6]

Other Americans followed suit:

> Many American advocates also argued that euthanasia might be a good way to save on medical costs. Dr. W.A. Gould, for example, in the *Journal of the American Institute of Homeopathy*, defended euthanasia as one way of resolving economic difficulties; he asked his reader to recall in this context the "elimination of the unfit" in ancient Sparta. Some offered more radical suggestions: in 1935 the French-American Nobel Prize winner Alexis Carrel (inventor of the iron lung) suggested in his book *Man the Unknown* that the criminal and insane should be "humanely and economically disposed of in small euthanasia institutions supplied with proper gases." W.G. Lennox, in a 1938 speech to Harvard's Phi Beta Kappa chapter, claimed that saving lives "adds a load to the back of society"; he wanted physicians to recognize "the privilege of death for the congenitally mindless and for the incurable sick who wish to die; the boon of not being born for the unfit."[7]

The "unfit" unquestionably meant those of no use to the market economy, the non-working members of the society. The connection between eugenics/euthanasia and the economic order is clear; those of no use to the economic order were marginalized. What was not clear is that the development of the market economy itself—the sole economic order—was to construct barriers that precluded segments of society from reaping any reward from it. It directly affected disabled people's ability to be productive members of the community.

THE VILE MAXIM AND THE SOCIAL DARWINISTS

Philosopher Herbert Spencer's proclamation that capitalism's "natural selection" process of individualism and competition weeded out the "unfit" by leaving the inferior in poverty to die fit in perfectly with laissez-faire capitalism, which from the very start would never be economically egalitarian and needed some credible public justification to explain why some prospered and larger numbers of "others" did not. If society viewed nonprosperity as the fault of the individual's shortcomings and not inherent in the design of capitalism, then capitalists were off the hook to admitting that class differences were a result of capitalism's economic structure and inherently exploitative nature.

Robert Proctor explains that:

When phrases such as "the struggle for existence" and "the survival of the fittest" became catchwords for the new social Darwinism, this reflected the broader social and economic structure of the times: this is what is meant when we hear that Darwin's theory cannot be understood apart from the Manchester economics of Ricardo and Smith and the dog-eat-dog world of mid-nineteenth-century British capitalism.[8]

Social Darwinists used the science of biology to support their undemocratic politics by upholding that heredity—race and genes—prevailed over the class and economic issues raised by Marx. Just as the "inferior" were not meant to survive in nature, nor were they meant to economically survive in society.

The social Darwinists elevated individual competition to the status of a "natural law." If the entrepreneurial business process, as explained by John D. Rockefeller, was "merely the working out of a law of nature and a law of God," then the rich capitalists were free to accumulate vast hordes of wealth and claim they were the "fittest." Free enterprise magnate Andrew Carnegie, a follower of Spencerian philosophy, expressed a sigh of relief when he said, "All is well since all grows better," getting off the moral hook with capitalism's "natural" law.[9]

While Hitler dismantled the democratic socialist Weimar Republic, the American social Darwinists did their best to prevent the formation of any social contract that would compensate for the injuries, occupational illnesses, high unemployment, and deaths propagated by industrial capitalism. Refusing to redistribute societal wealth and meet the pre-Nazi German democratic standard, the industrial class sought to prevail over the greater public's interests by using science as a political weapon. Laissez-faire sociologists and anthropologists used biological determinism to argue against implementing reforms that would better the living conditions of the poor, claiming that biology conferred a noncorrectable individual condition, that could not be solved by social reform. By erecting these "logical" barriers against humane social policy social, Darwinists could make the case for a bare-bones government, and use futility as a reason to curtail the role of government in society, to oppose socialized medicine, and to make public expenditures unpopular.

The elite social Darwinist's solution was to weed out the "unfit": the non-Caucasian races (particularly immigrants), the poor, the deaf, and the disabled. But clearly class rose above Spencerian "natural laws"; disabled offspring of the "fittest" (prosperous) class inherited the means to survive and did not starve to death, making it clear that "natural law" had little to do with survival, but man-made selection had everything to do with it.

Dissenters of the Spencerian view, such as sociologist Lester Frank Ward, spoke out against the social Darwinists' invocations by branding social Darwinist doctrine as:

> the most complete example of the oligocentric world view which is coming to prevail in the higher classes of society and would center the entire attention of the whole world upon an almost infinitesimal fraction of the human race and ignore the rest . . . I want a field that shall be broad enough to embrace the whole human race [not a select class], and I would take no interest in sociology if I did not regard it as constituting such a field.[10]

In the social Darwinist tradition, Charles Murray, co-author of *The Bell Curve*, made the class link when he wrote, "Some people are better than others. They deserve more of society's rewards."[11] It is the "fit" bourgeoisie busily concentrating their wealth and control over the means of production who deserve and get capitalism's rewards. The privileged who "deserve" more do get more under government policies (subsidies) that amount to a socialism for the rich, while the underprivileged struggle on Darwin's terms—capitalism for the poor.

Social Darwinism proved to be a convenient self-serving veneer for the masters of Smith's vile maxim, the Rothschilds, the Carnegies, the Harrimans, who benefitted from the sole possible economic order and did not want to see a more equitable system evolve. Social Darwinism provided the business class who controlled the means of production with the justification to leave the surplus population in poverty to die, rather than design an economic system that would accommodate all of society.

MISSING THE LINK: BLUR IN THE EUGENIC POLITICAL LINES

It must be noted that the "defect question" did not fall neatly into "left" or "right" camps of political thought either in the U.S. or in Germany. Alarmingly, elements on both sides supported euthanasia and eugenics. For instance, in the U.S. the turn of the century Progressive reformists viewed eugenics and euthanasia as positive social change:

> Eugenicists were an integral part of the progressive movement in the United States. Their policies were jumbled in with such other progressive issues of the day as electoral reform, government regulation of commerce, international disarmament, women's rights and suffrage, prohibition and birth control.[12]

The democratic movement saw eugenics as a secular, rational means to control what it perceived as meandering nature that interfered with the march of progress. It entirely missed the link to market capitalism, which de-valued disabled people's nonexploitable bodies. It missed the link to social Darwinism, where the "unproductive" of no use to building more wealth were disposable.

Unwittingly, the labor movement contributed to the ethics that propelled anti-humanistic eugenics. If work defines human worth and work is the central criterion for human validation, then the worker has his/her pride and the capitalist has their labor to exploit, two sides of the same paradigm. If work was to be the end-all of existence, then disabled people (who could not work) inevitably would be marginalized, and relegated to a corner of society.

In Germany, eugenics was seen as progressive in socialist circles:

> Many socialists identified eugenics with state planning and the rationalization of the means of production; many thus found the idea of a "planned genetic future" an attractive one...Alfred Grotjahn, for example, today considered the father of German social medicine and one of the leading architects of Weimar Germany's progressive health reforms, saw racial hygiene as a legitimate concern of medicine. He was one of those who defended the use of the term eugenics (rather than racial hygiene) in order to avoid confusion with racist notions of the political-anthropological variety.[13]

The vast majority of German physicians were not critical of euthanasia practices other than out of their concern not to do something illegal. A small group of doctors who were treating disabling diseases caused by economic, industrial, or environmental conditions heroically opposed the increasing power that Nazi biology and the insurance companies were exercising in the health care fields. The Marxist physicians, concerned that the poor, disabled, and unhealthy were getting the short end of the stick, stuck to humane principles that put care above profit and life above economizing and efficiency. Upholding that capitalism was the greatest malady afflicting industrial society, Dr. Ernest Simmel said that capitalism forces wage earners "to squander and waste the only thing they possess—their labor power and their health."[14] Forced into exile when the Nazi revolution took full root, their organization, the Association of Socialist Physicians, continued criticism from afar:

> The association marveled at the willingness of Nazi physicians to dismantle public medical services—services that had taken decades to construct, and for which Germany was world renowned. It ridiculed suggestions that such measures were designed to serve "the whole, rather than the individual" and deplored the Nazi contempt for the handicapped and the elderly—individuals who, in Nazi medical jargon, were nothing but useless "ballast lives," lives not worth living.[15]

But the majoritarian political spectrum simply missed the fact that social power relations control the nature of work and by having political power oppress those perceived to be of little use to their ends.

BEYOND "ADAPT OR PERISH"

"To aid the bad in multiplying is, in effect," wrote Herbert Spencer in *The Study of Sociology*, "the same as maliciously providing for our descendants a multitude of enemies." Allowing society to "foster good for nothings," Spencer claimed, is "injurious," for that "puts a stop to that natural process of elimination by which society continually purifies itself."[16]

Spencer held capitalism in regard for providing such a service, but one has only to look at Roy Cohn or J. Edgar Hoover, Michael Milken or Charles Keating, to see how individualism and competition have failed at weeding out "the bad." One could even say it has produced an unprecedented opportunity for the most "injurious" to prosper, through adaptation to obsessive capital accumulation. Take Robert Allen, CEO of AT&T, for instance, who became the poster boy for corporate greed by firing 40,000 workers and getting an accumulative $16 million in perks and bonuses for his dastardly deeds.[17]

Feudalism was toppled by capitalism, yet, as under feudalism, the world's billionaires—all 358 of them—own more assets than the annual combined incomes of 45 pecent or 2.5 billion of the world's people.[18] The sole economic order, set upon increasing the concentration of wealth and ownership of production, has done just that; the billionaires are the new feudal lords, the new masters keeping the hierarchy of wealth in place.

Adam Smith's "vile maxim" is the mantra of the 20th century business class. Our society is plagued with stock and securities fraud, medical billing fraud, telemarketing fraud, racketeering, price fixing, and unlawful labor practices. Political bribery is commonplace. Corporations like Nike, Disney, Wal-Mart, Reebok, and Kathi Lee Gifford Clothing take their manufacturing to Indonesia, Honduras, and Haiti where they can pay subhuman wages to young girls who work a grueling ten- to twelve-hour day for 28 or 40 cents an hour. The market society that glorifies efficiency and profit above principles of cooperation and equality has brought our "civilization" to an inhumane abyss.

Most dangerously, social Darwinist conditioning has paved the way for decision-making classes to successfully put the spin on welfare that it is the failure of the individual—not the economic system that benefits the few at the expense of the many. The critical link is that the capitalist market economy produces a negative social outcome: by fixating on the accumulation of money it produces social casualties.

In 1940 economist Karl Polyani warned of the dangers when markets dominate the affairs of society. He wrote:

> ...control of the economic system by the market is of overwhelming consequence to the whole organization of society: it means no less than the running of society as an adjunct to the market. Instead of economy being embedded in social relations, social relations are embedded in the economic system. The vital importance of the economic factor to the existence of society precludes any other result. For once the economic system is organized in separate institutions, based on specific motives and conferring a special status, society must be shaped in such a manner as to allow that system to function according to its own laws.[19]

Its own laws would produce a "market society" where human concerns and social orders get subsumed by a kind of economic tyranny, the inversion of what Polyani believed was needed to foster a cooperative and healthy society.

Perhaps it is time to get back to some of our precapitalist humane Enlightenment roots and ask, as did philosopher John Locke (whether we agree with his conclusions or not), "What is a civil society?" What is an economy for: to support market-driven profits or to sustain community bonds and elevate human participation? How can the realm of work be expanded to encompass activities precluded by the profit motive, and how can all members of society be included and rewarded whether they work or not?

The basic law of evolution is not about adaptation, it about self-transcending creativity. Moving beyond "Adapt or Perish," that is, beyond simply accepting one's environment as permanent and then adapting to it, is to move into a realm where one seeks to transform the inequalities. Our freedom lies in the fact that we are not at the mercy of some "natural law" but are part of a social order which is by no means fixed, but needs democratizing to offer a counterforce to the dominant market "society."

CHAPTER 6

THE ECONOMIC STRAITJACKET

Poverty is the worst form of violence.

—Gandhi

To try to change the outward attitudes and behaviors does very little good in the long run if we fail to examine the basic paradigms from which those attitudes and behaviors flow.

—Thomas Kuhn

Adam Smith exposed the class roots of our economic predicament when he wrote in *The Wealth of Nations*, "Till there be property there can be no government, the very end of which is to secure wealth, and to defend the rich from the poor."[1] Yet there have been social movements that have attempted to remedy persisting inequities by redistributing societal wealth to promote economic parity and insure social stability. The social contract as we know it came out of people's movements during the New Deal of the 1930s and the Great Society of the 1960s.

In response to social unrest, Franklin D. Roosevelt in his 1944 State of the Union address proposed an "Economic Bill of Rights" as an adjunct to the Constitution, stating, "We have come to a clear realization of the fact that true individual freedom cannot exist without economic security and independence." FDR rightly called for government to guarantee every citizen "a useful and renumerative job...the right to earn enough to provide adequate food and clothing and recreation...the right of every family to a decent home, the right to adequate protection from the economic fears of old age, sickness, accident, and unemployment, the right to a good education."

New Deal liberalism held that social injustices could be remedied by incrementalist reforms under the current system. By expanding the role of government in the economy, FDR in effect saved capitalism from socialism by positioning his liberal policies between the two opposing systems. The New Deal did offer some social security to the masses, but the meager concessions made by the U.S. government fell short of meeting the standards of democratic socialist countries such as Sweden, and came decades after those countries had implemented humane social policy reforms.

The story of the American social contract is a story of business beating back social justice at every turn. Smith wrote in the 18th century, "People of the same trade seldom meet together but the conversation ends in a consipiracy against the public..."[2] Still the same, American business interests exert strong control over U.S. policy; they fought FDR's expansion of government and kept liberal incrementalism in check then, as they do now. America's disabled population lives in an economic straitjacket, squeezed simultaneously by current social, physical, and entitlement policy barriers to employment and a national ethic that equates human value with work.

CONCOCTED CRACKS

Capitalist-dominated social policy has had disastrous economic consequences for the disabled in two areas—health insurance and public benefit programs—both impacting employment and standard of living.

Disability benefits in the U.S. lagged far behind the European social democratic countries, which set high inclusionary standards for public health programs in the early 1900s. It was not until 1956 that a grossly limited public disability insurance became available to Americans; Medicare was not available until 1972; and not until 1973 would the disabled poor who had no employment history obtain public assistance.

During the 1920s-40s, insurance companies experimented with disability benefits. Edward Berkowitz illustrates how private insurers tried to squeeze profits from disability insurance in his Twentieth Century Fund study, *Disabled Policy*:

> They [insurance companies] tightened the definition of disability, lengthened the waiting period before a disabled person could begin to receive benefits, refused to sell policies to women, and restricted benefits to those who became disabled under the age of fifty-five. In other words, they offered limited protection and attempted to take only the very best risks. Even so, they lost money.[3]

The insurance game is played like this: the industry first studies data and calculates rates that will assure profits. It then cherry-picks by denying insurance to bad risks. Although this excludes disabled people, it does provide some sort of safety net for those who start out nondisabled and become disabled later in life.

From the capitalist's point of view, there are two problems with private disability insurance. In insurance jargon they are called "adverse selection" and "moral hazard."

Adverse selection refers to a problem common to all types of health insurance. Since health insurance is costly, people tend not to purchase it unless they have reason to believe they might need it. The more bad risks the company takes, the more money it pays out, and the more costly the insurance becomes. The more costly the insurance, the more selective people are in purchasing the insurance and the worse the problem becomes.

Moral hazard, in plain English, refers to the fact that people cheat. They claim to be disabled when they are not. To protect against cheating, the insurance companies try to make sure that a policyholder will not receive more income from being on the disability rolls than he would if he continued to work ("over-insurance").[4]

Moral hazard theory put into practice by private disability insurers meant that the disabled person would get less than what was needed for a decent standard of living, so becoming disabled translated into a life of financial hardship, whether one had insurance or not, and generated a very realistic fear of becoming disabled.

These practices which left many "uninsurables" out of the private insurance loop made a strong case for public disability insurance. It would seem logical that insurance corporations would be relieved to support a government plan that would shift unwanted costs onto the public; however, going back to a class analysis, granting public disability insurance benefits meant distributing cash downwards, not into the pockets of business and the rich. In keeping, private insurance corporations were among the chief opponents of public disability benefits.

Businessmen formed the largest single group on the Social Security Board set up in 1938 and the advisory council in 1948. The private insurance industry, vehemently opposed to public disability insurance, wielded great political clout. In 1945 the social security committees of the Life Insurance Association of America, the American Life Insurance Convention, and the National Association of Life Underwriters entirely opposed the establishment of public disability insurance. Equally opposed were the Chambers of Commerce. This is not surprising. If workers were provided with a federal social safety net that protected them through unemployment, sickness, disability, and old age, then business would have less control over the workforce because labor would gain a stronger position from which to negotiate fair wages and safe working conditions.

The American Medical Association was also against public disability insurance because it feared socialized medicine (perceived to work against physicians' financial interests) would creep into America as it had in Sweden, France, Germany, Canada, and Spain. After the passage of the first disability insurance act, one AMA member whined in dismay, "This is the end of the medical profession."[5] Berkowitz explains the AMA's behavior during the disability insurance debate:

> The AMA, increasingly worried about the passage of national health insurance, took the lead in opposing disability insurance, arguing that it would perpetuate the condition of sickness and would work against rehabilitation. Further, the AMA said, the law would allow the federal government to supervise the doctors who examined the disability applicants. Who knew where that practice might lead? The solution to the problem of disability, the AMA claimed, was to eliminate it, not to encourage it.[6]

Cash benefits are a necessary support to participating in a rehabilitation program, but unfortunately, in its haste to forestall any attempt at socializing medicine, the AMA introduced the insidious argument that the motive for rehabilitation would be destroyed if disabled people were provided with income. The impossible promise of an end to disability has been equally damaging, creating in the public mind the false notion that funds spent on the disabled would be better spent on medical research to end disability.

Although FDR tried to pass disability insurance in the second phase of his New Deal, the Republicans (representing the capitalist interests) fought and delayed passage of disability insurance for about twenty years. The Democrats prevailed when a reluctant Eisenhower signed a much compromised benefit system into law in 1956.

This first disability insurance program, Social Security Disability Insurance(SSDI), applied only to injured workers over the age of 55, a limitation insisted upon by oppositional forces since the 1940s. Furthermore, since the states had leeway in implementing the federal program, SSDI administration was at the mercy of state politics, where business interests had more control. The result was an inconsistent dispersion of the "entitlement." In the 1960s eligibility was incrementally expanded to include younger workers and their children, but the public health care component, Medicare, often the only form of health care disabled people can get, would not be created until 1972.

CLASS, CHISELERS, AND CHEATS

So what about those with disabilities who were not injured workers? What about those who acquired a disability before they had built up enough quarters of work to qualify for SSDI? This group had no social security until 1973 when Supplemental Security Income(SSI), a needs-based program, was set up for them and for those elderly unable to qualify for retirement under Social Security.

SSI, the disability welfare system, is the humiliating lowest rung on the socio-economic ladder of disability benefits. SSI benefits averaging $470 per month[7] comprise about one-fifth of what a paraplegic veteran receives and roughly three-fourths of the $663 average that a disabled worker on SSDI benefits receives. In addition, SSI is means-tested, so one must remain destitute to stay qualified. In the U.S. disability social pyramid, the military disabled place at the top and the least valued members of our society—those disabled with no work history—place at the bottom. The resulting inequity: individuals with the same level of disablement receive different levels of public assistance and have different standards of living.

Originally the Democrats bestowed a decent standard of living upon the disabled worker through SSDI, but the program was subsequently devastated by a Democrat, Jimmy Carter. In 1979, responding to swelling SSDI rolls, Carter's Health, Education and Welfare secretary, Patricia Roberts Harris, claimed "disability is killing us"[8] and enlisted Congress to reform the program. The public disability program was accused of harboring chiselers who ripped off the system. The rationale used by the bipartisan Social Security Commission, backed by those conservative Democrats and Republicans always eager to cut back entitlements, was remarkably similar to the private insurance industry's moral hazard: if benefits were brought down to a level of significant hardship, the "lingerers" would get a job. As a result, the vast majority of those on SSDI, the deserving poor who could not work, were provided less-than-adequate aid to satisfy the public that a few able-bodied cheaters were not winning the game.

However, the Carter chiseling maneuver was rather disingenuous. In fact, the Carter administration held the view that entitlement programs "limited the ability of the president to manage the economy, solve social problems and achieve other national goals" and wanted the money going to disabled people to be freed up for other uses.[9] The fact that the administration accomplished this clearly demonstrates that the disabled are not held to have any objective "right" to a decent standard of living. Because disability entitlements are paid from the general fund and can be manipulated by politicians, any president's disability policy decisions are inseparable from their budgetary priorities and political ambition. The Carter administration changes to disability benefits marked the moral downfall of the SSDI system, for those truly disabled would have economic violence committed against them for their inability to work.

GURUS OF VIRTUE AND
THE U.S. WELFARISM SHORTCHANGE

According to *Left Business Observer* editor Doug Henwood, the American poverty line is set at a 1950s level with no allowance for changes occurring over the last thirty years. Research in the 1950s showed the average family spent a third of its income on food; therefore a "poverty income" was determined to be three times what experts thought the minimum food budget should be. That equation has never been adjusted to take into account the sharp rise in housing, medical care, and child care costs of the following four decades that have altered the average household's economic picture.[10]

The goal of SSI, to lift elderly and disabled people out of poverty by providing a national income floor, has never been reached. The federal

SSI benefit rate is about 74 percent of the national poverty guideline for an individual and 82 percent for a couple. Additionally, SSI recipients are allowed a much smaller income and asset level than is allowed to beneficiaries of any other entitlement program.

Studies by Patricia Ruggles of the Urban Institute show that if basic needs were refigured to the modern market, the poverty line would be pushed up by 70 percent, to a level nearly twice as high as the official rate, indicating that a quarter of the American people are in poverty.[11] If that adjusted poverty line was applied to the SSI benefit rate, people on SSI would be "living" at 35 percent below the poverty rate.

Anti-public spending forces have kept benefit payments so low that the 4.5 million disabled people on SSI find themselves in great hardship. They are expected to live on between $400 and $600 a month, depending on the state of residence. SSI must cover rent (unless subsidized), food (in states where SSI recipients are ineligible for food stamps), clothing, utilities, and transportation. By gross comparison, Representative Frederick Heineman, a member of the 1994 Republican freshman class, says his $183,000 yearly income makes him a member of the "lower middle class."[12] So which economic class does a disabled person who lives on SSI at $5,400 - $7,200 a year belong to?

The government has contained benefits, not elevated them to humane levels. When the 1994 SSI Modernization study made recommendations to raise the level of SSI benefits to 120 percent of the poverty level over five years and to increase resource limits from $2,000 to $7,000, the recommendations were shot down. Positive reform was made politically impossible by dis-information that equated entitlements with rampant fraud, fueling enough negative sentiment to turn the public against "welfare" in general. The trend has actually moved to cut back the meager SSI benefit amount. "Moderate" Republican Governor Pete Wilson in California, a rich state with the eighth largest economy in the world, has steadily chipped away at SSI and AFDC benefits. In 1995 he attempted to reduce benefits 4.9 percent for those living in high-rent areas and a whopping 9.6 percent for those in rural areas. Disability advocates in California decried that folks on SSI had adjusted to two meals a day from past cuts, and were Wilson to succeed they would be forced to choose between paying rent and utilities and eating.

Arianna Huffington, millionaire Republican, conservative opinion meister, and chairperson of the Center for Effective Compassion, says the SSI system should be "scrapped" and replaced with private charities.[13] Her belief in the morally driven philanthropy of the rich did not, however, bear up in her own experience. She and her husband tried donating private funds to start a benefit program for needy children when they lived in Santa Barbara, California, but could not sustain it. In a letter to the *Los Angeles Times* Henry Kramer from Santa Barbara wrote, "Even though the Huffingtons were generous and persuasive and had the ear of other prosperous people, their attempt to establish funds for needy children floundered. It did not outlive Mr. Huffington's senatorial campaign."

William Bennett, author of *The Book of Virtues*, cites an essay by Robert Rector, who claims that poor Americans live better than "the general population" in the democratic socialist countries of Europe, Bennett says, "[The poor in the U.S.] live in larger houses or apartments, eat more meat, and are more likely to own cars and dishwashers." These virtue gurus would have us believe that the American poor struggling to choose between food and shelter are well-off by the standards of other industrialized nations.

Are the poor in the U.S. living in larger or more adequate housing than the poor in social democratic countries? Affordable housing is hard to come by in the U.S. In most urban areas an entire month's SSI benefit will not cover a month's rent for a one-bedroom apartment. Federal housing has been in decline since 1992, and in addition, recent laws allow seniors-only federal housing that precludes young disabled people from living in their complexes. Getting a subsidized federal voucher can take up to sixteen years. Finding an accessible apartment in the private market and landlords who are willing to rent to disabled persons is tedious and difficult. Those lucky enough to have vouchers use up to one third of their SSI check towards rent. In high-rent areas like Los Angeles, some spend one week out of every month on the streets because benefits can't be stretched to cover housing and food for an entire month.

In Sweden, a democratic socialist country which Bennett would say is inferior to our less restrained capitalist nation, disabled people live in clean government housing, eat three meals a day, and are free to come and go. Disabled people don't have to be as poor as in the U.S. to receive housing assistance, because disability pensions are not counted against qualification for subsidized housing.[14] The Swedish government provides attendants, wheelchairs, and transportation as needed and maintains a humane universal health care system which focuses its cost-efficiency efforts on providing excellent preventive care.

What about the virtue gurus' common habit of connecting poverty (that we don't supposedly have) to an American unwillingness to work? When the U.S. is compared to other first world countries, we have the largest share of poor to rich, and the smallest middle class. The U.S. ranks first place in having the most poor, third place in having the most rich, and eighth in having the most middle class,[15] while Sweden has the fewest poor, ranks number one for having the most middle class, and has fewer grossly rich. Are the Swedes morally superior to Americans? Do they work harder and longer?

Sweden has higher unemployment yet maintains greater economic parity by redistributing far more than the U.S. does to boost all its citizens into economic security. A study by Jack McNeil of the U.S. Census Bureau which classifies groups according to earnings shows that in 1992, 22.7 percent or one fourth of the working population had an income under half the median. The poor work in America but are still poor.

A 1995 House Ways and Means Committee report found that the U.S. spent less on long-term disability benefits than Sweden, Germany, or the United Kingdom. That would indicate that the poverty of the disabled is due to government moral slackness. The U.S. is simply adept at being stingy when it comes to social spending and the virtue gurus are adept at victimizing the victims for outcomes attributable to public policy.

What the Swedes lack from the perspective of disability rights are civil rights to promote equality, access, and employment. But what is of great importance is that the underlying capitalist forces that control the social service system in the U.S. have been harnessed in Sweden by public sentiment, which is in agreement that all persons should have the benefit of public resources. The public good extends to the middle class in the form of child care, free university education, health care, vacations, and retirement benefits, and there is less resentment of public disability programs.

However, neither Swedish nor U.S. social service bureaucracies have dealt with disabled people's liberation. The medical model of disability, with its layers and layers of eligibility officers, social workers, administrators, medical professionals, and service employees in charge of policy design and implementation, prevails in both countries and runs counter to disabled people's empowerment. Both countries have all the paternalistic trappings of a civil service bureaucracy unaccountable to the citizens served.

LIVING UNDER THE SCREWS OF THE SYSTEM/ RISKY BUSINESS

What happens when disabled people want to work? Cartoonist John Callahan, author of *Don't Worry, He Won't Get Far on Foot*, found out when Social Security decided to kick him off the public dole.

Callahan, a quadriplegic, has an attendant provided through Oregon's Medicaid program. In order to remain eligible for his attendant, Callahan must remain eligible for Social Security (SS) disability. In 1991, anyone on disability benefits could not earn more than $300 (today it is $500) per month. But during one month of 1991 Callahan's paperwork showed that he had made over his $300 limit, triggering a termination of his benefits—including Medicaid. That termination came close to slamming him into an institution, ending his career, and dashing his hope for a decent life after disablement.

Medicaid paid his attendant about $1,200 a month, which Callahan would not be able to do on his own annual income of $7,400. For a quadriplegic, no attendant means imprisonment in a nursing home where, restricted to a "bed" area, he would not be drawing any more cartoons.

Callahan jokingly remarked that he might be compelled to become one of those beggars he draws holding out the tin cup that says, "Read George Bush's Lips." But then, he would have to become supercrip beggar number one to collect $1,200 for his attendant, another $500 for rent, plus food, utilities—about $2,200 a month— and still have enough to buy paper and ink to make cartoons in his "spare" time.

Contrary to volunteerism and Arianna Huffington's claim that charity can replace SSI, only the foolish would think private charity would come through on a shining horse with rent, food, an attendant to make Callahan's day. As it turned out, Callahan's income for the month that had severed him from his benefits was similar to all the previous months' income statements that had not terminated him. Callahan said that every time a new worker would be put on his case, they would make different determinations. It took an attorney who came through to sort out the paper trail, get credit for his overhead expenses, and get his benefits reinstated.

Building a career was supposed to be the point of the work plan that Callahan was on—to earn enough to wean off the system, something he greatly desired to accomplish. Who wouldn't?

Disabled people who try to make it on below-poverty "benefits" in America quickly realize that this is a dead-end street, as do single mothers on AFDC and others on welfare who want to get off. Charles Murray (*The Bell Curve*) would say poverty is the fault of the individual, not society. But it is not a matter, as Murray, the Republicans, and the neoliberal Democrats would have us believe, of taking "personal responsibility" for one's life, so often as it is a matter of being thwarted by convoluted policy, coupled with ineptitude, that punishes disabled people who do try to work, as in Callahan's case. Even if Callahan never makes enough to pay for all his expenses on his own, should he be thought a failure for not carrying the entire load? How many nondisabled people could afford to pay a personal assistant out of their paychecks?

John Callahan had the resources to fight the system; what happens to those who don't? Lynn Thompson, another quadriplegic living on SSI ($600 per month), tried to earn some extra money by stuffing envelopes at home. Unbeknownst to her, the work she did was in violation of SSI regulations. When she reported her income, Social Security responded that she had received an overpayment of $10,000, and that her benefits would be terminated until it was paid back. The Social Security Administration claimed that her MediCal and attendant benefits would also be cut off. Thompson didn't know that the SSA employees were wrong (as they so often are). Losing one's attendant is a ticket for a nursing home, but loss of MediCal is a death sentence. After a grueling and demeaning contest with SSA, Lynn Thompson killed herself. She left a recorded message saying that the reason for her suicide was that SSA had put her through hell and she could no longer live with the anxiety.[16]

Simply getting accurate information as to how work affects benefits can be a monumental task. One can call SSA several times and get a myriad of different answers to the same question; all answers can be wrong. The brutal truth is that the courts have held that SSA cannot be held accountable for dispensing inaccurate information. For disabled people living at below poverty with little savings, in need of public health care benefits, that risk is a work disincentive in and of itself.

Corporate government's legitimization of private insurance company underwriting practices is also a direct barrier to work. Insurance may exclude certain conditions or treatments from coverage, refuse to cover treatments for pre-existing conditions until six months or a year after enrollment, not cover the purchase of durable medical equipment such as power wheelchairs and respirators, or not cover attendant services.

Some of these concerns were to be addressed by the Portability and Accountability Act (the Kassebaum-Kennedy Bill), which is supposed to limit insurance companies' ability to discriminate against people with pre-existing conditions, but the bill allows insurers to exclude treatments for a twelve-month period. The Act was supposed to guarantee that people who have had health insurance for at least eighteen months can keep their health insurance if they lose or change jobs—regardless of their medical condition—but it imposes no limits on what insurers can charge. Associated Press reports that   insurers may be exploiting these loopholes. For instance, Kansas Insurance Commissioner Kathleen Sebelius told the House Ways and Means subcommittee that some insurers appear to be avoiding the law by telling employees that they will not get commissions for selling insurance to unhealthy people. According to Jay Angoff, director of the Missouri Department of Insurance, "We get reports of companies charging 500 percent of standard prices."[17]

Disabled people have forever been faced with these cherry-picking and high-rate practices of the private insurance juggernaut. Often a disabled person is locked into an economic straitjacket and out of the workforce by insurance exclusions and affordability: much-needed care becomes obtainable only through a public insurance program, such as Medicaid or Medicare, which imposes eligibility work restrictions and limits earned income.

In 1993 legislators made changes in SSA rules to make work "more attractive" for disabled people. These "work incentives" are so complex that in some cases SSA employees are not informing people of their work options or are turning down completely legitimate work plans because the employees haven't been trained to apply the regulations correctly. This kind of bureaucratic incompetence means that disabled citizens find themselves in receipt of incorrect letters of benefits termination, appearing before an Administrative Law Judge to resolve problems, or embroiled in appeals. Most recently SSA has attempted to scrap the Plan for Achieving Self-Support (PASS) program entirely.

Other dangers lurk in the world of work. Russell Redenbaugh of the Civil Rights Commission explains, "If a disabled person loses the medical benefits because of a job and then loses the job, reclaiming the benefits can take as long as two years. Not only that but there is a presumption that since you were working you must not be disabled at all."[18]

Take the case of Dr. Caplan, reported in the *New York Times*. Dr. Caplan became an amputee (leg aputated at the hip) in his fifties, yet continued his small medical practice until he was no longer able to get to his office. But unbeknownst to Dr. Caplan, he made the mistake of working three months too long.

Social Security Administration rules say that if a person who has been on disability insurance returns to work, s/he has a total of four years in which to decide if working with the disability is too difficult. If so, s/he can quit a job and reclaim benefits. But if s/he doesn't stop working by then, the federal government considers a person unhindered by the disability and therefore ineligible for benefits.

Dr. Caplan worked three months past this limit, so SSA informed him by letter that he was not entitled to the payments he had received; he had to pay back $24,813.90. In addition, being severed from disability meant severance from Medicare. He would have to reapply for disability benefits and would not have any health insurance until he requalified and met the 2-year "waiting period" for Medicare.[19]

WORK AS GOD

Just what does "disabled" mean? Social Security defines it as a condition which makes one unable to engage in any "substantial gainful activity" i.e., unable to work at any job for a period of twelve months.[20] This definition causes confusion today in light of the disability civil rights movement's foray into the world of work. Activists contend that disability oppression is about discrimination and lack of access. Since society grants status based on work, being able to work is a way to move beyond dehumanization. While the promotion of employment for disabled people is badly needed to counter inaccurate assumptions about disability, some go so far as to say that if barriers were removed and reasonable accommodations provided in the workplace, all disabled people could work. However, it is simply a gross overstatement to claim that all can work. Many on the rolls (if not most—we don't know) are disabled in accord with the Social Security definition and cannot physically, mentally or emotionally meet the demands of an eight-, four- or even two- hour work day.

Some say "You can't have it both ways," meaning you can't have the right to employment and the right to benefits because they are contradictory paradigms. In this view, all disabled must be mainstreamed into the workforce and into society, making disability unremarkable and thereby diminishing the difficulties associated with minority status. But we need to look at reality, not agenda-based rhetoric. In reality, there are disabled people who do work, there are disabled people who can work but are prevented from doing so for various reasons, and there are those who cannot work. It is discrimination to deny a disabled person who can work an opportunity to do so, but it is not "special" treatment for people who cannot work to be guaranteed a humane standard of living—rather it is a measure of a just civilization that they are decently provided for.

Others say such provisions would encourage people to claim they are disabled, essentially disempowering and discouraging citizens from taking "personal responsibility." In part, this is a struggle between opposing views of human nature, between those who believe that people want to be productive and engaged members of society (even if that doesn't include work in the narrow sense of contributing to corporate profits) and those who believe that people are fundamentally lazy and must be disciplined at all costs to work hard. The latter rationale is driven by a fear of losing control of the means of production. We in America have come to equate morality with financial productivity and immorality with laziness or non-productivity. Unfortunately, these equations don't derive from the intrinsic "good" or "bad" in either, but rather from the owning class drive to exploit labor for profit. The all-encompassing value placed on work is necessary to produce wealth. The American work ethic is a social control which ensures capitalists a reliable work force for making profits. American business retains its power over the working-class labor force through a fear of destitution which would be weakened if the safety net were to actually become safe.

In the humanist view, work is not the defining quality of our worth. Employability and aptitude for earning money are not the measure of what it means to live, to be a part of the human race. The goal of social justice is to ensure the dignity of each and every person. To buy into the capitalist propaganda that work is god, that people are laborers first and human beings second, serves only to oppress us all.

WRESTLING OUT OF THE ECONOMIC STRAITJACKET

We have only to look at social democracies like Sweden to see how punitive our system is and how badly America fails to meet the basic needs of its citizens. But just looking won't bring us the social justice we seek. The difference between Sweden and our country is that there was a class war that produced the system the Swedes have. The difference between a humane system and a punitive one hinges not on some cultural ability to see the light but on the struggle for social change.

We need to stop government from allowing insurance companies to cherry-pick and shift "non-profitable" people onto the public system. The business lobby, for example, won passage of a law, (USC 42 1395 y (b)), which allows private insurers and employers to rid themselves of their disabled retirees by dumping them onto Medicare. Such a requirement alone would bring down the insurance industry, since its profits have been largely assured by denying coverage to high-risk individuals and costly patients. A unifying public health care system designed to meet the needs of disabled and nondisabled, de-linked from employment, would also serve to erase many work barriers.

The social policy dynamic—that capitalists must be served by public policy—is behind all our social legislation. The real "chiselers" are businesses looking to exploit labor and prevent government from promoting the general welfare. As a consequence, with rare exception, American social welfare remains compromised, more punitive than just. It is time to stop government from "defending the rich against the poor." The political challenge upon us is the reaffirmation of the social contract and the strengthening of its legislative manifestations in the face of attacks by the austerity rollback forces.

CHAPTER 7

FROM TINY TIM TO JERRY LEWIS

CHARITY AND ECONOMIC RIGHTS ON A COLLISION COURSE

The rich have given to the poor a little food, a little drink, a little shelter and a few clothes. The poor have given to the rich palaces and yachts, and an almost infinite freedom to indulge their doubtful taste for display, and bonuses and excess profits, under which cold and forbidding terms have been hidden the excess labor and extravagant misery of the poor.

—Gilbert Seldes

The U.S. social safety net falls vastly short of humanely aiding those at the bottom of the socio-economic ladder. Large numbers of people remain unemployed, underemployed, and in poverty because our economic system perpetuates high unemployment and the corporate drive for high profits demands low wages. How would the elite address the needs of the "surplus" population, those for whom there are no jobs, those who cannot work, those who work at poverty wages, and those who have no health care? Rather than building a social contract that would provide health care for all and lift everyone to a decent standard of living, the elite would have Americans rely on private sector charity to "help the poor."

What's wrong with charity? Under the best of circumstances, charity becomes oppressive when it is used to buoy inequality, to benefit those "offering" aid, and to mask the greed that forestalls the establishment of economic justice. The mechanics of oppression are in full gear within the Muscular Dystrophy Association (MDA) cure charity, and can be used to illustrate that the charity "solution" really isn't a solution at all.

"HALF A PERSON" TARNISHES DISABLED

"As good as gold," said Bob, "and better. . . He [Tiny Tim] told me, coming home, that he hoped the people saw him in the church, because he was a cripple, and it might be pleasant to them to remember upon Christmas Day, who made lame beggars walk and blind men see." So wrote Charles Dickens in *A Christmas Carol*.

The stereotypical images of "cripples" as patient, saintly Tiny Tims waiting for God to take them home, or as totally distraught inferiors waiting for someone—or some charitable organization—to cure us, have contributed greatly to the oppression of disabled people. In either case, disabled people are good for one thing—to assuage consciences by being the object of charitable pity.

Hey, that's being useful!—for the charities that profit from disablement. The Muscular Dystrophy Association knows Tiny Tim is "as good as gold." The pity ploy theme, the hallmark of the cure charity telethon, has turned the MDA into a multi-million dollar nonprofit corporation that can afford to pay its top executive $384,000 a year with fringe benefits, deliver a bonus, build a plush new facility in Arizona, cover all of host Jerry Lewis's expenses, and have enough left over to keep some seventy vice-presidents on board.

In the same decade that the Americans with Disabilities Act acknowledges that disabled people are a target of widespread discrimination, Jerry Lewis perpetuates outdated images of disabled persons as leading tragic lives, as homebound victims waiting for cures. Fantasizing about what life would be like if he were disabled, Lewis told *Parade* magazine, "I realize my life is half, so I must learn to do things half way. I must have to learn to try to be good at being *half a person* [italics mine]."[1] What is Lewis's message? There is no life without a cure; disabled people are not capable of working, raising children, or participating in the majority culture in any "whole" sense. Lewis's exhibitions perpetuate the damaging myth that our disabled "half" lives are not worth living.

Lewis was further quoted, "I would put myself in that chair, that *steel imprisonment* that long has been deemed the dystrophic child's plight [italics mine]." To disabled people, the wheelchair is no imprisonment, it means liberty and freedom of movement, it enables us to participate in the majority society. And when Lewis refers to all people with MD as "Jerry's kids," including full-grown adults, how can anyone miss the paternalism? Disabled people do not want to be called "kids" any more than a black man wants to be called "boy."

Disability activists explain that Lewis's tactics tarnish all disabled people. Who is going to hire "half a person"? These paternalistic pity-parade telethons so focused on "cures" sabotage the dignity of the disabled and our acceptance as social equals. These two opposing images of disability, the charity model and the civil rights model, are on a collision course. While disabled people are intent on gaining dignity and equality, Lewis and other charities want to keep us back in Dickens's 19th century.

NOW COME THE UNGRATEFUL CRIPS

Dickens's ever-grateful Tiny Tim character (the orignal poster boy) sets the tone for the behavior of the proper "cripple" who must say, "Thank you, thank you, thank you" for what nondisabled people choose to give. The ungrateful crips, the activists, have gone public to stop the damaging misinformation transmitted to the 250 million viewers of the annual MDA telethon.

- Evan Kemp, former chair of the Equal Employment Opportunity Commission, who has a neuro-muscular condition, wrote in the *New York Times* that society sees disabled people as "helpless, hopeless, nonfunctioning and non-contributing members of society...the Jerry Lewis Muscular Dystrophy Association Telethon with its pity approach to fundraising, has contributed to these prejudices."[2]

- Chris Matthews, a former poster child, wrote to MDA that it was "expert in exploiting the worst side of disability and, with the eager assistance of Lewis, has made us out to be nothing more than pathetic burdens to society, whose only desire is to walk."

- Jerry's Orphans, an anti-telethon group spearheaded by Mike Ervin and Chris Matthews, went on *60 Minutes* to protest Lewis's fundraising tactics.

- Protests (some lasting the length of Lewis's telethon air time) have been ongoing in Los Angeles, Denver, Chicago, Austin, Boston, Nashville, Atlanta, San Francisco, Detroit, Louisville, and other cities for about seven years.

• In an open letter to Lewis called "The Disabled Need Dignity, Not Pity," Harvard graduate and new father Ben Mattlin described his poster boy experience:

> When I was about six years old, I was in a full-page magazine ad for the MDA: big blue eyes peeking though blond curls. The caption read, "If I grow up, I want to be a fireman." I didn't want to be a fireman, and knew then my diagnosis called for a normal life expectancy. Confused, I decided that I wasn't really one of "them" and denied a part of my identity, my connection to the only community where I could learn to feel good about my disability. I didn't know the word "exploitation" yet.[3]

False projections of death and physicalist attitudes are prevalent on the MDA telethon. Encouraged by the on-stage interviewers, the typical parent of a child who uses a wheelchair will usually express the unrelenting sentiment that "I want my kids to run, to jump, to play." Parents who join the MDA in placing so much importance on their children *not* being able to perform these physical acts are essentially saying that their children are what sociologist Erving Goffman has termed "failed normals." The children are getting the message that they are less than OK, that somehow they are a tremendous disappointment and a problem to their family—because they use a wheelchair.

It was interesting to listen to the children (when they were allowed to say something), because they did not reflect the same prejudices as the parents. One particularly offensive interviewer recently asked a young boy, "Ben, is it getting harder for you now that the time is coming?" She meant now that he was getting closer to death (had someone told her this?). Ben sat silent and dignified on the couch, while his father interceded with a reply. But this interviewer did not give up. She asked again, "Benjamin, is it getting harder for you? Does it hurt?" Ben looked at her questioningly and honestly answered, "No, not really." How damaging is it for a child to hear that these adults think they may die any day when, as in Ben Mattlin's earlier case, this is often false projection and many will have average lifespans?

The use of disabled children on the telethon is uncomfortably close to emotional child abuse. Some say you can't make money on a telethon without using the pity ploy. To this we must answer "No, thank you," and replace telethons with universal social policy that promotes dignity and enhances life.

CIVIL RIGHTS' HEAD-ON COLLISION
WITH CHARITY MENTALITY

Michael Winter and his wife discovered in 1995 that they could not get in the front door of the Planet Hollywood restaurant because there was no ramp. Staff led the Winters to the waiters' entrance and through the kitchen. "It was humiliating and demeaning to be sent to a separate and exceedingly unequal entrance simply because Planet Hollywood couldn't be bothered to comply with the ADA," Winter said. "I ended up with food and garbage in the treads of my wheelchair for hours after."[4]

Ironically, Planet Hollywood, one of the sponsors of the 1995 MDA telethon, was not accessible to those it purported to "help." It was willing to raise money to "help the cripples" but the owners are not willing to take our civil rights seriously. How could the owners—which include Sylvester Stallone, Demi Moore, Bruce Willis, and Arnold Schwarzenegger—claim an "undue hardship" exemption from the ADA accessibility regulations; how could they claim to be unable to afford to build a ramp over three steps?

Leslie Bennetts interviewed Jerry Lewis for *Vanity Fair* and confronted him with disabled activists' concerns about the telethon. Bennetts reported that when Lewis was asked if he thought his detractors made any valid points, he adamantly responded, "Fuck them," then told her to "Do it in caps. FUCK THEM." Bennetts described Lewis's reaction as "so hostile and paranoid it seems almost Nixonian." Lewis told Bennetts, "If you do anything to hurt my kids I'll have you killed, you understand?"[5]

Some of Lewis's supporters react the same way. In 1992 when protestors symbolically blockaded the gates to KTLA in Los Angeles (leaving one back entrance open to get in and out), a group of bikers decided that they would not go around to the open entrance. Screaming profanities at some fifteen people assembled peacefully in wheelchairs, the bikers charged. The *Los Angeles Times* reported that one woman was knocked out of her wheelchair by the bikers.[6] As one biker angrily crashed our demonstrators the hot exhaust pipes came dangerously close to burning my legs. To challenge the charity mentality is to risk collision with those who know little about disability but are filled with self-righteousness.

WHO BENEFITS FROM THE "BENEFITS"?

The question begging to be asked is, who really benefits from the charity business? Research reveals that little of the money donated to MDA is acutally spent on direct services or equipment that would assist disabled people in their daily lives. Bill Bolt reported in *In These Times* that:

> MDA does not provide the equipment needed to live independently —or, in some cases, to live at all. It does not provide respirators. It does not provide power beds. It does not buy computers, ramps, living-space access modifications, lifts for vans or vans themselves. It refuses to buy power wheelchairs for those not in school or not working—often the more severely disabled who really need a power wheelchair.[7]

So where does the money go? Bolt writes, "The facts are pretty shocking. The Annual Jerry Lewis Muscular Dystrophy Association Telethon raises more than $40 million dollars while MDA brings in a total of more than $100 million each year. Yet, according to the MDA's 1991 annual report, only one MDA dollar in six goes to research awards, grants and fellowships." Bolt further reports, "Another sixth of MDA revenues goes to services purchased for the disabled. The remainder of donations go to overhead, including more than $31 million in salaries, fringes and payroll taxes."

Paul Aziz of *Moving Forward* writes:

> The MDA annual report for '91 shows a total of $102 million in revenue from the public. Of that amount, $50 million was spent on "patient services." But the figures are deceiving, because it sounds like the patients are getting half the money the MDA is bringing in.

That is not exactly the case. In their report, only $28 million actually goes to the patients, the remainder of approximately $22 million is spent on salaries, payroll taxes, travel, lodging, office supplies, postage, contract and professional services and other miscellaneous expenses.[8]

When Aziz made several requests for a breakdown of the $28 million going to patients, MDA did not provide it.

The *Disability Rag* reported that more than $800,000 of the first million raised by MDA goes to the top five corporate officers. According to the *Chronicle of Philanthropy*, MDA executive director Robert Ross's 1992 salary was the highest in the "health" category of the not-for-profit organizations—$300,000 per year.[9]

Dianne Piastro, author of the syndicated column "Living with a Disability," asked the director of finance at MDA, "Who used the travel money and what type of travel did they do for the $6.9 million spent in 1990?"[10] Piastro said that MDA did not respond to these questions and failed to supply their tax returns; consequently, she had to file a complaint to get what is supposed to be on file and easily attainable public information.

In fact, charities often do more for *non*disabled people. They hire nondisabled employees, appoint nondisabled people to their boards, and contract with nondisabled service organizations who don't employ disabled people. Charities are supposedly set up to do "for" disabled people; in reality they are hierarchies of power in which the socio-economic status quo is perpetuated, with disabled people on the bottom.

Keeping the money and power out of the hands of those "served" and in the hands of the charity's bureaucrats seems to be an MDA priority, evidenced by a series of vitriolic responses to criticisms from disabled activists. Executive director Robert Ross wrote to Dianne Piastro, "We intend to take legal action against Ms. Piastro and her syndicator," and as a result many newspapers felt pressured not to publish her columns even though in the end MDA filed no lawsuit. When Evan Kemp criticized Jerry Lewis's money-raising tactics, Lewis wrote to President Bush accusing Kemp of "misusing the power of his governmental office" (then chair of the EEOC). Activists believed MDA hoped to get Kemp fired. In another instance, MDA threatened to hold Chris Matthews, co-founder of Jerry's Orphans, "personally and financially responsible for any and all losses" that might result from her publicly expressed opinions.

Clearly MDA does not work in partnership with the disabled and therefore can neither meet their clients' needs nor effectively contribute to national disability policy. Would changing the hierarchy solve the inequities? What if charities were forced to appoint disabled people—or members of any group served—to a majority on their boards? Some believe that those affected should make the decisions and set the policies and if they do not, then the tax-exempt status of the charitable organization should be lost. Their hope is that disabled people would direct the organizations to educate and empower disabled people. But despite entitlement-slashing rhetoric, *charities can never build an egalitarian society, simply because they arbitrarily pick and choose whom to serve. No one is entitled to anything from a charity*, rather one must be designated a "deserving" case. Anyone can be denied access to services at any time for any reason. That is not reliable assistance and it is not justice for all.

The Corporate Connection

The corporations that contract with MDA also benefit from the charity business. Since MDA itself is not in the business of health care or research, the dollars raised go to subcontractors: universities, medical providers, equipment companies, social service agencies, and other existing businesses. In 1991, nine million dollars went to "non-medical contract services and professional fees" alone. MDA is an empire that has been built around contracting services, and these businesses have a vested interest in seeing that MDA remains around year after year to renew those contracts.

The Alliance for Research Accountability in Los Angeles, critical of MDA profiteering, writes, "Forty-six years and hundreds of millions of dollars worth of [MDA] research have resulted in nothing but profits for drug companies and research labs. Hundreds, if not thousands, of children have been subjected to futile and dangerous experiments with nothing to show for it beyond giving steroids and immune suppressants for children."[11]

Anyone watching the telethon can see that businesses get a lot of TV advertising for the dollars they donate to MDA. Time and time again corporate representatives are called on stage by Lewis to deliver their checks. The name of each company is prominently placed in the background so viewers cannot possibly miss the connection. Often one donation will be split into several checks so executives come onto the stage several times to mete out their donation one piece at a time—garnering more advertising time.

BUSTING ALTRUISM: BENEFITS TO THE RICH

Dickens's ghost tells Scrooge, "If man you be in heart, not adamant, forbear that wicked cant until you have discovered What the surplus is, and Where it is. Will you decide what men shall live, what men shall die?" In both Dickens's story and the MDA telethon plot, the disabled child [surplus population] will die unless the haves donate money. In the end, Scrooge feels better about himself because he raises the father's salary and Tiny Tim's health improves because he is no longer undernourished. A Christmas Carol uses disability to wrench the hearts of the miserly but in the end it is the rich who retain control; they can be generous or they can be stingy, but Dickens leaves no doubt that in nineteenth century capitalist England, the vast majority of the poor and disabled were left to misery and squalor. Similarly, while the Tiny Tim tin cups rattle on the MDA telethon stage, the underlying social issues—poverty and a lack of entitlement to the necessities, like universal health care and living wage employment, that enable a quality life—are not addressed.

The charity system protects the privileged rich who, by donating tax-deductible dollars, appear to be generously concerned about the plight of the poor. However, their "solution" actually serves to keep the wealth, resources, and power in the hands of the few. Left Business Observer points out that:

> Altruism was rarely the motivating factor in establishing the large independent foundations—ones like Pew, Ford, MacArthur, Robert Wood Johnson that every NPR listener can name. The Ford Foundation was established to help keep the company in the family without paying estate taxes. John D. MacArthur, founder of Bankers Life and Casualty Company, never made any significant charitable contributions during his lifetime, but left his estate of nearly $1 bil-

lion to a foundation rather than to his estranged children. One of the trusts founded by the Sun Oil heirs, the J. Howard Pew Freedom Trust, was established to "acquaint the American people with the evils of bureaucracy...and with the values of a free market...to point out the false promises of Socialism..."[12]

"Nonprofits" also include "educational" organizations like the Kennesaw State College Foundation, which is under investigation for appearing to be a conduit for tax-deductible funds for Newt Gingrich's "Renewing American Civilization" college course, the stated goal of which was to "unseat the Democratic majority in the House."

In addition to serving as fronts for political agendas, nonprofits can create an illusion that they are mending the holes in our social fabric, when behind the benevolent front there is an enormous hoarding of wealth. *LBO* editor Doug Henwood observes, "In economic terms, the larger nonprofits could be thought of as giant stock portfolios, often with marketing operations grafted on." For instance, in 1992, the nonprofits held $1 trillion in financial assets. Nonprofits are managed independently, primarily by the wealthy elite, but they do not pay taxes. In 1991 the nonprofit revenue was $615 billion, or 11 percent of the Gross Domestic Product, none of which was taxed. Forty-two percent of "nonprofit" money is in stocks and 25 percent is in bonds, which means that the nonprofits also have a significant impact on Wall Street.[13]

Because donors to charities are entitled to a tax deduction, roughly one third of every dollar donated is subsidized by the federal government. That means public revenue which could be going to public welfare is lost to nonprofits. Gregory Colvin, an attorney specializing in tax law writes, "...$1.5 million raised and spent through the Kennesaw State College Foundation...could translate into a Treasury loss of about $500,000 in tax savings by Gingrich's donors."[14]

Arianna Huffington, a constituent of the right-wing Progress and Freedom Foundation, understands this connection. She would have those public tax dollars go into her nonprofit instead. She states, "We are targeting those who think taxes can take care of compassion and ask them to volunteer and to give money [to her Center for Effective Compassion]."[15] Huffington gets it. The law lets rich folks donate stocks to their own foundations, then deduct from income the current stock value, totally avoiding capital gains taxes in the process. Her nonprofit increases her ability (her husband is worth over $25 million) to invest on Wall Street and she determines how the profits are spent.

Jerry Lewis understands the Wall Street connection. When Kemp and other activists criticized MDA, Lewis told then-President Bush to "act to protect and preserve the invaluable American private-sector institution. . .with a categorical disavowal of Mr. Kemp's assault on MDA."[16]

However, the nonprofits, especially the charities, are rarely challenged. As James Cook put it in *Forbes* magazine, "Most Americans are astonishingly indifferent to how effectively charitable organizations use the money that comes their way. As they tend to see it, the righteousness of their cause assures the integrity of their conduct, and anyone who suggest otherwise had better watch out."[17]

At best, charities postpone societal questions about economic equality. At worst, charities serve as self-serving tax shields and allow right-wing ideologues like Newt Gingrich and Arianna Huffington to assault the "socialist" safety net while claiming that private charities will pick up the pieces. In the process the U.S. Treasury is robbed of dollars that could be put to entitlement programs. Charity, as we know it, is nothing less than an attempt to justify capitalism's inherent injustices, which makes it a euphemism for economic oppression.

ENTITLEMENT V. CHARITY: THE 20TH CENTURY BEGGARS

Laura Hershey, former poster child and a disability rights activist who initiated the "Tune Jerry Out" campaign, explains that a shift in thinking about disability is what is called for:

> The disability rights approach views disability as a natural phenomenon which occurs in every generation, and always will. It recognizes people with disabilities as a distinct minority group, subject at times to discrimination and segregation . . . but also capable of taking our rightful place in society.[18]

We need solutions which address reality. The scapegoating of vulnerable populations as costly consumers of tax dollars is reprehensible, and essentially false. The public resources that are distributed to the impoverished and disabled are redistributed in the community— to the pharmaceutical corporations, to the landlords, to the grocery store chains, to the utility companies. The argument that disabled people consume an inordinate amount of our social resources is similarly false; 80 percent of the world's resources are consumed by the wealthiest people.

Why do we still have twentieth century beggars like Jerry Lewis in a so-called civilized nation? The answers lie within the nature of capitalism itself. There is more profit to be made in the construction and equipping of national charity empires than in making public policy fill in the missing gaps. The advertising and contracting opportunities offered by an MDA telethon are more attractive to corporations who can afford the ante of a donation than the wider-spread universal benefit of increases in disability and welfare disbursements.

Just as in Dickens's time, we have not interwoven disability and poverty into the fabric of socio/economic policy so that entitlements replace begging, civil rights replace bigotry, and social justice replaces inequity. The nation needs to eliminate tax-free charity status and return the lost revenues to a democratic government to redistribute wealth in a democratic manner. That, afterall, is what constitutional "promoting the general welfare" is all about. Private and nonprofit charities doling out arbitrary services must be replaced with a sound disability-sensitive universal health care system that allows all citizens to live with dignity, and we must insist on a guaranteed income floor that leaves no one undernourished. Strengthening the social contract means recognizing its deficiences and making health care and sustenance economic rights, not luxuries. The reality is that neither Scrooge nor the disingenuous "thousand points of light" neo-liberal "volunteerism" will be the solution; the public wealth must be distributed more responsibly and a democratic government must be held to the task.

CHAPTER 8

THE FINAL (PROFITABLE) SOLUTION

MODERN INSTITUTIONALIZATION AND THE COMMODIFICATION OF DISABILITY

Nobody wants to go into a nursing home. That should tell us something . . .

—Wade Blank, co-founder of ADAPT

The truth has always been dangerous to the rule of the rogue, the exploiter, the robber. So the truth must be suppressed.

—Eugene Debs

The question for the entreprenuerial nation remained, what to do with the "unproductive," those not exploitable as laborers? And ultimately, how can disabled people be made of use to the economic order? The solution has been to make disablement big business.

Under the Money Model of disability, the disabled human being is a commodity around which social policies are created or rejected based on their market value. The corporate "solution" to disablement—institutionalization in a nursing home—evolved from the cold realization that disabled people could be commodified; we could be made to serve profit because federal financing (Medicaid funds 60 percent, Medicare 15 percent, private insurance 25 percent) guarantees an endless source of revenue. Disabled people are "worth" more to the Gross Domestic Product when we occupy a "bed" instead of a home. When we individually generate $30,000-$82,000 in annual revenues, the electronic brokers on Wall Street count us as assets and we contribute to companies' net worth. The "final solution"—corporate dominion over disability policy—measures a person's "worth" by its dollar value to the economy.

In order to optimize profits, the nursing home industry must maintain control over the lives of the disabled. Our current public policy predicament is an acknowledgement that the Money Model is well in place—but the prisoners of profit are intent upon revolt.

THE JAIL BREAK

Wade Blank, co-founder of ADAPT, Americans Disabled for Attendant Programs Today, began his long career as a disability advocate while he was employed by a Denver, Colorado, nursing home to set up a ward for young disabled people. His short-lived nursing home career fell within the years when legislatures were ending the old form of institutionalization by closing the doors of state institutions for the disabled, and nursing homes were finding that housing the displaced individuals could be very profitable.

The old sort, well documented by Wolf Wolfensberger in *The Origin and Nature of Our Institutional Models*, ran the gamut on social "solutions" for disability. Wolfensberger traces the original societal goals of institutions for mentally disabled people: first the professional's goal was to make the "deviant" un-deviant through behavior modification; that gave way to sheltering the deviant from society by isolation; and next, the goal was to protect society from the deviant through inexpensive warehousing, segregation, and sterilization. But eventually experience and research led professionals to a loss of rationale for all of the above practices. Wolfensberger concluded, "Today, of course, we know that most retarded adults make an adequate adjustment in the community, and that they are more likely to be the victims rather than the perpetrators of social injustice."[1] The experts realized that "deviance" was largely a social construct.

Disability historian Dr. Paul Longmore explains that the first widely held view of physical disability is the "moral model;" that is, society believed that disablement was a "deviance," caused by a lack of moral character or intervening supernatural forces, in any case, dangerous to society. The next historical view is the medical model—that disability is biological by nature but must be controlled by curing the "defects"—and resulted in medical and paternalistic social intervention such as sterilization, segregation, and institutionalization.[2]

The modern-day institution, the nursing home, made no deluded claim to "cure" or "protect" society from disabled people, rather the nursing home "solution" to disablement evolved from the cold realization that disabled people could be commodified; Medicaid providing an endless stream of cash.

When the state began unloading disabled people from its warehouses in the 1970s, many of the young "patients" were shifted into nursing homes for the elderly. Blank, sensitive to the displacement of disabled youths, first attempted to "reform" the nursing home so that people could have stereos, a pet, and some privacy amongst the dying and elderly. But Blank, being a witness to the emotional and physical abuse that the disabled suffered at the hands of the nursing home management (portrayed in the movie based on Blank's experience "When You Remember Me"), and being a veteran of the civil rights movement, knew that self-determination for these kids could never be accomplished in a nursing home environment. Activist Laura Hershey explains:

> In 1975, Blank proposed [to the nursing home he worked for] "that we move a few of them out into apartments, and we let the aides and orderlies punch in at the nursing home, then go to the apartment and give them service." That idea got Blank fired. "The nursing home saw where I was going, and they couldn't let me go in that direction."[3]

Where Blank was going was past "reform." He proposed to emancipate disabled people entirely from the nursing home by moving them into the community. Blank wisely saw that the disability movement must go beyond the independent living concept to "dismantle the plantation"—the nursing home plantations that routinely acquired disabled bodies and held them against their will—the root of institutionalized oppression. But the nursing home saw clearly that Blank's plan was counterproductive to its primary purpose. If people were to live in the community with attendants, Medicaid money would be going outside the nursing home. The fact that disabled people's freedom would cost the nursing home a loss of income proved to be the dividing line between Blank and his employer, and it is the dividing line between disabled people and the nursing home corporate complex today .

THE REBELLION

ADAPT protests and educates Americans about the inhumane, abusive, and imprisonment-like treatment disabled and elderly people have received in the so-called "protective" care of nursing homes. Those who have done time in nursing homes have exposed the rat-infested rooms, witnessed maggots crawling in open wounds, and counted the days inmates have lain neglected in feces.

Unnecessary decubitis ulcers, bladder infections, and respiratory infections have been tied to incompetent nursing home care. Investigations have exposed overdrugging of residents (sometimes slipped into the ice cream), the use of straps and shackles to restrain the inmates, and the physical and emotional abuse disabled people suffer in the hands of professionals. Activists have protested the rapes of disabled women, while these businesses try to hide "patient" abortions and sterilization from public scrutiny and offenders (often staff) go scot-free. Indeed the numerous stories of maltreatment have shown that neglect is a given in these "care-giving" institutions—requiring hospitalization to cure what the nursing home caused. Where is the "nursing" in that?

On the march with ADAPT, stories of physical and mental abuse behind the nursing home walls abound. Alan Gribos, a quadriplegic inmate whose simple night-time spasms resulted in a decubitis ulcer that ended up in the amputation of his heel told *New Mobility* magazine, "They were mainly interested in the $2,500 the Veterans Administration was paying them to house me each month. No one on the staff knew or cared about spinal cord injury and they didn't want to learn."[4]

It is not uncommon to hear of instances where those trapped inside these ghettos of care come to view suicide as the only out. John from Philadelphia, who wishes his last name kept private, recounted how one friend of his "saved up his sedatives each day until there were enough to do the job" because he was often "struck by staff and got tired of the tranquilizing, tired of being treated like a child, tired of the restraints."

The disability press has long condemned institutional entrapment where residents' rights and due process of law mean very little, crimes committed often go unpunished, and negligent practices remain unrectified. It has exposed the nasty little secret that fear and retribution lie behind these "safe" institutional walls. "Complain and you will suffer the consequences," writes Victoria Medgyesi for the *Disability Rag*.[5]

Disabled people aren't the only ones documenting the abuses. *Consumer Reports'* Trudy Leiberman conducted an investigation of nursing homes that led her to conclude that these "homes" range from inadequate to scandalous. Leiberman reports that about 40 percent of all facilities certified by the Health Care Financing Administration (part of the Department of U.S. Health and Human Services) have repeatedly violated federal standards, including critical aspects of patient care standards.[6]

The California Advocates for Nursing Home Reform (CANHR) reported that in 1993 alone 58 percent—over half—of California nursing homes were cited for violations. They received 1,515 citations and were levied $3.8 million in fines for violating state and federal regulations. They were issued 32,720 deficiency notices, averaging 22.9 per California facility. Facilities were issued 186 citations for verbal and physical abuse, with another twenty-three citations for sexual abuse. Fifty-two percent of California nursing homes received deficiency notices for failing to promote care that enhances dignity.[7]

Governor Wilson's office, in response to the federal inspectors being sent into California to uncover just such violations, called it "outrageous" that Washington "would deploy an army that sounds like the size of Operation Desert Storm" to inspect the state's nursing homes.[8] It seems that the federal government did not send an "army" large enough, because in 1995 the use of physical and chemical restraints increased dramatically. CANHR reported that 29,652 residents were physically restrained, another 32,103 were administered psychotropic medications, and chemical restraint use jumped 12 percent over 1994. These documented violations directly resulted in 19 deaths and indirectly in another 45 deaths.[9] These figures need to be viewed as the tip of the proverbial iceberg; many residents are uneducated as to their rights, many have no idea how to go about securing those rights, and many fear to make a complaint.

The de-institutionalization side of the disability movement focuses on the struggle for freedom: the freedom to choose where to live, how to live, and with whom. The most severely disabled are found on these front lines. Their motto is, "We'd rather die than go into a nursing home." Ironically, this movement is also about being safe from the "care-giving" industry.

The anti-institutionalization movement sees expanding the availability of community-based personal assistance services (PAS) as the solution to maximizing independence. PAS (not to be confused with home care provided by health care conglomerates) makes it possible for disabled people to live at home and participate in the life of their communities. ADAPT seeks a national PAS program that would be funded by redirecting 25 percent of the Medicaid dollars allocated to nursing homes, currently at $36.9 billion, to in-home care. Activists make the case that PAS, aside from being preferred by disabled citizens and increasingly by the senior population as well, makes better fiscal sense. The national average annual cost to house one aging and/or disabled American in a nursing home is $40,784, while the national average cost to provide Medicaid PAS is $9,692; the cost to house one person in a state institution for persons with developmental disabilities is $82,228, while the cost drops to $27, 649 to live at home with support services; the cost to house one American in a mental institution is $58,569, while the cost to provide community supports is $1,693; the cost to house one disabled veteran in a VA nursing home is $75,641, while the cost to provide services at home is $8,132.[10]

Public policy, however, is aligned with the nursing homes. For instance, government adjustments to the Social Security Act in the 1970s mandated states to provide nursing home care as an entitlement, but allowed PAS to remain optional under Medicaid. This bias in favor of institutionalization results in a patchy system where some states choose to provide PAS while others do not, some grossly underfund PAS, and some limit the number of people served. With no national entitlement, disabled people's freedom is annually at risk because PAS programs are subject to each state's budget axe, while nursing homes are guaranteed reimbursement.

ADAPT demonstates against institutionalization wherever the lobbying arm of the nursing home industry, the American Health Care Association, meets. Civil disobedience actions have resulted in massive arrests and publicity in cities all over the nation—Atlanta, Chicago, Orlando, Las Vegas, San Franciso, Nashville, and Houston. Recalcitrant former Health and Human Services Secretary Louis Sullivan (under the Bush adminsitration) was a target of ADAPT actions and President Clinton's Secretary, Donna Shalala, has been approached—yet the bias towards institutionalized care remains in place. Why the resistance to changing policy when the consensus among disabled citizens is for PAS in the home?

The answer is as horrible as institutional abuse and neglect: society sanctions profiteering on disablement. Eighty-eight percent of the nursing homes in California are for-profit corporations; they exist to make their shareholders money and they will cut corners of care to be "efficient" money-making machines. In spite of the cited abuses and confirmed substandard care in 1995, California spent 1.9 billion Medicaid dollars on nursing home reimbursements. Why? The calculating corporate players have steered public policies towards institutionalization and away from citizen-controlled community and home-based care because institutionalized "care" is big business.

THE INSTITUTIONAL ENTREPRENEURS:
LIFE IN THE FAST LANE

The health care industries have seen explosive growth over the past years; profits soar, stock market dividends are up, health care industry inflation runs rampant. Business is great.

This growth has provided unparalleled entrepreneurial opportunities for nursing home conglomerates to build empires of wealth. For example, Res-Care, which owns group homes in Colorado, Florida, Indiana, Kentucky, Tennessee, Texas, and Nebraska, owns 68 percent of HomeCare Affiliates, which has nursing and homecare services in four states. In its first full year as a public company it had a net income of $5.1 million, a 75 percent increase over its pro forma net income of $2.9 million the year before.[11] Making health care "pay" also provides CEOs with the opportunity to amass huge fortunes. Dr. Malik Hasan, the highest paid health care CEO west of the Mississippi, took home $20.5 million in 1995, the equivalent of $9,855 an hour, or 2,319 times the $4.25 federal minimum wage.[12]

Provider magazine, a publication of the health service industry, recounts the "big news" in 1994 for the top nursing home chains:

> The number of beds [that's disabled or elderly persons, but we are known as "beds" in nursing home jargon] operated by the top 10 in 1993 has increased by approximately 5,000 to 268,000. The 10

largest companies represent about 65% of the total beds in *Provider's* list. The number of beds of the remaining companies, however, has increased since last year by more than 11,000. . . .Reported revenues of the top 40 were about $10 billion this year, compared with $8.5 billion last year.[13]

The "big news" was that the industry's market expansion resulted in an influx of money available for aquisitions, mergers, and further expansion. Omega Healthcare Investment of Ann Arbor, Michigan, saw its net income jump from $4.4 million in 1992 to $11.5 million in 1993, an increase of 161.59 percent. National Health Investment of Murfreesboro, Tennessee, saw a net income increase of 82.85 percent, and California's Regency Health Services had an increase of 67.74 percent.[14] One of the top ten earners, Beverly Enterprises of Fort Smith, Arkansas, saw its net income jump from minus $10.1 million in 1992 to a whopping $57.9 million in 1993—a 673.05 percent increase.

The business press has no qualms about the health industry's profiteering mode. *Business First* magazine accounts for the remarkably high stock market earnings of the nation's largest chain of rehabilitation facilities, Healthsouth, by citing the corporation's three primary objectives: "1. increase net profit, 2. increase net profit, and 3. increase net profit."[15]

How to increase net profit is not illusive to cardiologist and Senator Bill Frist of Tennessee, chair of the subcommittee on disability policy, who owns $13.9 million in Columbia/HCA stock, a hospital corporation chain headed by his brother Thomas Frist, Jr. Senator Frist sits on several key committees including the Banking, Budget, and Labor Committees where he has influence over legislation that affects Columbia/HCA.[16]

Thomas Frist, Jr. set out to manage the Columbia hospital chain "like a Holiday Inn," amassing 240 hospitals and related business such as ambulance companies, laboratories, and laundries. Columbia brought a new vocabulary to the health business, referring to patients as "consumers." Between 1994 and 1996 Columbia's revenues grew 37 percent and profits before one-time items surged 62 percent. The medicine-is-money strategy paid off well for Senator Frist who, according to *IN FACT*, has become a millionaire several times over from his investment. As of this writing Columbia/HCA is being investigated for allegations that it has bilked the government by overcharging for services ranging from blood tests to hospitalizations and home health visits. That's health care corporate life in the fast lane—short on moral vision but keen on acquiring money.

The $70 billion nursing home industry is well aware of the vast public-money feeding trough that lies ahead. In 1991 the Congressional Budget Office estimated that the number of nursing home residents would jump from 1.7 million in 1990 to 2.5 million in 2010, to 3.7 million in 2030, and to 5.2 million in 2050. At a yearly base revenue of $40,000 per bed, this represents an annual $208 billion up for corporate grabs by the year 2050. And that does not include add-on billings such as medication, or inflationary increases in resident fees.

Other changes translate into more bodies for nursing home beds. As managed care corporations come to dictate rehabilitation practices, over-stay, which tends to dominate rehab now, stands to be replaced with under-stay or even no-stay. Under the fee-for-service payment paradigm, the rehab facility gets paid for each service, but under managed care rehab, providing service reduces profit. Managed care administrators will seek to dismiss quads and paras into convalescent or nursing homes—where the HMO has no financial obligation because Medicaid will pick up the tab— before they complete the rehab learning curve. That paradigm shift opens the door to a serious decline in quality rehab and to an increase in the number of newly disabled people stranded in nursing homes.

WHO'S IN "BED" WITH WHOM?

Both President Clinton and House Speaker Newt Gingrich promised to deliver a national PAS program, but the Money Model effect reaches into the halls of government. One story about Beverly Enterprises, the largest nursing home corporation in America (employs more people than all the U.S. automakers combined), provides a clue as to the whys and hows.

Alex Cockburn, writing for *The Nation*, uncovered a major scam, not reported in the mainstream (corporate) press:

> In 1989, with debts of $850 million, Beverly Enterprises was facing bankruptcy. Its strategy for survival was to sell off some of its 845

nursing homes throughout the country as quickly as possible for as much as possible. Forty-five of those homes were in Iowa, and in August of 1989 Beverly sold them to Ventana Investments, a company owned by a man named Bruce Whitehead, an entrepreneur/hustler from Amarillo, Texas. But Whitehead didn't make a straight deal. He also set up a charity called Mercy Health Initiatives, whose nonprofit status he used to wheedle $86 million in tax-exempt bonds out of the Iowa Finance Authority. When Whitehead approached the authority for the money, he insinuated that if the state did not comply he would pull out of the deal and the nursing homes would most likely close, tossing some 3,000 old folks out of their beds. The state came through with the money Whitehead said he needed to buy the homes, and Mercy Health threw in $6 million in promissory notes for fees to Whitehead and the underwriters, bringing the tab for the deal to $92 million. This transaction gave Beverly an immediate cash infusion of $10 million. It landed Whitehead a profit of $6.5 million, personal ownership of four homes worth $1.8 million and a $5 million contract for a construction company he owned.[17]

Cockburn goes on to explain that in the end Mercy Health was burdened by a debt because the value of the homes was overinflated, while Whitehead and Beverly made off with their profits. This enterprising caused Judge Gene Needles to call Beverly and Whitehead "unconscionable" profiteers.[18] Nonetheless, Beverly is still in business and the story does not end in Iowa.

A similar deal was initiated in Arkansas. According to Cockburn, "the Governor's [Bill Clinton] wife and friends stood to gain handsomely from brokering an $82 million ADFA bond deal over Beverly's nursing homes. The Arkansas deal alone represented perhaps $800,000 to Rose Law." One of Rose Law's partners was Hillary Clinton, and ADFA (the Arkansas Development Finance Authority), Cockburn says, "[was a] money machine set up by Bill Clinton when he was still governor of Arkansas whereby Clinton was the . . . ultimate arbiter of the pools of money that could be dispensed by ADFA." The Arkansas deal fell through when the Arkansas attorney general accused Beverly of offering Clinton a $100,000 bribe.[19]

Is it any wonder that in 1992 Governor Clinton's state budget proposed deep cuts in PAS hours that would have meant sending 1,000 disabled people into nursing homes? ADAPT of Arkansas protested the cuts by occupying state offices until Clinton conceded that no one should be denied access to the program, but the concession came only after a prolonged and bitter standoff.

The Beltway insiders say, "You've got to pay to play." Corporations set aside dollars for political action committee and soft money contributions and wealthy board members and stockholders contribute to politicians' coffers to assure that their bottom lines are protected by those politicians. Delving into who is paying to play, we discover that Andy Turner, CEO of Healthsouth, the nation's largest chain of "rehabilitation" facilities which are licensed as nursing homes, was the biggest single contributor to Newt Gingrich's 1994 campaign.[20] Gingrich promised ADAPT that he would pass a national PAS program several years ago—but as of this writing, hasn't.

The political action committee of the American Health Care Association(AHCA), which represents the for-profit nursing home chains, is one of the top contributors to federal candidates, distributing $475,000 to politicians in the 1996 elections.[21] AHCA contributions to individual politicians for nineteen months (1995 through July 1996) totaled $392,738, of which $165,233 went to Democrats and $227,505 to Republicans. Other PACs making contributions include: Living Centers of America, $3,075; Genesis Health Ventures Inc., $14,250; Health Care & Retirement Corp., $2,700; Hillhaven Corp., $13,250; and Manor Healthcare Corp., $48,500.[22]

In Texas alone, representatives of for-profit nursing homes contributed some $150,000 to state officeholders in the last election cycle. In California, nursing home entrepreneurs can contribute as much as they want to politicians because there is no monetary limitation for individual contributions. Is it any wonder that California has the largest number of nursing home regulatory violations in the nation? The 1996 Republican-controlled California Assembly Health Committee blocked all nursing home reform legislation designed to ameliorate the horrible conditions described in this chapter. Although $3,868,162 in fines was assessed in 1995, the state only collected $730,575. 44 percent of the fines were waived, reduced, or dismissed. CANHR concluded, "The Governor's and the Attorney

General's lack of leadership on the prosecution of elder abuse in nursing homes has left residents unprotected and more vulnerable."[23]

In this "democratic" political system is it any wonder that the Republican-led 105th Congress ended federal protection by rolling back nursing home regulations? Repeal of the Boren Amendment, which regulates Medicaid payments to nursing homes, will place residents in greater danger by undoing the standards and practices that make it possible to control some of the abuses. The GOP proposal to deregulate the industry and allow nursing homes to provide free-market "care," unfettered by federal oversight, became a bipartisan goal: Bill Clinton also sought to repeal the Boren Amendment.

In these neoliberal times, if Clinton and Gingrich reach an agreement with ADAPT on in-home care, most likely it will be a version where costs are contained and the disabled individual will not be in control. A national model under their tutelage could even lower the standard by requiring less than what is available in some states now. And it will likely be a model where the "consumer" will not be setting policy, the nursing home industry and medical-industrial complex will dominate the program, setting up nursing-homes-on-wheels where companies manage our care and send the attendants to the home.

Indeed, corporations have already privatized some state PAS programs and contracted to manage attendant services. In Tulare County, California, when National Home Care (now Addus) contracted to provide PAS for the county, an investigation by Legal Services backed up by the State Department of Social Services found that quality of care declined. National set attendant hours for tasks performed—so much time to take a bath, comb the hair, dress, etc. Advocate Maggie Dee's investigation revealed:

> . . . the central theme of fear was the lack of participating in what the disabled individual enjoyed doing: shopping with their PAS, errands, split shift allowing for an education, p.t. work, volunteering . . . . EVERYTHING WAS DOCUMENTED so there was no sense of privacy. Not only every task but every negative statement was reported. Those who refused to go along with the program found themselves waiting days, even weeks, before someone was sent out to assist them on a regular basis. The Health Department had to go out to one of the recipients' homes where they found maggots in food on the coun-

tertop and slime in a mop which was consistently used over and over to mop the woman's floors without cleaning it . . . . all because National Homecare offered $1 million to Tulare's General Fund to get the contract.[24]

Corporate in-home care is not what disability activists view as ultimately liberating PAS social policy. Since corporations (and unions) are likely to set hours that are convenient to running a business, they could even "manage" away our freedom . As Nancy Becker Kennedy, a quadriplegic comedian in Los Angeles, puts it, "I can't report home for milk and cookies at 5 pm. That would end my . . . . career."

Our freedom is threatened when home care agencies, nursing homes, and government form a menage a trois where each gets a piece of the action while liberating social policies are ignored.

THE FINAL SOLUTION

The business solution to disability is to maximize the economic worth of the disabled by making us a commodity. Accordingly, any policy that slashes corporate profits will be opposed with corporate dollars (and contributions to politicians' campaign coffers). Government may be robbing us of our freedom by not responding to our true need—for self-determination—but corporations and financial speculators are paying them to do it. For now the nursing home-industrial complex and government are "in bed" with one another and that does not promise emancipation for disabled people.

Our collective effort must be to stop the over-medicalization of disability and commodifying of disablement. The way for disabled people to avoid becoming road kill in the entrepreneurial fast lane is to bypass the nursing homes, "tear down the walls" of the institutional bias, and replace that with citizen-controlled long-term care policy. When disabled citizens get in the driver's seat, we can own our dignity, make our own choices, hire our own assistants, agree upon hours, and put the money towards decent individual worker wages instead of into middleman or shareholder pockets. We must break out of the corporate jail and refuse to have our freedom paper- traded away on Wall Street.

CHAPTER 9

THE ADA
IN THE NEW WORLD ORDER

FREE-MARKET CIVIL RIGHTS
IN A PUBLIC RELATIONS ERA

*The value of dissent is not purely negative; it does more than
protect us from error. It often points to the truth.*
                                        —Carey McWilliams

But wait a minute, now that we have the Americans with
Disabilities Act (ADA)—our civil rights—isn't everything fine?

Unfortunately, the ADA has some extraordinary limitations, as a
direct result of the political climate in which it was produced and as a
result of skillful public relations maneuvering. It is supposed to address
discrimination in the private sector, yet was signed in an era when
business controlled the "public" agenda. This being a given, it is difficult to feel very comfortable with the thought that we have "won" as
much as we would like to believe.

THE SHRINKING EMANCIPATION DREAM

When George Bush, trumpeter of the New World Order, declared
that we needed a "kinder, gentler" nation in the late 1980s, he was
using public-relations-speak from his CIA covert action training: never
let on what you really mean, just tell them what they want to hear.
"Kinder, gentler" may apply in practice to the upper 5 percent who
benefited from Reagan/Bush policies designed to enrich the business
class. But to the working mother of three children making $10,500—
who paid more in taxes in 1983 than Boeing, General Electric, Du
Pont, Texaco, Mobil, and AT&T combined paid on their profits of
$13.7 billion—it meant "leaner, meaner" deception.[1]

The philosophical momentum for social justice behind the Civil
Rights Act and the following progressive court decisions of the 1960s

was spent. On the way out were civil rights and entitlements, coming in was the notion of "big bad government." The Republican agenda, implemented by Presidents Ronald Reagan and George Bush, was bolstered by corporate goals of promoting globalization and political dominance of government. Reagan and Bush dismantled the entire Community Services Administration, which had driven most of the 1960s social change agenda by advancing human services, occupational safety, consumer protection, and environmental laws. The Republicans vigorously reined in democratic victories that had forged a civil rights movement, established an Office of Economic Opportunity, and started the War on Poverty during the Great Society.

Disability progress was not left untouched. Reagan, viewing regulatory activity as burdensome to business, unsuccesfully sought to kill Section 504 of the Rehabilitation Act, the first civil rights bill that protected the disabled from federal discrimination. His administration succeeded in its target on social service spending: it undercut 75 percent of the housing subsidies which allowed many to live outside of institutions; unjustly dumped 490,000 people from the Social Securiity disability roles; gutted SSI to the extent that 33 percent of those needing the program were no longer being reached,[2] and cut Legal Aid services .

Corporate interests increased their political presence and applied pressure to shift spending away from the public good. Michael Parenti in *Democracy for the Few* explains how:

> Corporations of the Fortune 500 financed conservative think tanks to churn out policy studies and pro-business propaganda. They opened new lobbying offices in Washington. In 1971, less than two hundred firms had registered lobbyists in the capital. A decade later the number had grown to two thousand. By 1979, the American Petroleum Institute, an organization of oil, gas, and petrochemical companies, was spending $75 million a year in lobbying efforts. The entire oil industry employed over 600 people to pressure Congress and government agencies. Lockheed, a big defense contractor, currently maintains 135 lobbyists in Washington.[3]

Billions of public dollars still flowed from the big bad government but Reagan and Bush redirected the money away from public need and lavished it on corporate subsidies and the wealthy. While disabled people and others were living on "benefits" that forced them to choose between buying food and paying utilities, Reagan adjusted tax policy so that the top one percent saw their average incomes soar by 85.4 percent while the incomes of the bottom fifth declined by 10 percent.[4] The New World Order delivered over a quarter of the world's total assets to the top two hundred corporations.

The ADA passed both houses of Congress and was signed by Bush in 1990. Congress stated that society has tended to isolate and segregate disabled people; that discrimination persists in critical areas such as employment, housing, public accommodations, education, transportation, communication, recreation, instititutionalization, health services, voting, and access to public services, but that unlike individuals who experience discrimination on the basis of race, color, sex, national origin, religion, or age, disabled people had no recourse to redress discrimination. Congress found that some 43 million Americans have one or more physical or mental disabilities and that those disabilities confer an inferior status resulting in social, vocational, economic, and educational disadvantage.

Given the shift from a people-centered society to a corporate-centered society described here, it is necessary to question whether the ADA is the hoped-for emancipatory legislation that would pave the way for disabled people's social and economic parity. John Dewey said that politics is the shadow that big business casts over society. The shadow has grown over the last twenty years to global proportions and it is hanging over the ADA.

READING THEIR LIPS

Historically, Republicans have not supported civil rights because their agenda is business-driven. Republicans like to point to Lincoln as an example of one of their best in that he freed the slaves, but Lincoln himself stated:

> I have not meant to leave any one in doubt...My paramount object in this struggle is to save the Union, and it is not either to save or destroy Slavery. If I could save the Union without freeing any slave, I would do it. . . .[5]

Similarly, Republicans have been adept at exploiting the appearance of "moral" superiority by championing family values, democracy in Third World countries, and even minority rights to their public relations benefit.

Casper Weinberger, Secretary of Health, Education, and Welfare (and later indicted for perjury) under President Ford, savvily advised, "Presidential statements and conference-related activities highlighting the President and concern for the handicapped could be advantageous for the Administration in an election year."[6] Bush polished this idea to a fine art while seeking election in 1988. By promoting the rights of disabled people he not only garnered moral credit but as Taylor Humphrey, CEO of Louis Harris and Associates concluded, "The shift in the disability vote helped elect George Bush."[7]

Lip service and meaningful action are two different things, as Humphrey, who has profited from commissioned studies on disability issues over the years, made clear when his company refused to hire a qualified blind applicant for a telephone interviewer position in 1984.[8] While "concern for the handicapped" brought a sense of humanity to the Bush presidency, in reality, contrary to the "kinder, gentler" PR rhetoric, Bush's disability policies were cost-driven and in line with the GOP goal of reducing big, bad government.

THE REPUBLICAN PLOY

So why would a Republican administration that was beating back civil rights and social spending in all other areas pass another civil rights law? After all, the National Association of Manufacturers, the Chamber of Commerce, and the National Federation of Businesses were all opposed to the ADA. The answer lies in how the idea was sold to George Bush while he was Vice President.

Reagan appointed George Bush to spearhead his Regulatory Relief Task Force in 1980. Its goal: to derail regulations that placed "burdensome and expensive" requirements on business. One of his first targets was Section 504 and the guarantees of education for disabled children. According to author Joe Shapiro, who documents this period in *No Pity*, Evan Kemp, Jr., a disabled Republican attorney, intervened to stop the undoing of Section 504 through White House legal counsel, and heir to the R.J. Reynolds Tobacco fortune, C. Boyden Gray. Kemp framed the issue for Bush this way:

Disabled people want independence, Kemp told Bush. They wanted to get out of the welfare system and into jobs. They did not need a paternalistic government to help them. The "eye-opener" for Bush, according to

Gray, was that disabled people were seeking self-empowerment rather than looking for "some captured bureaucracy in Washington, D.C., which usually was the thing that Washington D.C., interest groups wanted."9

What could be a more Republican-based ideology than this? Getting disabled people off welfare, reducing government spending— this disability rights thing was a Republican wet dream if there ever was one. And disability rights would be a PR bonanza because "civil rights" could be softened with language like "bringing disabled people into the mainstream." Who could object to that? All the while, ways could be found to decrease the "captured bureaucracy" of disability entitlement programs.

A cost-benefit analysis prepared by David Stockman makes clear the connection between policy-making and paring down entitlement spending:

> David Stockman's Office of Management and Budget drafted a new White House position [on Section 504] that applied a cost-benefit analysis to proposed disability benefits. To the bean counters at OMB, it seemed sensible. The less disabled a person—and presumably the more likely that person was to work and live independently —the more help and rights he or she got. The more disabled someone was, the less he or she was guaranteed.10

Those who could labor for the capitalists were thought worthy of aid and those unable to were devalued because they could not, a clear example of survival-of-the-fittest-capitalism applied to social policy-making. As Shapiro explains it, Stockman's proposal was killed by Gray out of concern for the effect it would have on his new friend Kemp, who is severely disabled. But, while Gray was having these conversations with Kemp and Bush, the White House money managers were gutting social services and entitlement spending.

It is my conclusion (not the Beltway party line) that when George Bush signed the ADA in 1990, a bargain was struck. Disabled people's civil rights would be tolerated by the anti-government GOP, the party of business, as long as the ADA cost the federal government next to nothing and promised to get people off entitlements. The Bush administration was gambling that plenty could be gained for very little outlay if disabled people could be removed from the growing disability roles

Corporate America, which dominated the Bush White House, anticipated that the ADA would be all show and little substance. The legislation was drafted by thirteen politically conservative members of the unnoted National Council on the Handicapped, all of whom had been appointed by President Ronald Reagan.[11] In concert with a Republican president, they made sure that business had nothing to fear from the ADA; employment discrimination provisions are lax, there is no mandated affirmative action, and there are loopholes to delay and stall access. In short, compliance is largely *voluntary*.

FREE-MARKET CIVIL RIGHTS

President Bush, after vowing to "bring disabled people into the mainstream," insisted on a substantial weakening of the ADA before he would sign it.

ADA access requirements were fought by the National Retail Federation, the American Banking Association, the Baptist Joint Committee, the American Bus Association, the American Institute of Architects, Health Facilities Management Corporation, American Association of Homes for the Aging, and the YMCA, which sought exemptions and narrow regulations that would be to their advantage but affect all such organizations.[12] When the National Association of Homebuilders wanted to avoid the required minimal form of access in all new apartments and condos, it successfully lobbied Vice President Quayle's Council on Competitiveness to get the rule weakened.[13]

Congressional Republicans watered down the ADA by extending compliance dates into the future. For example, only newly purchased buses are required to have lifts, old ones can remain inaccessible until they wear out (Congress now allows companies like Greyhound to defer compliance *indefinitely*). Only new buildings or those undergoing renovation must be made accessible, and the Act was tailored to exempt or postpone small business employers from compliance.

A gaping loophole exists under the exemption from "undue hardship." Any business can claim that it will be a "significant difficulty or expense" to conform with the law. Since compliance was left to courts, lawyers, and state governments, those more concerned with business interests than civil rights often determine what is an "undue financial burden"; a too-expensive "right" can become no right at all.

By far the most serious dilution of the ADA occurred in the employment provisions. Activists and the more progressive supporters, like Senator Tom Harkin, recognized the harmful connection between employment and current insurance underwriting practices that allow insurance corporations to refuse coverage for or jack up premiums to employers that hire a disabled employee. They sought to reform health care delivery through the ADA, but Republican private insurance proponents insisted those reforms be dropped in order to pass the bill. The former director of the President's Committee on Employment of Persons with Disabilities, Rick Douglas, who has multiple sclerosis, explained that as a result he could obtain work only with a large corporation or government agency that could absorb the costs of insurance for him—that's not exactly an open ticket to the job market.

Bush dealt a killing blow to the already weak employment provisions when he vetoed the 1990 Civil Rights Act, which would have allowed disabled people to join women and other minorities in suing companies for damages for discrimination. The bill he did sign in 1991 placed a cap on the monetary damages available *to disabled persons* bringing employment bias suits under the ADA, although no such cap exists for discrimination based on race. Bush simply sidestepped our biggest obstacle—employment discrimination—by protecting American business from financial repercussions. The post-civil rights era ADA conformed with the spirit of "free" enterprise; disabled people had civil "rights" only if business *agreed* it could afford to extend them. Businesses recognized the ADA's shortcomings and responded in some instances like this:

> "Forewarned is forearmed," advertised one workshop on the ADA sponsored by a California city's Chamber of Commerce. The workshop explained how businesses could minimize the law's effect.[14]

LAX FUNDING AND ENFORCEMENT PUTS ONUS ON DISABLED

The fact that the ADA is largely non-funded haunts our progress today. Local and state agencies, calling the ADA an "unfunded mandate," delay compliance, and "enforcement" is monitored by federal agencies like the Equal Employment Opportunity Commission (EEOC), which oversees employment issues, and the Department of Justice (DOJ), which handles access issues.

Initially, there was little money allocated for enforcement. In 1992 the *Disability Rag* questioned poor funding, pointing out that the feds awarded a little over $12 million for ADA "education," and got this retort form Evan Kemp, Jr., who had by then been appointed by Bush to head the EEOC:

> The U.S. Equal Opportunity Commission, whose mission is strictly dedicated to enforcement of civil rights laws, is earmarked to receive an additional $32.5 million and 250 staff above its current resource level. The requested dollar increase is the largest one-year increase in the history of EEOC! The magnitude of this requested increase of EEOC is a reflection of the Administration's strong commitment toward ensuring that a rigorous law enforcement program is undertaken regarding ADA and other civil rights statutes which the Commission enforces.[15]

By comparison, in 1996 when Social Security requested money for Continuing Disability Reviews to determine if those on benefits are "still disabled," Congress awarded it $320 million. *Thirty-two million dollars was appropriated to "protect" us from discrimination in employment so that we can get a job and—ten times that—$320 million was awarded to get us off entitlements.* What does that say about the corporate state's priorities?

The increase Kemp applauded fell grossly short of what it would take to do the job. Between 1992 and 1995, 39,927 ADA employment complaints were filed with the EEOC, generating the largest backlog of employment bias complaints in history, an increase of 42 percent since 1990.[16]

Business Publishers reports that "two out of three cases filed under the ADA with the Justice Department are returned because the department does not have the time to investigate them."[17] According to David Burnham, author of *Above the Law*, only 2 percent of civil rights cases filed with the DOJ result in findings of guilt for those charged with violating citizens' civil rights. By comparison, 86 percent of those charged under immigration statutes receive guilty verdicts.[18]

This lack of commitment plays out in all areas. For instance, the *Los Angeles Daily News* ran a 1995 headline that read, "City faces deadline on handicapped access, $500 million in work should be done by Jan. 26"[19] and reported that only 20 percent of the city's 450 government buildings complied with federal access requirements. The article stated that "there are no funds set aside specifically to retrofit buildings for ADA compliance." Yet Liz Savage of the Justice Department was quoted as saying that they will work out a solution "without invoking penalties," even though the city had been subject to earlier laws and had been out of access compliance for over 22 years. The DOJ's solution in Los Angeles was to propose changes to the ADA that would extend the compliance period to the year 2005. The upshot: we could be colonizing other planets before seeing curb cuts in a smaller town like Muskogee, Oklahoma.

There are other consequences of the legislation's weak design. Disabled individuals are the ones who must file complaints to see the law enforced. This places the onus on us to make private business and local governments conform to the law, which insidiously undermines our social standing. Disabled people will continue to be viewed as costly to society because government opted out of taking financial responsibility for removing barriers in a directed and planned manner.

BACKLASH

If it isn't such a strong law, then why the backlash and all the bad press the ADA has gotten over the past few years? The *American Spectator* and *Reader's Digest* called it "A Law that is Disabling Our Courts." Pat Buchanan has called for its rollback, Newt Gingrich vowed, "I will dismantle the ADA" on *Meet the Press* in the spring of 1995 and Congressmen Mickey Edwards (R-OK) and Tom DeLay (R-TX) have called for its repeal.

Nowhere but in America could there be an upheaval over such a weak law, over such a small social contract. There is no logic to the GOP-led attack, but such frenzy is to be expected in an era when every regulation that protects the public is under fire from the "Republican revolutionaries." Their campaigns against unfunded mandates and affirmative action, and for regulatory "reform," welfare "reform," and environmental "reform" all seek to weaken or eliminate existing law. The ADA is just one more target in the shooting gallery.

But the backlash also flourishes from misunderstandings and outright misreporting. For instance, Rick Kahler of the *Rapid City Journal* in South Dakota wrote an article called "ADA Regulatory Black Hole,"[20] claiming that the ADA "imposes heavy fines and jail sentences for those who don't [make their businesses accessible]."

Concluding that business was hamstrung, he wrote, "laws like the ADA make getting out of business look more profitable all the time."

Justin Dart, Jr., one of the primary movers behind the ADA, responded that the black hole was there, but it was in Kahler's source of information. He explained to Kahler:

> ...[the ADA was] written in cooperation with a business oriented Republican administration, it is a *free enterprise* civil rights law. It empowers the local business owner to decide, to provide equality to people with disabilities on a case by case basis, in ways that make common sense for the individual customer and business. [italics mine]

Kahler then issued a second article confessing, "I Blew it on ADA." Kahler is right that there is a black hole, but it is the voluntary and extended compliance options, the lack of federal funding, and the lack of strong employment provisions. There have been and will be benefits from the ADA, but not nearly what is necessary to achieve economic parity.

A Revolution Thwarted

It *is* revolutionary to alter the American landscape with architectural changes brought to bear under universally accessible design. To see ramps replacing steps is visually symbolic of our slow progress, at least on the ramp, restaurant, and recreation fronts. For that class of disabled persons with the money, life has improved. They can attend more concerts, use the restrooms in more restaurants, purchase great lifts for their accessible vans, get on airplanes and fly across the country with relative ease, and go to more movies.

But what good is the freedom to sit in a United Artists theater if one cannot afford the price of a ticket? When asked by the *Washington Post* how the ADA had affected him, Morris Turner, 32, of Wheaton said, "It is still almost impossible for me to get a job." Turner has cerebral palsy and is unemployed. "Maybe there are a couple more curb cuts and a couple more accessible buildings, but overall my life is not that much easier."[21]

The ADA will be successful only to the degree that it is instrumental in securing economic justice. It *would* be revolutionary to force corporate America to hire disabled people and it *would* be revolutionary to prevent corporations from firing employees upon disablement. *It is the economic arena—beyond ramps—that is central to breaking out of the underclass that has kept us on the bottom socio-economic rungs of the capitalist pyramid.* Unfortunately, the ADA has not been given the power to fully deliver on its revolutionary promise.

Like any other civil rights legislation, the ADA is supposed to equalize the playing field for job applicants, but disability rights free marketeers concluded that all that was needed was an "equal opportunity" to employment, as opposed to affirmative action to rectify past patterns of discrimination.

Dr. Larry Scadden of the National Science Foundation, who is blind, says that he encountered discrimination during the eighteen months he spent trying to land a job. "I am convinced that it is easy for most businesses to turn a candidate down and make it look like the disability had nothing to do with it," says Scadden.[22]

"Potential employers often disguised their prejudices about blindness by offering excuses such as another applicant had more experience, another applicant would do a better job or all of a sudden I would be told that the job was closed," Dr. Scadden explains. He says that it is not discriminatory to want the best person for the job, that's the way it should be, but adds that proving that the nondisabled person who *was* hired had fewer qualifications under the ADA is really tough to do.

Jim Stewart found a less-than-receptive welcome mat for disabled job applicants when he got his bachelor's degree from San Diego State in 1991 and attempted to land employment as a civil engineer. During his two years of job searching, Stewart encountered numerous obstacles. "I could tell people were apprehensive as to what I would be able to do," he says, "I could tell by their body language that they were not expecting someone in a wheelchair."[23]

Stewart, recognizing that he would need to forge his own success story, said, "I got so frustrated that I went to Caltrans [California Department of Transportation] and pretty much forced my way in there." Stewart worked as a volunteer for two months until the employees at Caltrans got to know him and recognized that he was capable of doing the work. "Then they did whatever they could to get me hired as an engineer," Stewart explained.

The assumption that Stewart and others like him cannot not do the job remains a huge obstacle. Women and people of color have had some employment successes through affirmative action, particularly in getting government jobs. But the disabled do not have mandatory pre-ferred group status under affirmative action as other minorities do; rather the Labor Department "urges" employers to hire us. In Stewart's case, Caltrans, which is a public employer, had to be pushed to take him seriously.

Instead, the ADA has modified the job interview process so that employers cannot ask about the applicant's disability but may ask if the applicant can do the job with or without a reasonable accommodation. The ADA instructs employers to judge applicants on the basis of their qualifications for a particular job; the theory is that by not focusing on the disability, hiring can be conducted without prejudices affecting employment decisions.

But the fact is that disability discrimination is as rampant as ever, and it's really hard to prove. After passage of the ADA, most personnel officers have obtained enough training to avoid making the kind of bla-tant mistakes that would land them in an ADA lawsuit. A potential employer would have to discriminate openly to lose a suit brought at the hiring stage. And since the burden of proof is on the applicant dis-criminated against, he or she must have superior evidence to prevail.

To bring suit, one must go through the EEOC, which polices the process. Like a cop, the EEOC directs traffic, giving a green or red light to one's case by issuing a "right to sue" letter before private attorneys can take the matter to court—postponing decisions that immediately affect one's financial status and unduly extending the length of time the whole process takes.

Disabled citizens filed more than 12,000 charges of ADA violations with the EEOC in the first year alone. By 1994, 33,000 ADA employ-ment complaints had been filed, 11 percent alleging discrimination in the hiring process. But the *EEOC greenlighted only 28 discrimination cases and only three alleging discrimination in hiring*. That means that three new-hire cases were pursued out of 3,630 complaints, not enough to begin to make a dent in helping people get jobs. As of December 1995, about 20,000 disability cases were unresolved by the EEOC due to backlog.[24]

Such low activity indicates that the EEOC is reluctant to use the power of the office to say to American business that government will not tolerate disability discrimination. And other indicators point to a less than enthusiastic White House under Bill Clinton. The *Washington Post* reported that Gilbert Casellas, Chairman of the

EEOC, said, "Nobody gives a crap about us," after his repeated attempts to meet with the White House over the problems the EEOC is facing in light of lack of funding and the backlogs.[25] The official unspoken message to business is "go ahead and discriminate because we aren't going to prosecute."

By comparison, when President Johnson signed a 1967 Executive Order banning sex discrimination in federal employment, the National Organization of Women filed over one thousand suits against U.S. corporations in a concerted effort to make it clear that they intended to see the law enforced.[26] Contrast that to our free enterprise lawsuit apologists who in reply to business's concerns say:

> Fact: No avalanche of lawsuits. There never will be because the ADA does not allow million dollar judgments. In five years there have been just 650 public and private lawsuits under the ADA. At that rate it would take 50,000 years to sue every business and community covered by the ADA.[27]

Where court action was vital to the Civil Rights Act of 1964, it is seen a killer to our "progress." So, are we to be comforted that since the regulations took effect lawsuits are not breaking business's back? What about disabled people's backs oppressed into poverty? Women's accomplishments came through tough-minded organization, protest, and non-apologetic legal actions. On the other hand, disability rights leaders are so co-dependent on "free enterprise" politics that they are afraid to rock the corporate boat. Without a guaranteed equality of results will we be better off in years to come? What if the African American community had left it to business to "do the right thing"? What if affirmative action for women and minorities never happened?

ROCKING THE PR BOAT: CORPORATIONS LIE

In 1994, then director of the President's Committee on the Employment of People with Disabilities (PCEPD) Rick Douglas said that it was clear that a majority of medium to large companies had implemented ADA procedures, but truthfully concluded that they were not hiring people with disabilities. Alan Reich, president of the National Organization on Disability, summarizing a study by Louis Harris and Associates, Inc. (commissioned by his office) that found two-thirds of working-age disabled people unemployed, said, "A wide gap remains to be bridged." It is still true that "not working is perhaps the truest definition of what it means to be disabled," concluded *Business Week*.[28]

But this bit of truth was bad press, both for the corporations engaged in ADA PR campaigns and the PCEPD, whose job it was to promote employment. In 1995 another N.O.D./Harris study focused more on the corporate party line and less on the failure of the ADA to secure employment for the disabled. Louis Harris and Associates reported that 90 percent of the executives surveyed "support provisions of the ADA that prohibit discrimination in employment"; 70 percent thought that the law "should not be changed" (between the lines, that means not be strengthened); 66 percent said that litigation has not increased since the ADA's passage (the government is seeing to this). Harris explained that the reason corporations were not hiring more people with disabilities was because there was a "lack of qualified applicants." "Unqualified" like Dr. Scadden or Jim Stewart perhaps?

In an article titled "Rulings Terrorize Small Business," writer Michael Fumento commented on the survey: "No CEO in his right mind would want to be listed somewhere as disapproving of an act which everybody thinks is supposed to help Stevie Wonder and Jerry's kids."[30] Fumento criticized the ADA for having too broad a definition of disability, which is contestable, but he cut through the public relations fog to serve up one bit of indisputable truth: corporations lie.

Is it any wonder that in 1995, Rick Douglas, who in 1994 had acknowledged that the disabled were not finding employment through the ADA, was replaced at PCEPD by former Congressman Tony Coelho?[31] Soon after, Coelho issued a report that claimed corporate America was hiring disabled people. This PCEPD-commissioned survey of CEOs and human resources managers from Fortune 500 companies found that all of the 300 companies interviewed supported the ADA and almost three-fourths were hiring disabled people. The PCEPD claims that 11 million disabled people want to work. If each corporation that responded positively hired one disabled employee, that would leave 10,999,775 unemployed. If each corporation hired 10, that would leave 10,997,750 without a job; if they hired 100 that would leave 10,977,500 unemployed. It is naive to rely upon reports prepared and commissioned by corporate executives and disability leaders who have much to gain by promoting the success of the ADA. The essential question is, do we want public relations civil rights or civil rights that deliver?

EMPLOYMENT FOR ALL

Seven years after its passage, it is obvious from our persistently high jobless rate that disabled people did not get enough from the ADA to jolt us out of our historical unemployment predicament. Russell Redenbaugh, a Philadelphia-based member of the U.S. Commission on Civil Rights, who is blind, told the *Washington Post* in 1995, "The [ADA] goal of increasing employment opportunities for those of us who are seriously disabled has not been met at all."[32]

Newsweek reports that 85 percent of the discrimination claims under review at the EEOC are brought by people already in the workplace and that the law is primarily aiding injured or impaired workers who must be retained when they become disabled on the job. *Newsweek* explains that dissent has come both from businesses who object to having to retain the workers and from disabled activists who:

> fear a backlash by business that will hurt the people the law was intended to help. Says Michael Auberger, co-founder and national organizer of ADAPT, a Denver-based disability-rights group: "It's going to have to change. Otherwise, there's going to be a wholesale slaughter of the law." Already, Russell Redenbaugh of the U.S. Commission on Civil Rights is calling for hearings to examine whether ADA's scope needs to be narrowed.[33]

But this is where the ADA is to be commended for working. Companies want to unload disabled employees because they mean extra insurance costs and may no longer be as physically exploitable for profit-making. Is it not possible for a disabled employee, say someone who had polio as a child, to get carpal tunnel syndrome from overuse or be further disabled in some other manner on the job? The ADA allows the injured employee to challenge firing upon disablement, instead of being forced into a workers compensation "buy-off" which usually benefits the employer more than the injured worker. It is counterproductive to the best interests of any disabled person, employed or unemployed, to seek to weaken the ADA's effectiveness in the workplace.

If anything, the ADA needs to be *strengthened* to make it impossible to fire someone who becomes disabled, so that corporations cannot profit from creating work environments where employees are abused and injured on the job. Wouldn't it be appropriate to join with those forces that would like to reform business exploitation practices that ignore safety, rather than capitulate to the demands of profiteers who do not have their workers' interests in mind and would like to dump them when it is convenient? If work-related disability were to cost capitalists profits, then more attention would be placed on safe working conditions and all would benefit.

Since Nixon signed the Occupational Safety and Health Act into law in 1970, enforcement in the workplace has steadily declined. Occupational injury rates are sky high in the 1990s. Repetitive stress injuries are up from 22,600 cases in 1982 to 302,000 in 1993. Chemical and toxic poisoning is on the rise. Some 6,000 Americans die on the job every year; that's 20 people a day. Nearly two million workers have been permanently disabled and over two million have died from diseases incurred from workplace conditions. Only a few employers have been prosecuted and just one, a builder in south Dakota, was sent to jail (for 45 days).

The *Newsweek* article further reported, "Auberger would like to see recovering alcoholics, drug abusers and some people with back pain excluded from the ranks of the disabled." Wake up, Auberger, you sound like Newt Gingrich. The people you want to eliminate from the ranks of the disabled are not taking jobs away from you; corporate America is doing that. Perhaps people with "traditional" disabilities aren't successfully using the law yet because it doesn't work for them. Use ADAPT to strengthen the ADA to ensure the quality of results so that more disabled people get newly hired.

Of great concern is that now that we have our civil "rights," society expects the disabled to get off public benefits and government is poised to undo entitlements. We need to educate the public to the simple truth that ensuring disability rights and benefits provides a just working environment for all Americans. And we need to re-focus our business-dominated society on people, to place the public welfare at the center of our community efforts.

PART III

ENDING THE SOCIAL CONTRACT

No one has ever tried survival-of-the-fittest capitalism for any extended period in modern democracy, so we don't know how far rising inequality and falling wages can go before something snaps…if the democratic political process cannot reverse the trend to inequality, democracy will eventually be discredited.

—Lester Thurow

The world may be moving inexorably towards one of those tragic moments that will lead historians to ask, why was nothing done in time.

—Ethan Kapstein

CHAPTER 10

LET THEM EAT UNENFORCEABLE CIVIL RIGHTS

PROMOTING THE GENERAL WELFARE IN A DOWNSIZED AGE

The majority of men prefer delusion to truth. It is easier to grasp. Above all, it fits more snugly than the truth into a universe of false appearances.

—H. L. Mencken

One spin on the ADA was that disabled people would "become a strategy for profitability—a new competitive advantage in the search for capable workers."[1] On the heels of a 1987 Department of Labor "Workforce 2000" study, the Hudson Institute predicted growing labor shortages and concluded that U.S. employers of the 1990s would have to look to new sources of high-quality workers if they were to remain competitive. *Business Week* concluded, "One of the hidden keys to profitability may be a large and growing bloc of Americans-people with disabilities . . . in a decade in which willing and able workers will be increasingly hard to find, the nearly nine million working-age Americans with disabilities now outside the job market may be one of the best sources of new employees—period."[2]

Given what has occurred—massive layoffs, a deskilling of the labor force into low-paying service sector jobs, downsizing, factory shutdowns, corporate carting of jobs overseas, high unemployment, NAFTA, GATT—is it possible this Hudson Institute was serious? Or, decoded, did "willing and able workers" mean a more exploitable workforce, i.e., cheaper, nonunionized, and less uppity?

Disability advocates misunderstood that corporate America, via the globalization of capital, was downsizing the country towards

Third World inequality—not towards "equal" anything. They miscalculated when they left it to a "benevolent" free enterprise system to make reparations; our jobless rate is 65-75 percent worldwide regardless of any civil rights. Even *Business Week* concluded, "Many of the barriers confronting them [disabled people seeking jobs] do not appear amenable to ready resolution by the ADA alone."[3]

It becomes imperative to look at the economic inequalities that remain after 30 years of civil rights, like the persistently high numbers of underclass minorities living in poverty for whom there are no jobs, regardless of affirmative action, and the growing numbers of displaced nonminorities facing increased job insecurity, lowered career expectations, and poverty wages. Civil rights, although necessary to counter discrimination, may not be radical (get to the root) enough to change our predicament. Questions arise such as, how do economic rights factor into a globalized market that leaves greater insecurity in its wake and threatens to enlarge the "surplus" population? What happened to universal concepts like full employment and a guaranteed income? Will civil rights solve the inequities imposed by globalization?

A TELLING KISS

How is it possible that thirty years after passage of the Civil Rights Act of 1964, African-American unemployment is still high at 11 percent nationwide. In South Central Los Angeles, it is 60 percent. How can it be possible when, as in the case of that civil rights movement, hundreds of thousands of people were actively pushing for betterment of their condition? One answer is that a movement may begin as a strong voice for the people but be successfullly co-opted by power, by government. Historian Howard Zinn writes about the 1963 March on Washington:

> When black civil rights leaders planned a huge march on Washington in the summer of 1963 to protest the failure of the nation to solve the race problem, it was quickly embraced by President Kennedy and other national leaders, and turned into a friendly assemblage.[4]

And Malcolm X cut through the facade to explain it this way:

It was the grass roots out there in the street. . . . [It] scared the white power structure in Washington, D.C. to death. I was there. When they found out that this black steamroller was going to come down on the capital, they called in. . . . these national Negro leaders that you respect and told them, "Call it off," Kennedy said. "Look, you all are letting this thing go too far." And Old Tom said, "Boss, I can't stop it because I didn't start it.". . . . They said, "These Negroes are doing things on their own. They're running ahead of us." And that old shrewd fox, he said, "If you all aren't in it, I'll put you in it. I'll put you at the head of it. I'll endorse it. I'll welcome it. I'll help it. I'll join it."

This is what they did with the march on Washington. They joined it . . . . became part of it, took it over. And as they took it over, it lost its militancy. It ceased to be angry, it ceased to be hot, it ceased to be uncompromising. . . . No, it was a sellout. It was a takeover . . . . They controlled it so tight, they told those Negroes what time to hit town, where to stop, what signs to carry, what song to sing, what speech they could make, and what speech they couldn't make, and then told them to get out of town by sundown.[5]

Arthur Schlesinger in *A Thousand Days* explains, "The conference with the president did persuade the civil rights leaders that they should not lay siege to Capital Hill . . . in 1963 Kennedy moved to incorporate the Negro revolution into the democratic coalition."[6]

Author Joe Shapiro recounts the corresponding disabled people's march on Washington:

Blank's [ADAPT] discreet line to the White House had given ADAPT new power. Several months before the Washington march, ADAPT had taken over the federal building in Atlanta to demand that the Department of Transportation agree not to fund any city purchases of buses unless they had lifts. Some city bus lines were trying to buy the cheaper buses before the ADA went into effect. A curious thing happened in Atlanta: police dragged ADAPT protesters out of the federal building only to be ordered to escort them back in to stay overnight. The police even provided blankets to keep the demonstrators warm as they slept in the lobby and hallways. A call had come from the White House on behalf of the president. Transportation Department officials were then flown to Atlanta to negotiate the temporary ban on inaccessible bus buys that ADAPT had sought. *In Washington, ADAPT had returned the favor by refusing to chain themselves to the White House gate. Patrisha Wright had urged them to do so, arguing that Bush could do more to pressure House Republicans to support the ADA.*[7] (Italics mine)

A connection to the White House is interpreted as more "power." What would Malcolm X have to say about that? He would say, "The crips were told where to go, when, and how. And then they were told to accept this weak ADA because it was all they would get and to get out of town. What these crips had was an illusion of power. The government was in charge and Tiny Tim said, 'Thank you' for his crumbs and left the next day."

President Bush patted and *kissed* Evan Kemp, Jr. on the head when he signed the cornerstone of disabled people's "freedom," the ADA. By contrast, Martin Luther King, Jr. was under FBI surveillance during his struggle. Calling King a "communist," the FBI sought to discredit him as the leader of the African-American movement in the hopes of replacing him with someone whom the black community would admire, and the white power structure could control.

Disability rights leaders Evan Kemp and Justin Dart, Jr. were an FBI civil-rights-leader-dream come true. Kemp, the ultimate insider, is part-owner of Invacare, a medical equipment supply company, and Dart is an heir to industrialist Dart Sr.'s Rexall Drug fortune. There was no need for FBI surveillance of our top leadership because Kemp and Dart posed no threat; they were Republicans fostering business interests. President Bush's kiss symbolized this melding of purposes.

The government used the leaders as a buffer between those truly hurting at the bottom and business seeking to preserve the status quo. In 1963 and again in 1990 with the passage of the ADA, the grass roots had been maneuvered into believing that they were getting a good deal, when in fact the business class had won again. Kennedy and Bush extended only as many "rights" and only as much "equality" as was necessary to quell the fire.

LET THEM EAT UNENFORCEABLE CIVIL RIGHTS

The U.S. adopted a policy of civil rights incrementalism that was never intended to erase inequality. Only after Europe had charged the U.S. with racism did President Truman set up the first Committee on Civil Rights in 1946, to push Congress to pass laws against lynching, to stop voting discrimination, and to "suggest" laws that would remedy racial discrimination in employment.[8] It was 1954 before the Supreme Court struck down the separate but equal doctrine upheld since the 1890s. Even then, desegregation was not enforced. Civil rights were passed in 1957, 1960, 1964, and 1968. The government would extend a small bit of "equality" but not seriously attempt to enforce the anti-discrimination laws, and years later the same problems remained. It took the insurrection of African Americans in the early 1960s, like the lunch counter sit-ins all over the South where some 50,000 people demonstrated and some 3,600 were arrested, to see that "separate but equal" was challenged in practice.

The greatest number of urban riots in American history—a total of 131—came three years after passage of the Civil Rights Act. To the hungry it must have seemed that "Let them eat cake" had become "Let them eat unenforceable civil rights." None of the half-measure civil rights bills passed by Congress seemed to better the poor conditions surrounding their lives. The War on Poverty brought down the numbers of those living below the official poverty line by half, but *as pressure from the leadership waned, poverty rose again accordingly*. The ghettos remained intact.

Affirmative action proved to be another bit of incrementalism that has not solved the need. Attempting to remedy the ongoing effects of discrimination, affirmative action applies to under 4 percent of college applicants; the approximately 96 percent of remaining college slots are left to traditional admission practices. Affirmative action is largely voluntary for business and local governments; only those that have a history of discrimination have been forced by the feds to formulate affirmative action programs. Although affirmative action has paved some important inroads to equality, commentator Richard Rodriguez points out it has had little effect on the lives of the poor:

> The embarrassing fact was that the primary beneficiaries of affirmative action were mainly middle-class. And worse: Those on the inside

gained their label of "minority" because of their supposed relationship to a larger number of people on the outside. Which led to a guilt. Middle-class undergraduates knew that they were gaining on the backs of the poor.[9]

Economic oppression is linked to racism and it is linked to physicalism but it is above all linked to class. Writer bell hooks explains that she was on a panel with other prominent black artists but that:

> I was the only person willing to argue for there being major class conflicts in black life and challenging the notion that being victims of racism solidifies us, so that we are not tearing one another apart on the basis of class. This is a popular fiction that denies the growing gap—not just between black people in privileged classes and those who are poor, but the differences and contradictory similarities in attitudes and values that are separating those groups.[10]

Minorities have rightly come forward to challenge the values of a disability movement that fashionably promotes civil rights at a time when "reform" to Medicaid, SSI, and welfare threatens the stability of programs that affect poor minorities. At the opening session of the 1995 Developmental Disabilities forum in Washington, John Sanford said:

> Traditionally, the disability movement has carried a *middle-class white agenda*. It has only been recently that this movement is beginning to tolerate issues affecting people of color.[11] [italics mine]

Sanford is justified in naming race as an issue, but he is heroic to name class as a dictator of opportunity in our society. Racism is rampant but it can be mitigated with class power. The same holds true with disability. The rich crips now have access laws, and if they come across a barrier they will have the means to get it removed. They will rely on their connections and insider schmoozing to get a job or to influence Congress on their issues. Christopher Reeves, for instance, advocates raising insurance company caps on benefits that affect his class's lifestyle, but increased benefits without affordable universal coverage won't touch the lives of the growing numbers who are unable to pay for private insurance (64 percent of the uninsured say that they are uninsured because they cannot afford the premiums).[12] He lobbies for more research money to cure his spinal cord injury by saying, "Our government spends about $8.7 billion a year *just maintaining* these members of our family" [italics mine]. Make no mistake, Reeves means that the uncurables are a drag on public resources. Reeves sat in his wheelchair on the stage with the other liberals at the 1996 Democratic Convention and obfuscated reality by telling the American people that the Clinton administration does not want people to "have to fend" for themselves. This was just after Clinton signed a welfare "reform" bill that threw thousands of impoverished children into deeper poverty and reduced poor children's food stamps meal budget from 80 cents to 66 cents. What about the 300,000 disabled children severed from SSI and Medicaid who will have to "fend" for themselves because of Clintonite "reform"?

Poor disabled people cannot rely on the few disabled members of the elite who may speak at the Democratic Convention, hold an executive position with Wells Fargo Bank, or have a job as a newscaster, to change the reality for those on the bottom, any more than the black community could rely on the middle class that abandoned the ghettos once they had the means to get out.

King eventually understood that civil rights could not provide enough jobs at a living wage or obliterate poverty, and organized a Poor People's Encampment in Washington. He sought to get at the roots of economic inequality but was killed before he could fight this battle. Like King, disabled people must go beyond ramps, with a piercing gaze that can see through the agents of oppression into those economic and undemocratic dynamics that have created inequities. Civil rights incrementalist history tells us that it may not be so wise to rely on a system to generate equality when that system's goals—increasing concentration of private and corporate ownership—are in conflict with the principles of equality.

CORPORATE ZEITGEIST SINKS BOATS

Corporate profits are up overall 40 percent; according to *Fortune*, 1995 profits were up 54 percent over the last year's. "Life in corporate America," concluded the *Wall Street Journal*, "is about as good as it can get." Between 1980 and 1993, corporations increased dividends to stockholders over 250 percent. With the richest 1 percent owning 46 percent of all stocks, and the richest 10 percent owning 90 percent of all stocks, the wealthy clearly have benefited more than anyone else from this version of an economic boom.[13]

There is little evidence that the average citizen is benefiting from corporate America's prosperity. Soaring profits do not translate into full-time living wage jobs for unemployed Americans. The Bureau of Labor Statistics puts the unemployment rate at 8 million, but according to the Council on International and Public Affairs, another 31 million work part-time, 4.6 million took part-time work when they would have preferred full-time jobs; and 6.2 million who want jobs are off the recording charts because they gave up looking.[14] The real jobless rate is closer to 15.9 million or 12.5 percent of the population— more than twice the official rate. If the 11 million disabled that the President's Committee on Employment of Disabled Persons claims want to work are added in, 27 million remain jobless in the U.S.

Corporate profits are way up but are not translating into decent workers' salaries. America's average inflation-adjusted weekly wage is down 20 percent. Real wages have fallen for 80 percent of the workforce; *Business Week* reports the going rate is $7.40 an hour. The *Los Angeles Times* reports that in California over 700,000 workers find that they must hold down more than one job to support themselves.

It is obvious that a rising tide, contrary to the party line, does not lift all boats. The U.S. has the widest gap between rich and poor of any of the world's industrial nations. A report by the Organization for Economic Cooperation and Development found that an American adult in the 90th percentile—the high-wage group that earns more than 90 percent of all Americans—takes home 5.9 times what an adult in the 10th percentile or lowest-earning group does. By comparison, in Finland, a higher wage adult earns only 2.59 times as much as the lower group. In addition, U.S. household incomes have been dropping for all groups, except the richest.[15] For instance, take American CEO pay. In the 1970s, CEOs of major corporations made 40 times the salary of an average worker. In 1995 the ratio was 187 to 1; by 1996 CEOs could make 200 times the worker's mean salary. The average CEO pay jetted up from $329,000 a year in 1970 to $3.7 million in 1996.[16] In 1996 Morgan Stanley President John Mack took home $10.67 million, an estimated 500 times what the company's lowest-paid worker earned. Wealth is being dramatically concentrated and redistributed upwards.

Low wages are only part of the economic order imposed by the transnational corporate zeitgeist. The capitalist/worker relationship has been altered; labor is becoming less important to wealth acquisition. According to Jeremy Rifkin of the Foundation on Economic Trends in Washington, corporate America is eliminating two million jobs a year. The corporate sector has learned that massive "downsizing" (euphemism for firing) pushes profits up; firing workers generates Wall Street bonanzas. Thanks to paper trading on Wall Street, corporations can increase capital simply by "restructuring." For instance, stock options owned by Lucio Noto, CEO of Mobil, rose in value by $24 million on the day he booted 4,700 workers. When AT&T went public with its layoff of 40,000 "nonessential" employees, Wall Street cheered; the announcement alone caused a $2.63 per share increase in AT&T stock, netting four billion dollars on the New York Stock Exchange. Yet the company offered fired workers, some of whom had worked there for over 20 years, a measly $12,000 *if* the employee would sign a paper promising not to sue the company. The old implied contract—that a loyal worker will have a solid job with a company—is a social contract broken in the oligopolistic economy of the 1990s.[17]

CEOs playing the downsizing game reap huge rewards for putting people out of work. Scott Paper's Albert Dunlap cut 10,500 jobs in 1994 and saw his earnings jump from $618,000 to $3,575,500. Kodak's George Fisher fired 14,100 in 1993-94 and saw his salary rise from $1,890,000 to $3,901,000. Michael Jordan at Westinghouse Electric fired 4,900 and doubled his take-home from $713,400 to $1,357,000. Louis Gerstner of IBM got rid of 36,000 jobs and got a $1,800,000 raise on top of his $4,600,000 salary. James Mellor of General Dynamics dropped 35,465 jobs between 1990 and 1995 and made $11.3 million in 1994.[18]

Downsizing makes a mockery of Reagan's "trickle down" theory that if the rich are doing well, the middle class and poor will benefit. The merger of Wells Fargo and First Interstate Bancorp drove both stocks to record levels, making its major stockholders, like billionaires Warren Buffet and Walter Annenberg, a bit richer in 1996 but severing several thousands of workers from their jobs. "Downsizing for growth" means growth of stockholders' wallets, not growth that would create jobs. The bottom line is that the few are greatly benefitting at the expense of the many.

DOWNSIZED, OUTSOURCED, AND "UNFETTERED"?

There is a price our society pays when investors and Wall Street have dominion over our lives; greater profits mean greater social insecurity for the masses. For instance, from 1983 to 1992 U.S. transnationals increased jobs overseas by 345,000 and eliminated 783,000 jobs in our country. Then Secretary of Labor Robert Reich said, "We are faced with the spectacle of CEOs pocketing multi-million-dollar bonuses and stock options after abandoning their employees and communities—indeed, precisely *because* they have abandoned their employees and communities."[19]

Subtler forms of abandonment lie within the "leaner" company walls. Studies show that corporations are insisting, whether spoken or not, that workers put in more hours to keep their jobs. Salaried professionals find they must work 12-hour days and weekends to compete. Workers in manufacturing are scheduled more overtime to compensate for smaller, leaner workforces. In 1995, California production workers averaged 30 percent more overtime than in 1985, largely due to fewer employees to do the work, and the rate continues to climb. California Governor Pete Wilson backed a law that removes the requirement to pay time-and-a-half for overtime after eight hours, so that now employers are only required to pay after 40 hours. At some factories, the 8-hour day, 5-day week has given way to schedules that management deems efficient, even if that ignores the calendar's seven-day cycles and community patterns of work, sleep, and play. Overwork and less leisure time have become standard fare in the 1990s.[20]

In the process of making more "flexible" capitalist machines, businesses are abandoning employee health benefits and pension plans and unloading the burden of having full-time employees. *Business Week* reports that in 1980, 95 percent of large to middle-sized companies offered health insurance but today the figure is down to 80 percent. Harper's Index puts the percentage of U.S. working men who are covered by employer-provided health insurance at 55 percent, women at 37 percent.[21] Workers are hired part-time or on a temporary basis so companies do not have to pay benefits. Experts estimate that by the year 2000, these "contingent" workers will make up 50 percent of the workforce. While temporary agencies are banned in

France, the Netherlands, Italy, the United Kingdom, and Greece, the largest private employer in the U.S. today is Manpower, Inc.

Pundits frame these structural changes as the inevitable result of a deterministic market or as "technological shifts" inherent in the Information Age, and pitch them as an opportunity for "individual" achievement. In this view, being downsized (fired) is a chance for "self-determination," a chance to get away from the "paternalistic" nature of secure employment.

One way to get this "unfettered freedom" is to become an independent contractor in the subcontracting netherworld. Corporations can unload the cost of full-time employees and bust what little power unions have left by outsourcing work. The result: a more desperate (and controllable) contingent workforce where job insecurity is compounded by isolation; former employees pitted against one another for a smaller piece of the pie; the dispersed self-employed's wages undercut by squeezing them to do the work for as little as possible. This scenario means that individuals must pay for their own health care, try to replace no longer existent pension funds, and be in constant search of work.

Experts claim disabled people are likely to have an advantage on the self-employed track since they are often trained to be "techno-aristocrats" and computer-related employment, the fastest-growing occupation, is estimated to jump by 60 percent nationwide.[22] But the kicker is that these jobs are going to people sitting at computer terminals in India, where they can be had for 50 cents an hour or less. Ending the social contract as we know it means devolving workers' rights worldwide by de-securing people and bringing the workforce down to the lowest common denominator.

WORKING ON A CHAIR GANG

Section 504 of the Rehabilitation Act of 1973 established that federally-financed institutions are required to pay a "fair" wage to disabled workers, but they are not required to meet even minimum wage standards.[23] The traditional sheltered workshop is the prototype for justifying below-minimum wages for disabled people, based on the theory that these workers are not able to keep up with the average widget sorter. (One such workshop was reported to pay as low as 11 cents an hour.) How "fair" is a sub-minimum wage under any circumstances when one cannot live on it? Any employer is allowed to pay below minimum wages to disabled employees under federal law, if the employer can show that the disabled person has "reduced productive capacity," and there is no mandated time frame in which they must prove it. The disabled can be trapped in assumptions about their abilities while others benefit by their entrapment.

The GOP, always the guardian of profit, is looking for a domestic slave labor workforce, one that is nonunionized, unorganized, and desperate for any work at all. For example, Senator Phil Gramm of Texas talks about forcing the poor to work for $2.50 an hour and suggests making prisons into industrial parks. Disabled people do promise a cheap source of labor, maybe not as cheap as in India or Haiti, but cheaper than nondisabled people. According to a 1992 Census Bureau report, on average, a severely disabled person makes $1,562 per month, while a non-severely disabled person makes $2,006. A nondisabled person makes on average $2,446, or 33 percent more than the severely disabled individual and 20 percent more than the non-severely disabled individual. This indicates that employers either devalue disabled employees or that they take advantage of us financially. According to the 1992 Census Bureau report, the earnings of men and women with disabilities have decreased since 1981 compared to nondisabled employees.[24]

Republican legislator Baugh in California latched onto the subminimum wage concept for disabled workers by offering legislation in 1996 that would allow employers to hire disabled workers at a "special minimum wage" (that word "special" again), without the minimal and very subjective "protection" of having to show that the prospective employee is "less productive" than a nondisabled one. Theoretically, any disabled person could be considered "less productive," and this sub-minimum wage could be used to exploit any disabled worker.

The existing minimum wage for a 40-hour week, even with recent hikes, is not a living wage. The California GOP proposal, by suggesting that disabled people can somehow manage to live on less than anyone else, lacks even the most rudimentary understanding of disability (or cruelly ignores it), because we often have more expenses than nondisabled people do.[25]

Is it so coincidental that a sub-minimum wage is proposed when the state keeps reducing SSI and the federal government is looking for ways to get disabled people off benefits, now that we have our civil "rights"? Vocational rehabilitation (VR) agencies have offered incentives to employers for years, like partial reimbursement of wages and picking up the cost of on-the-job training. Now other incentives are proposed, such as allowing VR agencies to collect our disability checks (instead of us) for a period of time after they get us a job.[26] There won't be much of an incentive to find quality jobs because any job at all will allow them to collect the money. McDonald's will have all the sub-minimum wage workers it could possibly need.

A few years back a blind woman called me to say that she went to a job interview where the prospective employer said to her, "Why should I give you a job when you can get benefits and others cannot?" The employer's attitude was that others were more deserving of employment because they did not have the "advantage" of living on below-poverty benefits, so this disabled applicant was expected to accept her lot gracefully and go away. The employer, typical of the majority, was certainly ignorant of how disabled people fare in the U.S., and she will certainly be ignorant when the benefits are cut even more. But I would wager that if she could get this blind applicant for sub-minimum wages and Medicaid would pay for health care, her attitude would change in a flash.

Imposed poverty wages are not unique to disabled people in the age of welfare "reform." Another group to flood the overcrowded job market, be subsidized by government, and be similarly positioned for lowly jobs are those on Aid to Families with Dependent Children. The Personal Responsibility and Work Opportunity Act will force two to four million women into the job market. Is it any wonder that the National Restaurant Association adopted welfare "reform" as one of its pet projects? Uneducated women pushed off AFDC will make perfectly desperate waitresses. The bonus: the government will partially pay the wages of welfare workers (workfare), bestowing upon employers a cheaper workforce. The Clinton White House heralded the Act as going "in the right direction." The right direction for whom? The workfare gulag is designed to bolster business's interests, not to promote education or training that might result in career jobs or even stable employment for these women. And since the Act does little to create more jobs, those coming off AFDC are often competing against low-wage workers and, in some cases, displacing workers with a job onto unemployment or welfare.

Disabled people may get yet another chance to join an oppressed group of workers—prisoners. The feds have filed a class action suit to improve the conditions for hundreds of disabled inmates who cannot currently do the most basic things, like take a shower, go to the library, or take a prison job, because there is no wheelchair access. Some have even been denied the use of a wheelchair because the cells are too small for one.

Representative Frank Wolf introduced legislation that would allow prisons to conduct "pilot programs to test the feasibility of providing increased employment for federal prisoners by producing items for the private market, in conjunction with private U.S. firms, that would otherwise be produced by foreign labor." According to *CounterPunch*, billionaire Bill Gates has a chain gang. *Prison Legal News* exposed the fact that Microsoft used prison labor at the Twin Rivers Correctional Center in Monroe, Washington, to pack Windows '95 and Microsoft Office software, as well as thousands of Microsoft mice, through a subcontractor, Exmark.[27]

Just ask Gates what this means to corporate America: below-minimum wages, no overhead, no medical costs, no retirement benefits, no local taxes, no workers compensation. The taxpayers absorb the costs of doing business. Is it any wonder that since 1980 the number of working prisoners has increased 360 percent, making prison labor a boom industry in the U.S.?

Phil Gramm says that all prisoners should work a 40-hour week. Well, the "three strikes" law provides an endless labor supply, forces are at work to extend sentences, prisoners have no rights, strict "bosses" can beat laborers or put them in solitary confinement if they become uppity, prisoners are not able to unionize or to vote, and Social Security disability benefits are not collectable while in prison. Checkmate!

With the assistance of Attorney General Janet Reno's class action lawsuit to make prisons accessible (a plaque in her office reads "All furniture in this office was built by federal prison inmates") and the EEOC enforcing equal opportunity, disabled people can make use of what inmate Dan Pens calls the three strikes retirement plan and set up the first chair gang in the world.

The job climate where disabled people seek to exercise their employment "rights" is one which is downsized, outsourced, low-wage, reduced benefits, increasingly temporary, hostile to union organizing and exploitive of the desperate. A quarter of the workforce now works part-time, temporary, or contract jobs; seven million work more than one job to make ends meet.

While being disabled does not necessarily mean that one cannot work 12-hour days or more than one job to make ends meet, in many cases it is well beyond the physically possible. Indeed, that is so for nondisabled workers, as unprecedented stress levels plaguing our society and erupting in violence have shown. This rising leaner and meaner workforce dynamic is where disabled people will be pressed to "compete." It will behoove us to join with others who are working to stop the corporate plundering of the workforce.

THE FEDERAL RESERVE VS. THE PEOPLE

Liberalism's "equal opportunity" presents the illusion that it can resolve these matters. If we can rid the world of discrimination then everyone can work hard, get a job, and make it to the top, right? Far from it. The economic paradigm that creates the surplus population and leaves large numbers of people in poverty is designed that way. It is what Professor William Vickery calls "one of the most vicious euphemisms ever coined," the so-called 'natural' unemployment rate.[28] Vickery is referring the fact that 6-7 percent of the people are left jobless because those forces in command hold that unemployment is necessary to maintain the health of the economy.

This belief is so widely held that when news of the creation of 705,000 jobs in February 1996 hit the press, it shocked Wall Street so much that the Dow Jones Industrial Average tumbled 3 percent in a matter of hours. The Wall Street Journal clarified matters: "Fears that employment data will confirm that the economy is growing at a faster rate than central bankers find acceptable continue to weigh on the market . . ."[29] The telling words are what the banks "find acceptable," specifically the Federal Reserve Bank, an independent bank that sets interest rates and essentially runs the economy of the nation. Although the Fed's official goal is to keep inflation down and employment up (as demanded by the Humphrey Hawkins Act), it does quite the opposite. Noam Chomsky explains:

> If you are investing, say, in bonds, your biggest enemy is potential inflation, which means potential growth. Therefore you want to move away from places which are going to be stimulating the economy. The Federal Reserve interest rates will tend to go up to prevent stimulation of the economy and the possibility of inflation—the two tend to go together. So they've had a dampening effect on economic growth, also on jobs. They want unemployment to go up, basically. So underemployment goes up, the labor costs go down. There's less pressure for wage increases. So the commitment to full employment, which was originally at least part of their formal commitment, has disappeared.[30]

High unemployment is not the result of some "natural" force; it is social policy adopted by "God," the Federal Reserve.

Chomsky explains that the government has known for a long time that there are ways "to slow down the movement of financial capital and to protect currencies and to maintain stimulative policies by government."[31] For instance, Nobel Prize-winning economist James Tobin pointed out in 1978 that the increasing flow of financial capital would have the effect of driving down growth rates and wages, which would increase inequality by concentrating the wealth in narrower sectors of the population—a perfect description of what has occurred. Tobin's answer was to tax the flow of capital to stop the inevitable destructive results of such speculation and to shift the money to productive investment. According to Chomsky, even though this plan could benefit those private capital sectors in the long run, the Tobin tax was ignored because the overriding intention of the business class, which has unprecedented power internationally, is "to use the fiscal crisis of states to undermine the social contract that's been built up—to roll back the gains in welfare, union rights, labor rights, and so on," around the world.[32]

Job cuts or company shutdowns cost nearly 30 percent of U.S. workers their jobs from 1990 to 1995, according to the annual Corporate Report on job demographics by Cognetics Research.[33] The salient questions get back to what is work, who controls it, what is its purpose? If work is controlled by investors and Wall Street looking to make ever higher profits from people's labor, and that system is not working for all, then clearly the paradigm must be challenged. Who are the investors and the banks to say who has a job and who does not? It is clear that justice will not be possible as long as social policy is controlled by financial speculators.

PROMOTING THE GENERAL WELFARE

Inequality is a social construction that benefits a small group: the business elite. The good news is that the multinational economy that leaves the people's interests to the nonexistent mercy of capital is only possible because social policies allow it. Laissez-faire capitalism—the kind that Spencer claimed "naturally" resulted in death for those "unfit" at the bottom—has never existed. The so-called "free" market has always been controlled by banks and corporate forces intervening in government policy to their advantage.

It comes as no surprise that the U.S. has traditionally lagged behind other industrialized societies when it comes to the health, education, and welfare of all its citizens. The Organization for Economic Cooperation and Development (OECD) reports that low U.S. social welfare outlay generates "the highest poverty rates among nonelderly households" of the OECD's member countries. Access to food, housing, education, employment, health care, and transportation is necessary for all, yet not available to all. What if the U.S. practiced an equality of results where every poor person in this rich country—white, red, yellow, black, and disabled—was guaranteed a livable annual income in addition to civil rights? Would racism diminish? What if all—as in the social democratic countries of Europe—had access to health care, housing, food, a college education, regardless of whether the economic system was providing enough jobs for them? Would we have a less divided, less violent nation today?

Capitalism is not God-made; the socio/economic inequalities it generates are created by men and can be changed by the people. In a true democracy, government can be used as a social justice intervention tool to prevent the huge inequalities that result when business interests maintain such power to manipulate resources at the public's expense. If work is labor that is pushed into generating more output at the expense of the laborers, rather than providing people with decent salaries, and rewarding and creative use of their time, then that paradigm must be altered to promote work that enhances our lives, not that destroys communities, consumes lives in the pursuit of Dow Jones Averages, or leaves millions in poverty. In Europe CEOs make 20 to 30 times what the average worker makes, compared to U.S. CEOs at 200 times. Government can be used to impose a maximum wage that is linked to the minimum wage, so that if those at the top get a raise, so do those at the bottom.

Finding justice for all will mean a departure from the traditional concepts of economic growth. Our environment is stretched to its bio-physical limits. Development in the sense of a continual over-consumption of finite resources will need to be replaced with a sustainable economy—one that serves all but is not built on growth at the expense of destruction of our planet. Full employment and economic parity will need to occur within boundries. Even though the majority of societies tend to organize around the accumulation of wealth, which usually means greater output for greater profit, that paradigm will not serve humanity in a world where our natural resources are shrinking at an alarming rate. In short, the profit motive tied to increased production will have to be shattered and replaced with values other than materialism, for the human race to survive. Perhaps it is time to think about production for use, less output, more quality for the betterment of humanity, and find the means to equitably include all people as participants.

Civil rights ignited indignation over issues of exclusion and inequality, but the future calls for a *stronger social contract* to ensure the general welfare. We must ignite indignation over the injustice of the few benefitting greatly at the expense of the many.

CHAPTER 11

ENDING THE SOCIAL CONTRACT

CAPITALISM BEGINS TO EAT ITS OWN

What some financiers and politicians see as nothing more than fiscal prudence other people see as social homicide.

—Jonathan Kozol

Social Security is a part of the social contract, the Keynesian welfare state, that benefits the entire population. Today seniors like to separate Social Security retirement benefits and disabled people like to separate disability benefits from the body of "welfare," but all came out of a universal attempt to redistribute wealth to promote the public good—to mitigate hardships like high unemployment, disability, poverty, and aging. The fact that both identity groups believe that their programs will be politically contaminated if included in the same boat with welfare is indicative of just how far the right has come since FDR and even since Nixon, who signed the original welfare disability legislation, SSI.

The climate has changed to such an extent that former Governor Richard Lamm of Colorado said on *McNeil-Lehrer*, "The New Deal is unsustainable...Social Security is obsolete...Medicare is unsustainable."[1] Americans are told by government and the corporate media that all will have to "sacrifice."

Noam Chomsky explains that due to strong popular support for social programs, the monied class has been restrained politically to do more than contain the expansion of existing programs.[2] Reagan, a long-time opponent of Social Security, feared to directly attack the safety net in the 1980s, but the right has found an opening in the 1990s. Professor Chomsky writes:

> . . . changes in the international economy in the past 25 years, accelerated by the end of the Cold War, have enabled the decision-making

classes to move from containment of the threat of democracy and human rights to rollback of the despised social contract that had been won by long and often bitter popular struggle.[3]

Political theorist Antonio Gramsci defined the state as the entire range of activities and institutions by which a "ruling class" both coerces the people and wins their consent to its agenda. One way to adjust the political climate is to use cultural and educational institutions, the media, the education system, and religious organizations to put a public relations spin on an issue to elicit support.

Spin doctors cry that draconian cutbacks are *inevitable* in the interests of "fiscal prudence" and "austerity" and "balancing the budget." For instance, the Organization for Economic Cooperation and Development explains, "What was once . . . considered as a central achievement of the welfare state is now being evaluated differently;" the International Monetary Fund holds that "to assume that real 1980 benefit levels can be held constant is not realistic;" the *Christian Science Monitor* surmises, "As the world's finance leaders meet in Washington this week for the joint annual meeting of the International Monetary Fund and the World Bank, many of the world's governments—from industrialized Europe to even a few in Latin America—are looking for ways to reduce their costly role as provider of a safety net to the people," and says outright, "political leaders know that their toughest challenge is galvanizing the necessary public support at home for trimming various social expenditures."[4]

Think tanks such as Citizens for a Sound Economy, a chief supporter of that rollback doctrine of the century, the Contract with America, aim at ending entitlements, doing away with regulations that protect our health and safety, and lowering taxes for the rich. Citizens Chairman C. Boyden Gray (regulatory hatchet man for the Bush administration and former White House disability liaison) leads the effort with financing from Fortune 500 corporations. In keeping with corporate goals, Citizens' Vice President Nancy Mitchell proclaims, "We cannot do it [get rid of the deficit] unless we are willing to take on the 800-pound gorilla called entitlements."[5] Citizens is a member of the "Coalition to Save Medicare," which supports reducing Medicare funding; *CounterPunch* reports that Citizens has an arm totally devoted to lobbying for legislation that the think tank develops. The editors write:

> This dubious arrangement allows Citizens' business supporters to pay it to throw up the intellectual scaffolding needed to support corporate America's legislative program and then use the lobbying network to press for its approval.[6]

According to the National Committee for Responsive Philanthropy, Citizens produced more than 130 policy papers, conducted 50 different advertising campaigns, appeared on 175 radio and television news shows, placed 235 op-ed articles, and received coverage in more than 4,000 news articles in 1995 alone. From 1992 to 1994, twelve conservative foundations controlled assets of $1.1 billion and awarded $300 million in grants to the right-wing political agenda—privatization of government, deep reductions in federal anti-poverty spending, industrial deregulation, and the transfer of responsibility for social welfare to state and local government and charities.

The right defines the "problems"—welfare, children's SSI, food stamps, Medicare, Medicaid, benefits for immigrants. Hand in hand the Cato Institute, Robert Rector of the Heritage Foundation, and Newt Gingrich enshroud welfare with the stigma of individual pathology, as fostering "dependency," rife with "cheaters"—even anti-biblical—and claim falsely that Social Security is headed for bankruptcy.

The response of government, the corporate state, has been to adopt the austerity rhetoric rather than to refute it. David Korten, author of *When Corporations Rule the World*, predicts a crisis of immense proportion. He writes on the failure of current government to intervene in behalf of the public good:

> It is more than a failure of government bureaucracies, however. It is a crisis of governance born of a convergence of ideological, political and technological forces behind a process of economic globalization that is shifting power away from governments responsible for the public good and toward a handful of corporations and financial institutions driven by a single imperative—the quest for short-term financial gain. This has concentrated massive economic and political power in the hands of an elite few ...[7]

The "revolutionary" Republicans make it overtly clear that they intend to privatize public programs so that business will be the beneficiary of taxpayer dollars. For instance, the plan to privatize Social Security promises to be a boon to a salivating Wall Street, not only in fees to be collected by brokers investing Social Security retirement dollars ($240 billion by the year 2010, according to the *Washington Post*) but in the billions that would be added to the corporate investment kitty. Economists like Robert Kuttner may warn that there is no historical proof that the high stock market (at 8000) is sustainable, but will Americans' *unfounded* faith in the market make privatization a fait accompli? Will a public program designed to protect against capitalism's shortcomings, ironically, become dependent upon the market?

Both political parties serve the elite few. Conservative Douglas Besharov of the American Enterprise Institute wrote in the *Washington Post*, "Bill Clinton is as responsible as the Republicans for what is happening to welfare in America."[8] The neoliberal president trumpets that "the era of big government is over;" his motto is "more empowerment, less entitlement;" his slogan is "from welfare to work." The Democrat Clinton signed the Personal Responsibility and Work Opportunity Act that throws millions of mothers onto the job market, but he never answered the question "where are the jobs?" Clinton allowed $50 billion to be siphoned from food stamps, removed the cost-of-living adjustments for food stamps and took another $20 billion from aid to legal immigrants. He has done nothing to undo Reagan's slashes to SSI, rather his 1997 budget seeks to save $596 billion during the next seven years by tightening SSI eligibility rules.[9]

Clinton says that he hopes that his legacy will be to "reform" Social Security and Medicare. Social Security has already been hit dead center. When Clinton ended "welfare as we know it," he *eliminated* Title IV of the Social Security Act and so ended the 60-year federal protection for the poor guaranteed by FDR. Clinton took the first significant step to undo New Deal entitlements—which only a Democrat could get away with. The Urban Institute estimated that welfare reform will increase the number of persons in poverty by $2.6 million. The Clinton legacy? The "liberal" president moved his party to the right of Richard Nixon.

The debate is no longer over cuts versus no cuts, it is over "how much and how can we sell it?" The upshot of bipartisan consensus is that Clinton and the GOP are both undoing the social safety net. Liberalist reform, which used to mean routing out corruption, enacting civil rights, and improving the health and welfare of the citizenry, now means squeezing the most vulnerable citizens. As one employee of the Los Angeles County Department of Social Services explains, "Due to cuts and the political climate we are being instructed to do things here which we know will harm the public, which would not have been thinkable in years past."[10] Consensus, the holy middle, only underscores the defeatist nature of a "two"-party corporatized state. It is a false consensus born from suppressing the alternatives, in a system where both parties represent the same interests.

Social Security benefits have already been reduced by changing tax codes. Eighty percent of the pensions are now taxed as ordinary income—the check is worth less. The question is, what will happen, in the name of "reform," to disability benefit programs? In keeping with the neoliberal thrust to shrink government spending and echoing Vice President Gore's "Reinventing Government" mantra (resulting in fewer federal jobs and leaner outcomes), the Social Security Administration is brewing major changes to disability benefits which, like those cooked up for welfare, would alter "disability as we know it." Disability entitlements are a means of redistributing wealth and as such they are subject to political manipulation. While reform that is meant to *improve* disability programs is needed, given current corporate state directives to undo welfare in general, the very real danger is that the deficit-meisters will disingenuously "reform" Social Security at disabled people's expense. Already government is severing whole categories of disabled people from the rolls.

THE CONTINUING DISABILITY REVIEW REVIVAL

The Carter administration reacted to a *growing* program when it reduced benefits in the 1980s. More people were becoming disabled than government was willing to accommodate, so lawmakers changed the rules to dissuade enrollees. Applications for disability benefits rose from 1.5 million in 1988 to 2.7 million in 1994, singling disability out as the fastest growing entitlement program in the nation. Bob Dole proclaimed that "disability will soon become the nation's number one health care and social welfare issue."[11]

The GOP-led Congress, in keeping with pegging entitlements as the cause of the nation's ills, has accused the Social Security Administration(SSA) of not controlling the growth of the program. It has charged SSI and SSDI as being rife with abuse and in need of repair. In response, SSA proposes to both revive and increase the number of controversial Continuing Disability Reviews (CDR), mandated by President Carter every three years to determine whether one remains disabled. Commissioner Shirley Chater received more money in 1996 to remove people from the rolls than ever before in SSA history—$320 million—pushing up her total budget to $720 million. SSA expects to conduct 1.4 million reviews over a two-year period, five million by 2002.[12]

What disabled people experience at the hand of government is largely underreported and consequently unforeseen. One story to make it into the corporate press in 1993 was a CNN report alleging that SSA spent a record $32 million on employee bonuses from money Congress had designated for speeding up the disability application process. What CNN did not report was that Congress granted SSA these additional funds on the tail end of a 1991 Ways and Means Committee investigative "Report Card" which found that SSA made the average citizen wait three months for a claim determination, that those who appealed when benefits were denied had to wait a full year for a reply, and that 63 percent of the appealed denials were reversed after a hearing before an independent judge.

Congressional reports described the consequences of this decline in service in graphic detail: some qualified citizens were forced onto public assistance, others attempted or committed suicide, still others lost their homes and property, and many were forced to go without medical treatment since public health care is tied to disability benefit eligibility. In 1991, Congress gave SSA an "F" for its administration of disability benefits. Today? According to Commissioner Chater, the number of days for processing a disability claim stands at 348. She hopes to make that 262 days.[13]

Similarly, there was little media attention when Reagan arbitrarily dumped 490,000 disabled people from the rolls, until that process resulted in deaths and tragedy. Then the reports came from all over the country telling of hardship and suffering. The *New York Times* criticized the administration's actions on the front page: "In the last seven months, the Reagan administration had ended disability insurance for more than 106,000 families, including some who are almost certainly entitled to them."[14] The *L.A. Times* reported that eleven people died in 1982 as a result of the loss of their benefits. Jack Anderson wrote, "Reagan's money managers have been scrutinizing the federal budget with eyes as cold as the marble around them."[15] The *Southwest Times Record* out of Fort Smith, Arkansas, ran an article titled "Social Security Cutbacks Border on Terrorization." The *Philadelphia Inquirer* reported on the case of Kathleen McGovern, who committed suicide when she was dumped by SSA. The *Baltimore Sun* reported that Vietnam vet Roy Benavidez, awarded a medal of honor by Reagan, got terminated from the rolls.[16] Reagan intervened to make sure that Benavidez did not "fall between the cracks," but the cracks were wide and the cracks were intentional for the 489,999 who did not know the president.

The politics surrounding disability issues in the 1990s are strikingly similar to the political climate around disability during the 1980s. The current Congressional focus on growing rolls, rising costs, potential savings, and cheaters on the system, all point to what some disability advocates see as the prelude to a repeat of the Reagan bloodbath.

BACK TO THE FUTURE?
CHEATS AND COSTS MAKE POLITICAL HAY

•   Then: By the time Reagan took office the disability rolls had stabilized and appeared to be under control, but policy analysts from the General Accounting Office (GAO) and SSA Office of Assessment questioned how many people remained on the rolls who might no longer be disabled. They first concluded (incorrectly) that as much as 20 percent of the caseload no longer belonged there and that SSA was paying out $2 billion a year to people who were not eligible. Later SSA issued a report that as many as 26 percent—more than one quarter—of recipients were illegally collecting benefits. Reagan's Office of Management and Budget projected savings of $900 million for FY1985 by removing the "cheaters" from the rolls.[17]

•   Now: Rep. Jim Bunning (R-KY), who chairs the House Ways and Means Subcommittee on Social Security, says, "SSA is doing a terrible job getting people off the rolls." He adds, "Of the 4 million disabled workers currently getting benefits, roughly half—almost 2 million—are long overdue for a continuing disability review. The CDR backlog grows by 500,000 a year." Some testified before a 1996 hearing on Disability Work Program Disincentives that individuals are abusing the SSA system in "significant" numbers. Congress charges that SSI and SSDI are rife with abuse and in need of repair citing, once again, individual pathology in the form of cheaters and lingerers. It calls upon SSA for "reform" and tougher "enforcement."[18]

The GAO tells Congress that disability benefits are going to "deplete" the Retirement Trust Fund. The director of income security issues at the GAO testified that SSA could save $1.7 billion by increasing disability reviews. Experts say that for every $1 spent on a CDR, $3 will eventually be saved.

THEN: THE QUESTION OF DUE PROCESS

Under Reagan, SSA bean counters systematically shed tens of thousands of persons from the disability rolls by using an internal paper case-review process that randomly pulled names from the Baltimore computer. *The administrators doing these reviews did not directly come in contact with the person that they were deeming no longer disabled.* Nonetheless, SSA contended that 490,000 persons' medical conditions had "improved" and that they were able to work, sent the lot a termination letter, and three months later just stopped sending checks.

One career SSA employee commented, "All they knew there was 2 billion dollars to be saved" and once the effort to save this money began, it was "gargantuan, difficult to stop."[19] As one state disability determination office worker reported, "We are now in fact meeting a quota system, to satisfy the administration higher-ups and keep our jobs."[20] Public disability "insurance" was subjected to political and administrative manipulation, completely severed from the citizens' interest.

Some discarded persons managed to challenge SSA by filing appeals with the court. As the cases were heard before administrative law judges, some were found to no longer qualify, some were determined to never have met the standard, but it became apparent that 200,000 people, or about 40 percent of those cut off, still had severe physical or mental disabilities that prevented them from working. SSA had claimed that 26 percent or approximately 1 million of the individuals receiving disability benefits were doing so fraudulently; in the end, SSA was able to eliminate 290,000 people, or 7 percent, from entitlement.

The federal government's rationale was that it was following the CDR law and that it was necessary to control the growing cost of the disability program. It took attorneys like Elena Ackel of Los Angeles Legal Aid to bring the grim realities of the unjust inner workings of SSA to the 9th Circuit Court (federal), where conservative Judge Alan Grey put a stay on the entire CDR process in 1982. Even then, Health and Human Services (HHS) Secretary Margaret Heckler objected to the stay, saying that unless the order was nationwide she would not abide by any court orders. Judge Grey put out a warrant for her arrest and as Rob Peters, director of Mental Health Advocacy in Los Angeles, put it, "That is when the CDRs ceased."[21]

After this inhumane ordeal, Legal Aid attorneys, like Michael Pritchard of Arkansas, concluded that SSA could not be entrusted to act justly on the behalf of disabled citizens and pushed through new law which made it a legal right for a disability applicant to have a lawyer. The political backlash pressured Congress to pass a 1984 due process law prohibits SSA from removing a citizen from the rolls unless it can be determined that their medical condition has improved; the burden of proof would be on SSA. Disability became a more secure entitlement, but many paid a huge price to get it.

NOW: THE RISE OF THE MEDICAL "MILLS"

It is difficult to accept that government could inflict such unwarranted pain on the disabled population. It is equally difficult to imagine that SSA could be capable of acts of this magnitude again.

SSA Commissioner Chater stated in a press release announcing the funding request that she was "committed to protecting the rights of those whose cases are being reviewed." She pointed to "safeguards" in the CDR process: screening out cases that have a high likelihood of continuing eligibility; adhering to the statutory standard requiring SSA to show medical improvement; and allowing appeals through the administrative law judge process. But how comfortable can we be when cost-cutting is the goal? As mentioned earlier, SSA plans 1.4 million reviews in two years, 5 million by the year 2002[22] and it expects the reviews to produce a "cessation rate" of 14 percent—meaning an estimated 196,000 recipients would be declared ineligible for benefits in two years time.[23]

Already there are ominous signs. Recipients are being evaluated for "medical improvement" by doctors under contract to SSA. Rob Peters of Mental Health Advocacy in Los Angeles describes one medical evaluation (Certified Exam) done by an SSA examiner for a client who has been with his clinic since 1972. The client has indisputable documentation of his disabling condition, schizophrenia. Peters says, "The CE was about a five-minute event. The client was asked who is the president of the U.S., what day is this, and then the doctor found this person able to work."[24] What was worse, Peters explained, is that the SSA-contracted doctor never saw this client's medical records, although required by law to do so before making a determination.

Attorney Joel Liedner of Los Angeles, a specialist in Social Security law, relates another case in which SSA's doctors did not get the records from the treating physician before concluding that his client was "able to work."[25] SSA did not rely on the treating physician, who knew his client's medical history of a psychogenic disorder that produces uncontrollable seizures, but rather relied on the SSA-paid physician's CE. Another client of Leidner's who is an amputee was told by an SSA examiner that his stump had grown, which is medically impossible. Recalling an earlier Social Security case, Liedner reported that one of his clients had been sent to a "doctor" who turned out not to be a licensed physician at all.

According to Peters, it costs $95 to conduct one CE, so most of the $720 million funded to SSA for CDRs will go to what he calls the "medical mills" to do evaluations. Since SSA contracts with bulk provider conglomerates that operate many clinics, the potential exists to make millions a year. These businesses know it is lucrative to get and keep a CE contract from SSA. The individual "doctors" hired by these businesses know that too. Is there any doubt that this arrangement means that determinations will be favorable to SSA's get-them-off-the-public-dole goals?

There are also incentives for private physicians to return patients to the workforce. Proving disability to SSA is a time-consuming process that promises additional paperwork burdens for office staff on future patient visits. When a person is deemed disabled there is a two-year "waiting period" before they are eligible for Medicare. Reimbursements for treatment are less than through private insurance companies, and a physician who overstates a disabling condition to insure a patient's continued receipt of SSDI is subject to reprimand. The only incentive a private doctor would have to submit a finding of continuing disability to SSA is insuring proper care of a patient's condition. SSA's use of outside contractors for CDRs shows the degree to which cost-cutting now outweighs citizens' security.

The Reagan administration opposed the medical improvement standard, claiming that it would be "difficult" for SSA to prove that a condition had improved. The situations described by Peters and Leidner would indicate that SSA has found a way to duck the medical improvement standard, by rushing people through these "mills" where medical accuracy is overrun by "efficiency" and profiteering.

"It's going to be another bloodbath, because it is going to be so hastily done," says Peters. "It is a slow process to come onto the system, it needs to be a slower and more careful process going off."[26]

In addition, SSA is cracking down on the ability of the administrative law judges who hear individual appeals to reverse decisions that the medical examiners make (ALJs reinstated half of those who were cut off under Reagan). SSA has instructed judges, " An administrative law judge is bound to follow agency [SSA] policy even if, in the administrative law judge's opinion, the policy is contrary to law."[27] This directive means that the judge is to disregard federal law if it conflicts with SSA policy geared to get people off the rolls. The implied threat? The judges may forfeit their jobs if they do not abide by SSA's wishes.

The SSA order to the ALJs could also result in the denial of present and future individuals' disability benefits in application appeals. For instance, law established by the federal courts requires that pain be a consideration in determining disability, but SSA does not consider it and the courts say that the treating physician's opinion must be a "considerable or controlling weight" in determining disablement, but SSA does not treat it so.

Leidner warns, "SSA does not pay the legal fees of attorneys to protect these disabled people being told they 'can' work."[28] How many barely making it on disability benefits can afford an attorney? Or find a Joel Leidner who will represent them for free?

DISABLED CHILDREN SCAPEGOATED

The Personal Responsibility and Work Opportunity Act of 1996 contained a clause that had nothing to do with "personal responsibility" or "work opportunity" but did affect disabled children on SSI. The clause changes the eligibility rules for SSI by reengineering the process by which disability is determined. The Congressional Budget Office estimates that up to 715,000 children could lose their SSI benefits beginning July 1, 1997, as a result.[29] Other estimates put the figure closer to 300,000. How the GOP succeeded in cutting children's SSI exemplifies scapegoat politics.

According to Rep. Jim McClery (R-LA), a leader of the "reform" effort, Congress targeted children's SSI for cuts because "[SSI is] a program that's gone wrong."[30] Rep. Gerald Klecxka (D-Wis.) said, "It is a program growing out of control."[31] Republicans claimed that poor parents were coaching their children to fake disabilities in order to collect SSI. *Newsday* reported that Gingrich told the U.S. Chamber of Commerce that parents were not only coaching their children but were beating them if they did not succeed. "They're being punished for not getting what they call crazy money, or stupid money. We are literally having children suffering child abuse so they can get a check for their parents," said Gingrich.

Gingrich had plenty of help from the media. *CounterPunch* reported that the *Washington Post* started what would become a "lynch mob" with a story about children's SSI in February 1994, and all the richest journalists in the country joined the attack:

> The *Post*'s piece set off a hue and cry against children's disability, and led to an all-important ABC *Prime Time* report last October. No fewer than three of the network's millionaire correspondents disparaged the program: Wallace, chief correspondent for that segment, called it a "taxpayer scam"; Diane Sawyer said it was "a program designed to help disabled children but parents are helping themselves"; and Sam Donaldson—who receives tens of thousands of dollars of federal agriculture subsidies annually for his New Mexico ranch—marvelled at "how easy it is to get on the receiving end of what some are calling 'crazy checks.'"[32]

Marilyn Holle, an attorney with Protection & Advocacy in Los Angeles, who has worked with disabled children on SSI, says, "It's important to know that the studies by both the GAO and Social Security itself really underscore that these stories are apocryphal," and that "there are procedures in place to insure that children who do not really meet the SSI standards are not going to get benefits."[33] And Leonard Rubenstein, director of the Bazelon Center for Mental Health Law, answers charges of fraud by explaining, "SSI has been scrutinized; it's been studied; it's been analyzed; and guess what, there isn't a lot of abuse."[34]

Holle further explains that eligibility is not based just on a child's performance at one test or in a particular setting, rather "to qualify for SSI one must show both a severity and long-term character of the disability."[35] She emphasizes that such evaluations are conducted by trained professionals such as psychiatrists, physicians, psychologists, and social workers.

So what about the charge that SSI is "growing out of control"? The GAO reported that the number of children on SSI rose from 300,000 in 1990 to 900,000 in 1996. What are the reasons for the increase?

In 1991 SSI was expanded in response to the Supreme Court's Zebley decision, which required SSA to better evaluate children's physical and mental impairments. Children who had disabilities not included on SSA's formal list of disabling conditions could be assessed individually under Zebley. In addition, children inappropriately denied SSI since 1980 were encouraged to re-apply, so more children became rightfully eligible for benefits and were put on the rolls.

What is the value of the Zebley test? "It is only by looking at people individually and seeing how combinations of impairments impact their daily life that you can really evaluate the disability,"[36] explains Holle. She believes the individual evaluation is a better measure of the impact of a person's disability than the listings themselves. For instance, Holle says, "Think about someone who tests at an IQ of 71 and who has another impairment, although not one on the listings. By eliminating the individual assessment, you are saying to this person, we're not going to look at you as a whole person, we're not going evaluate how the combination of impairments come together and impact on you. We're going to exclude you." Yet that is exactly what the nation has done by reversing Zebley.

Jonathan Stein of Community Legal Services in Philadelphia, who was key counsel in the Zebley case, dispels the myth that children with minor behavioral and other conditions now get SSI as a result of Zebley. "The fact is that prior to Zebley," says Stein, "a number of children, such as kids with cerebral palsy, cystic fibrosis, mental retardation, and spina bifida were not being fairly evaluated."[37]

Claims of children receiving unwarranted benefits fly in the face of the facts. New rules which took effect in 1991 resulted in half the children claiming SSI being denied, nationally totalling over 800,000. Since then allowance rates have sharply fallen, so that 2 of every 3 applicants are denied. The system was already working to keep out children with minor conditions.

Stein believes that misconceptions and myths about fraud have not only fueled the Republican charge against SSI but that their extreme position is what influenced the Childhood Disability Commission to agree to eliminate the individual test. "The spill-over of an extremist position like the House's is lowering the common denominator of what people feel we should be doing. This is more of a political judgement than a policy judgment," he says.[38]

Despite efforts to stop it, the scapegoat campaign succeeded. The Consortium for Citizens with Disabilities (CCD) estimated that 38 percent of kids with pulmonary tuberculosis, 33 percent with mental retardation, 29 percent with developmental disabilities such as autism, 29 percent with burns, 25 percent with head injuries, 22 percent with arthritis, and 18 percent with epilepsy will no longer receive benefits as a result of not being able to meet the restrictive medical listings.[39] The estimates vary on just how much will be "saved" by no longer sending a check to the parents of these children. If we use the CCD estimate of those to be dropped from the program—335,000 (about 27 percent)—and the 1995 figure of $25 billion for the total cost of the program, eliminating the individual evaluation could mean a "savings" to taxpayers of approximately $8 billion.

Children who lose SSI are targeted to lose their Medicaid health coverage as well. It is sure to follow that fewer parents will be able to care for their disabled children at home, and more children will be institutionalized at higher cost. This is the outcome of scapegoat politics, saving a little here but ignoring that the social need does not disappear. For disability activists, it is painfully clear that one spinoff of welfare "reform" will be that fewer parents will be willing to have a disabled baby .

THE POLITICS OF THE DEFINITION OF DISABILITY

One day you are disabled, the law changes, and the next day you aren't. How can that be? Historically, the definition of "disability" has been kept flexible precisely so that government could restrict or expand the program in response to economic or political directives. When HHS Secretary Joseph Califano complained that entitlement programs left too little in the general budget for the government to accomplish other goals,[40] the motivation for the Carter "reform" surfaced: cutting disability benefits freed up money which could be used by the executive branch for its priorities, making disability "insurance" one more volleyball to be batted about by political forces.

Now that the rollback forces are in power, definitions are being used to reduce the disability rolls. Children's SSI is a perfect example; the new definition tightens the requirements to "a finding of a listed impairment that results in marked and severe functional limitations and that can be expected to last for 12 months or result in death."[41] Those not meeting this standard will no longer receive public aid. Governors have decided that they would like to define "disability" and efforts are ongoing to reform Medicaid to such a purpose. As Senator John D. Rockefeller IV put it, "This will allow new definitions to be concocted that could deny benefits to those in desperate need."[42]

Another way to squeeze out numbers is to make determinations based on "severity" of disablement. If disability entitlements are to be cut, the question becomes, "Who is still worthy of assistance?" Who are the "deserving" disabled? When this question filtered through the California Department of Rehabilitation, the resolution was that people who are "severely" disabled on the basis of functional assessments are the most deserving of state resources. Who is functionally "severely" disabled? As Rocky Burks, director of Independent Living Services, pointed out, "That would mean the majority of the developmentally disabled would be included as 'severely' disabled. But a paraplegic, for instance, considered able to work but who might not be able to perform the same job as before their injury might not be 'severely' disabled enough to qualify for rehabilitation benefits because of 'functional' ability."[43]

Paul Seifert, director of government affairs with the International Association of Psychosocial Rehabilitation Services in Columbia,

Maryland, says, "Either we construct a back door to the programs or Congress will create a trap door that will drop people into situations of homelessness."[44] The intent of the rollback Congress is to do both: backdoor people out via CDRs and frontdoor eliminate them via definitions of disability. The impetus is on narrowing eligibility, changing the way determinations are made, time-limiting benefits (without any guarantee of employment), and decreasing cash benefits. The political climate that kept the emphasis on entitlement has been upstaged by cost-cutting goals.

BOTH PARTIES DUMPING WHOLE CATEGORIES

One of the first major moves in the trap door direction came when neoliberal President Clinton, not to be be outdone by the right, signed GOP legislation attached to the Contract with America Advancement Act (four days after it hit his desk) that eliminated drug addiction and alcoholism as disability categories. When he signed welfare reform Clinton eliminated another category, disabled legal immigrants on SSI.

The right, in the form of the "tough love" American Enterprise Institute, backed by Charles Murray, and the Progress and Freedom Institute, has campaigned for the demise of SSI in its entirety. Tough love proponents seem to ignore that the cutoffs promise greater social costs in their wake. The International Union of Gospel Missions reported a 60 percent increase in the number of people needing shelter and services from food kitchens. Food stamps cutoffs and future benefit cutoffs promise more than volunteerism can handle. Without Medicaid, addicts will be financially unable to seek treatment. They will, however, still have addictions and still seek to support those addictions, often through violent crime. Health care costs will increase as addicts and others cut from disability benefits use emergency services as their medical "plan." An addict living in Iowa gets $330 per month plus Medicaid, but hospitalization or imprisonment for only one week would easily cost ten times that amount.[45] Tough love could actually backfire.

MAKING THE ADA PAY

With the momentum once again on costs, the simple desire of individuals with disabilities to make a choice to work without foregoing public health care or untimely loss of other benefits has been jumped on by "Return to Work" (RTW) policy-making proponents, including government, disability groups, and businesses looking for a contract with government.

Advocate Frank Bowe (who is deaf) writes:

Congress and the president hoped that millions not now working would start working after the ADA was enacted. . .we ourselves will see our rights recede in time if Washington concludes that there are few or no societal benefits to be gained from our civil rights.[46]

Those "societal benefits" Bowe refers to are the $20,000 in combined savings to Social Security programs and in new tax income garnered annually by moving one person off benefits and into a job. Multiplying tens of thousands of dollars times millions of people yields tens of billions in savings and new tax revenue. The message is that disabled people should try harder to get off the dole and work because now that we have the ADA we owe it to Uncle Sam—or else.

Bowe confirms the deal disability elites cut with President Bush; we got our civil "rights" in exchange for getting disabled people off entitlements. Has any other minority had a price tag put on their heads for freedom and independence? Must we accept that our civil rights come with indebtedness?

Making the ADA pay has other meanings. SSA proposes to form public-private partnerships to further its goal of "addressing program growth." For example, Mark Dakos, vice-president of Work Recovery Inc., told the Social Security Subcommittee that his company can "objectively" assess an applicant's ability to work and promised that his ERGOS Work Simulator would greatly reduce disability claims coming into SSA. It's no surprise that companies are jumping on privatization as a means of solving the return-to-work issue. Vocational rehabilitation agencies seeking contracts with SSA stand to collect between $15,000 and $50,000 in federal funds by taking SSDI/SSI dollars that now go to the disabled individual.[47]

It seems clear that money saved through disability reviews, preventing disabled people from getting benefits, and dumping whole categories from the rolls won't go back into job development for disabled people. According to the *Los Angeles Times*, "If officials can slow the growth of the disability program, some of the money saved could be used to help bail out the retirement fund."[48] Cutting disability benefits is likely to turn into a zero sum game, where the money goes back into the general fund (remember Jimmy Carter) at disabled people's expense.

Disabled people have long been made into commodities to be bought and sold by entrepreneurs in cahoots with government; SSA "reform" may be a backdoor way to make the ADA pay for everyone but us. Instead of placating Washington budget-cutting bureaucrats, advocates must turn the emphasis on full employment for all; we must ensure that disabled and nondisabled alike are able to get and keep living wage jobs—or are provided a humane subsistence in the absence of those jobs.

THE REDESIGN RACKET:
DUMPING FIRST—EMPLOYMENT?. . .WELL, MAYBE LATER

People are being booted off benefits before policies are in place that will prepare the way for secure employment. Has disability policy changed so that those cut off from benefits will be better equipped to manage on their own? Have financial penalties been removed? Has the private health care system been revamped so that it does not discriminate against disabled people? Are there more work opportunities for disabled job seekers? Are there jobs available at wages that make it possible for disabled persons to support themselves? Is there less discrimination? What is the ADA's performance for new hires? Are employers mandated to provide a "reasonable accommodation"? Has rehabilitation provided adequate opportunities? Is assistive technology affordable and readily available? Is personal assistance a part of national policy? At the time of this writing the answer is a resounding "no."

The bean counters are now looking at RTW as a budget-balancing device. Social Security Subcommittee Chairman Bunning says he favors "short-term" rather than "lifetime" benefits as an "incentive" to return to work; he means limiting benefits to three years (without any guarantee of a job). Some, like George Waters of the Washington state-based Return-to-Work Group, expand on this position by proposing to end the "severely" disabled category. They contend that all disabled people can work and they support limited benefits—three years and you're off the dole.[49]

Time limits would unilaterally sever millions from entitlements. But disability does not adhere to Congressional time clocks. A time-limit solution is based on a false understanding of a disability as necessarily curable, or subject to improvement. Such proposals revive the notion that people linger on the rolls because they are enjoying the good life on disability benefits. Is it really credible that someone living at 74 percent of the federal poverty level on SSI at $470 per month would want to remain impoverished if there was an alternative? Those who claim that people "fake" disability to get out of some hellish job must not understand how hellish SSI is; no one wants to end up on it. For disabled people SSI is a Faustian bargain, an awful solution to which many have no alternative.

Who is "able" to work and when is still an unanswered question. The Return-to-Work Group claims that as many as 40 percent of the disabled population can work (and that Congress would reap a net savings of $40 billion in the next ten years);[50] the President's Committee says that 11 million want to work; the GAO says, "Almost one of every two beneficiaries may not be realistic candidates for return to work because of their age or because they are expected to die within several years;"[51] and census data show that 51 percent of people with disabilities believe that their disabilities prevent them from working.

Rob Peters of Mental Health Advocacy says the disability qualifying standard is tough enough to meet and adds that 85 percent of those on SSI for more than two years will be legitimately disabled for the rest of their lives. "These are people who may take some marginal jobs to make a hundred dollars here and there, but they are never going to be fully employed because they cannot manage that," explains Peters.[52]

Numerous individuals testified before the Committee on Aging June 5, 1996, that 15-30 percent of people on the SSA rolls are able and willing to work. But United Cerebral Palsy responded, "This figure startled us. We believe it to be a very low estimate and suggest that with access to supported employment, assistive technology, personal assistance, health care and other supports, this figure would be much higher. It is difficult to believe that 70-85 percent of the current case load of SSI/SSDI beneficiaries are incapable of and/or unwilling to work."[53]

There is no proof that 70 percent, 40 percent or 10 percent could work. Government's past attempts to dictate such determinations has proved incompetent and unjust. Who is "able to work" may never be answerable by "experts." Disabled people are the best judge of what they can do, yet government has never devised a system that would allow disabled people to work without fearing the loss of financial and medical support.

Disability leaders believe that once work disincentives are out of the way, disabled people will have "equality of opportunity" and become employed. This is double-think. The system is designed to keep large numbers out of the workforce; 6 percent are compulsorily unemployed in order to keep wages low and profits high. While removing disincentives will help disabled people take jobs, it will do nothing to see that there are 11 million jobs to be taken.

What if that $720 million going to boot people off benefits was used to create secure, decent-paying jobs with health benefits instead? Would we see disabled people "walk off the rolls" then?

EQUAL PAIN? EQUAL GAIN?

Gore Vidal warns that the elite in America are surprisingly successful at convincing people to vote against their own interests, and, even more astoundingly, to think against their own interests.

The GOP-led Congress has thrown austerity bait at the American public and we have swallowed the lies: that entitlements fuel the deficit, that the budget-meisters' intent is genuine and the pain of deficit reduction will be equally shared among all. That logic completely ignores the fact that the decision-making classes and special interests are fighting for a greater piece of the budget pie and have no intention of giving up anything.

The balanced budget agreement proposed a $200 billion cut from entitlements. Meanwhile, 1997 tax cuts will cost the government $85 billion over five years. The average tax cut for middle-income families and individuals will be less than $200, yet the richest 1 percent will have their taxes reduced by more than $16,000 each year. The 1.8 percent of the population that is rich enough to pass along money to heirs will not have to pay as much in inheritance taxes. The capital gains tax cut, 85 percent of which benefits the already wealthy, will provide yet more revenue for their class. (According to the Center on Budget and Policy Priorities, the real cost of the tax cut will be $250 billion..[54])

In light of this, proposing "savings" by cutting people off benefits or reducing benefits across the board (one suggestion: cut SSI by 10 percent) qualifies as vile. How much more "austere" can one be than $470 (SSI) or $682 (SSDI) per month? Yet Trent Lott (R-MS) proposes to adjust the Consumer Price Index upon which yearly increases are based downward and to reduce the Social Security cost-of-living increase. This, in effect, would be a backdoor way to balance the budget on the backs of the disabled and elderly. The disabled who don't have a lifetime of earnings to make up for the loss in Social Security income would be especially hard hit.

There has always been some opposition to public benefits for the disabled. The austerity ruse is simply a re-emerging denigration of disablement in general, an expression of the ongoing resentment of those who do not "perform" and cannot be used to "produce" in a capitalist state. Yet some of our own leaders would prep disabled people to accept the decision-making class'es pitch to reduce government's role as a safety net provider. Professor Frederick Thayer of the Graduate School of Public and International Affairs of the University of Pittsburgh sums up the situation this way:

> The holy war on "entitlements" is based on the theory that there are too many old, sick, disabled, poor and unemployed Americans, and too many students in high schools and colleges. Society cannot afford to support all of them, and many must now find work or suffer deprivation.[55]

FDR, in his first inaugural address in 1933, refuted the elite's austerity rhetoric that hard times were "inevitable":

> Plenty is at our doorstep, but a generous use of it languishes in the very sight of the supply. Primarily this is because the rulers of the exchange of mankind's goods have failed, through their own stubborness and their own incompetence . . . Practices of the unscrupulous money changers stand indicted in the court of public opinion, rejected by the hearts and minds of men .

Wealth is as abundant as ever. Over the past 15 years, Standard & Poor's 500 Index, the reading for how blue-chip corporate America is doing, rose 574 percent. There is no need for any austerity to be imposed upon the disabled, the elderly, or impoverished families. Just as in FDR's day, the wealthy have devised ways to benefit at the public's expense. Will the "money changers stand indicted in the court of public opinion" in the 1990s, or will they be allowed to get away with their greed and short-term gains at the expense of the rest of us?

Disability leaders hail Clinton as a protector of our programs. While Clinton did insist on preserving the Medicaid disability entitlement when the House wanted to abolish it, he also waffled on block grants, conceded that cuts are necessary to entitlements, and proposed to put a per-capita cap on Medicaid benefits. When welfare reform legislation eliminated over 300,000 children from SSI (and from their only source of health care, Medicaid), Clinton did not insist that the misplaced provision be dropped because it was part of the Social Security disability regulations for children. Instead the Democratic President remarked that the Personal Responsibility Act "had serious flaws that are unrelated to welfare reform" but he believed it was his "duty to seize the opportunity it gives us to end welfare as we know it."[56]

We need to follow the lead of the French, who do understand the class dynamics behind austerity. When the corporate-controlled government in France proposed cutting pension plans, hundreds of thousands of the French simply turned out into the streets to say "non."

Social Security, disability, and health care must be secured as protected funds that are not subject to federal budget negotiations. This would prevent the budget-meisters from conveniently changing the rules to dip into Social Security funds for their own political purposes. And, with entitlements out of the spotlight, future budget battles would expose where the real money in the general fund is going—to corporate subsidies and the military.

CHAPTER 12

BURSTING GRAND ILLUSIONS

MOTHER TERESA, "REVOLUTIONARIES," DEVOLUTION AND PERSONAL RESPONSIBILITY

All animals are equal, but some animals are more equal than others.

—George Orwell, *Animal Farm*

I can't stand the pompous among us who complain about welfare. The biggest welfare recipients in the United States are the richest people.

—Larry King

The 104th Congress's attempt to undo the social contract needs to be characterized as what it was: the foul birth of pernicious neglect, cousin to that 1980s Orwellian oxymoronic policy termed "benign neglect." The rollback doctrine attests to the unspoken agreement between our representatives and their wealthy business sponsors: public money can be manipulated to benefit the wealthiest and charity can keep the poor conveniently impoverished scapegoats, while mean-spirited "flexibility" wreaks havoc on the population.

MOTHER TERESA AND CHARITABLE NEGLECT

Mother Teresa made waves in disability circles when she refused to comply with disabled access laws requiring an elevator in her homeless shelter in New York City. She based her refusal on the "religious grounds" that elevators constitute a luxury. Disabled activists were quick to point out that Mother Teresa and the nondisabled sisters do use elevators in other New York buildings. Begging poverty, MT held that the elevator money could be better used on soup and sandwiches.[1]

One evening I attended a gathering to hear Christopher Hitchens talk about his book about Mother Teresa, *The Missionary Position*. I wasn't surprised to learn that MT was connected with the likes of businessman Charles Keating of S&L scandal fame or that her global income far exceeds what she spends on charity.

Hitchens revealed that MT asked presiding judge Lawrence Ito of Los Angeles to grant clemency to Keating when he was charged with fraud because Keating had been "kind and generous to God's poor." When L.A. District Attorney Paul Turley replied to MT's letter, explaining that Keating had defrauded 17 individuals out of more than $900,000 and 17,000 out of $252,000,000, and that her charity was in receipt of stolen money, he asked MT, what would Jesus do if he had money that was stolen? Turley wrote:

> I submit that Jesus would promptly and unhesitatingly return the stolen property to its rightful owners. You should do the same. You have been given money by Mr. Keating that he has been convicted of stealing by fraud.[2]

MT did not respond to the DA's letter and no money was returned. Is it possible that Mother Teresa did not install that elevator because, like Keating, she was most interested in illusions?

In fact MT and the sisters sit on a vast treasure trove which they barely tap to do their "good work." While her clinics for the poor in India lack adequate medical staffing and supplies and her proposed homeless shelter will lack an elevator, MT collects enough capital globally to more than finance state-of-the-art medical faciltes and many New York elevators. According to Hitchens's sources, just one of her checking accounts holds about $50 million.[3] It seems MT was more interested in accumulating capital than in providing an elevator that would provide dignity to the disabled. Is that "benign neglect" or "pernicious neglect"?

At the Hitchens gathering an elderly woman who had attended an event when Margaret Thatcher was Prime Minister of England related that Thatcher had said that one billion people would have to be eliminated from the population by the end of the century. She added that when Thatcher was asked how, she responded "benign neglect".

"Benign neglect," calculated policy under Thatcher and Reagan, went like this: leave the poor, the unemployed, and starving to be objects of charity and without hope. In step, MT says, "it is very beautiful for the poor to accept their lot, to share it with the passion of

Christ. I think the world is being much helped by the suffering of the poor people."[4] In the elevated spiritual state of poverty, MT does not concern herself with the lack of decent jobs, low-income housing, social security, or disabled access.

Many Republicans and too many of their Democratic colleagues advocate replacing social services with charities and volunteerism. The elite promote MT as a saint because she serves monied interests. She mythologizes and justifies "benign neglect" spiritually for them; the poor are meant to suffer, and consequently the rich do not need to redistribute their hoards of wealth to anyone. And disabled people—in MT's picture—are to silently accept their lot and be carried by able-bodied saints who know what's best.

Both the right and neoliberals are spinning complementary illusions—that money is short for social spending—as they put the squeeze on the poor and disabled via pernicious neglect. The deficit actually fits well into the plans and ideology of the right—corporate-dominated social policy determines the "scarcity" of public funds while the missing money is being amassed by the wealthy and the multinationals.

THE DIRTY LITTLE SECRET

It's no secret that Republicans have never favored Social Security, welfare, Medicaid, Medicare, unemployment benefits, public education, subsidized housing, or disability spending. David Stockman, after leaving his position as President Reagan's budget director, explained the less obvious: "Why the conservative anti-spending party [GOP] ended up ratifying a half trillion dollar per year Welfare state" is "the modern dirty little secret of the Republican Party." Wrote Stockman, "The conservative opposition helped build the American Welfare State brick by brick during the three decades prior to 1980."[5] What better way to wipe out social spending than to design it for failure?

During the 1980s, Thatcher and Reagan called for a "new" approach to governance: reduced public spending, tax cuts for the wealthy and corporations, deregulation, privatization of publicly owned undertakings, and tough monetary targets. They heralded the "free" market as the salvation for all social ills. In fact the abandonment of Keynesian economics in favor of a policy of "benign neglect" produced a sharp rise in unemployment, and higher inflation in both nations, and, thanks to Reagan, made the U.S. the largest debtor nation in the world. Were the money managers in Reagan's White House incompetent? Why was the debt allowed to go unchecked by the Reaganites?

Economist Walden Bello, describing the GOP's goals during the Reagan regime in his book *Dark Victory*. wrote, "The…[goal] was the dismantling of the New Deal's 'social contract' between big capital, big labor, and big government."[6] Market theorist Friedrich von Hayk said in 1985, "Reagan thinks it is impossible to persuade Congress that expenditures must be reduced, unless one creates deficits so large that absolutely everyone becomes convinced that no more money can be spent."[7] What better way to get rid of the welfare state than to get rid of the funds for it?

Stockman, the insider, validated Bello's theory and von Hayk's observation in an interview with author William Greider, when he revealed that Reagan-era budget deficits were intended to place the GOP in the position to claim that they had to "logically" slash social spending to avert a national financial crisis and "balance the budget."

The GOP "revolutionaries" of the 104th Congress pressed onward, falsely placing the blame for the deficit on the welfare state and entitlements. Bob Dole, who has had his health insurance paid for by the federal government for 39 years,[8] bragged to the American Conservative Union, "I was there fighting the fight, voting against Medicare [the only health care for many disabled]. . . Because we knew it wouldn't work in 1965." The GOP sought to dismantle AFDC, Social Security, Medicare, and Medicaid via the "Contract with America." House Speaker Gingrich admitted as much when he said that his proposed changes to Medicare would allow it "to wither on the vine."

By 1990, 80 percent of all government borrowing went to pay the interest on the debt. By 1992 the debt was $4.2 trillion and serviced by bondholders.[9] Essentially, deficit borrowing redistributed the people's tax dollars into the banks, the investment firms, and their clientele of wealthy investors. When those financial institutions, like the savings and loan industry, deregulated by Reagan, took bad risks, the taxpayers footed the bill. In the case of the S&L failures, the bill was $500 billion and the CEOs, developers, and real estate moguls made off with their profits virtually unscathed.

There is a difference between going into debt for good reasons and for bad ones. The debt itself was not at a precarious level under Reagan (at $2.7 trillion) relative to the GDP, and it is even less so today. The case can be made for running up the debt when it benefits all of society. If the money were to be spent, for instance, on job creation which in turn would enhance societal wealth, that would be a socially justifiable debt because subsequent increased wealth would eventually overtake the deficit, as FDR proved in the 1930s.

The benefactors of the deficit are attempting to undo the New Deal and replace it with a business deal. Thatcherism and Reagonomics have produced a society where childhood malnutrition and disease are on the rise; where one in every three British babies and one in every four American babies is born into poverty. Reagan, Bush, and now Clinton have wasted public resources on the military, subsidies for business, and Wall Street bail-outs. The anti-spending proponents have no qualms about giving government handouts to benefit the business class.

"REVOLUTIONARY" DEVOLUTIONARIES

Randolph Bourne, socialist and writer with a disability, who is most famous for his 1911 prophetic conclusion that "war is the health of the state," once said, "The purpose of an education is to know a revolution when you see one."[10] The purpose is also to be able to spot a pseudo-revolution when you see one; Republican "revolutionaries" are running through well-worn ruts. Historian Robert McElvaine explains:

> The idea that the central objective of government ought to be to make the rich richer has been the basic thrust of conservative political parties in the country from Hamilton's Federalists through Henry Clay's Whigs and William McKinley's Republicans of Bryan's era down to the present. The Reaganites gave this hoary theory a new name when they spoke of "supply side economics," and Gingrich and   his followers now dub the same idea "revolutionary."[11]

The pseudo revolutionaries mirrored Reganomics in their 1997 budget deal by proposing to eliminate the estate tax entirely for those wealthy enough to have an estate. But they settled for a capital gains tax cut—the majority of the cut going to families with incomes over $200,000. The capital gains tax reductions, estate tax cuts, and reduction in the corporate alternative minimum tax all disproportionately benefit those at the top of the economic ladder.

The "deficit busting" Congressional tax cuts balloon each year, resulting in a loss of income for government programs of $15.7 billion in 2007. In addition, Congress gave the military $7.4 billion more than it asked for in 1995 and $11 billion more in 1996. The 105th Congress proposed to end the minimum corporate tax altogether. Longstanding corporate deductions such as three martini lunches, the $110 million granted to McDonald's and other corporate giants to advertise overseas, and subsidies to arms merchants for advertising and promoting arms sales to developing countries, were left untouched.

Voodoo economics similarly decreased taxes for the wealthy and corporations, increased military spending, and brought on high inflation and high unemployment in the 1980s. There is no guarantee that the deficit busters will not leave a greater problem, like recession or depression, in their wake. Frederick Thayer, professor emeritus at the Graduate School of Public and International Affairs of the University of Pittsburgh, explains:

> Whenever the deficit is reduced as a percentage of GDP, the rate of economic growth declines not long thereafter. Sometimes the decline becomes a recession. There are no contrary cases. Economists tend to say that economic decline causes a reduction in revenues that, in turn, creates a deficit, but the cause-effect relationship is in the other direction.[12]

Ironically, the "revolutionaries'" one original move, enacting a balanced budget amendment to the Constitution, is their worst. It promises momentous change resulting in social and economic disaster, because an inflexible balanced budget amendment would permit no leeway to adjust public spending to bolster the economy or help the people in the event of a recession or depression.

NEWTSPEAK DEVILS IN THE DETAILS

Revolutionary lingo—like welfare "transformation" and "personal responsibility"—is Orwellian Newtspeak that masks the reality of what House Speaker Gingrich (*Time* magazine's Man of the Year in 1995, under ethical violation charges in 1996, fined $300,000 for lying to Congress in 1997) would do to our people under the guise of "flexibility." Central to Gingrichite philosophy is devolution, the transferral of authority for regulation and spending from Washington to the states via block grants, said to "empower" state governments to become more "efficient" through greater flexibility over rules and regulations.

An examination of "flexibility" reveals the true nature of states' rights/local control proponents' intent. For example, block granting of Medicaid would put the states in charge of the design of health programs, including eligibility and the amount, scope, and duration of services. In actuality, the 1995 GOP plan to devolve Medicaid to the states sought to end the guarantee of service for the disabled, pregnant women, and children under 12.

The finer details tell the story. Senator John Chafee (R-RI), a defender of disability protections, fought for and won an amendment to the Senate's draconian Medicaid plan that would preserve the entitlement for the disabled, pregnant women, and children under 12, preventing states from opting not to provide Medicaid to them. But 24 Republican governors signed a letter to Senator Dole complaining that this version retained too many "onerous federal mandates on the states" and demanded that the Chafee protection be taken out.[13]

Justice for All, a disability organization, responded to the governors' position by asking, "What difference does it make? If they plan to protect the interests of all their citizens what difference does it make if a few words are added to ensure that people with disabilities are protected?"[14]

The governors maintained that mandating coverage for disabled people, pregnant women, and children under 12 "will militate against the states' ability to implement reforms." If that is the case, then the intent of "reform" must be to limit eligibility. As Rep. Edward Markey (D-MA) put it, "Will states re-write their definition of disability when they meet up with an economic crunch? Who will be defined away first?"[15]

The governors wanted to allow the states to define disability, meaning there could be as many as 50 different definitions. The Association of Retarded Citizens explained, "With less money, one clear reason that the governors would want to set their own definitions would be to limit eligibility."[16]

The governors further wrote that entitlements "create both a huge potential cost shift to states and unlimited potential for litigation..." This resulted in the removal of the right to sue clause in the Senate

Medicaid bill. Since private lawsuits allow citizens to hold state government to their obligation to provide federally mandated services, the governor's objection was a thinly veiled desire to restrict access. The protection provided by the Chafee amendment would ensure a citizen's right to services and to the courts. The governors did not ask the most logical question, if block grants mean a cost shift to the states that the states can not absorb, why support devolution at all?

Senate Majority Leader Dole dropped Chafee's amendment even though the Senate Finance Committee passed it 17 to 3. According to the *Washington Post*, GOP leaders explained, "While there may have been some confusion on the part of Chafee and other committee members, they never really intended to vote for the disabled guarantee." Despite a transcript that proved Chafee's amendment had been adopted, Dole rewrote history and said, "It wasn't included. I think it was just an honest misunderstanding."

This prompted Senator Rockefeller, a member of the committee, to ask, "Where am I? Is this the United States Senate or the Twilight Zone?"[17] Disabled people may conclude that if state government excludes us from guarantees of public health care when private insurance discriminates against us, we will be in the twilight zone.

Thwarted in 1995 but still intent on reform, the National Governors Association (NGA) presented its own Medicaid reform plan in 1996 which, although claiming to "guarantee health care to our most needy citizens," belied that assertion. Families USA explains:

> Significant numbers of very vulnerable groups will lose existing or future coverage—including people with disabilities, seniors, older children, and families receiving public assistance. All guarantees of meaningful coverage will be eliminated. New and unaffordable cost-sharing requirements may be imposed. Federal standards for quality of health care will be nullified And the ability of program beneficiaries to enforce remaining rights will be weakened.[18]

Save Our Security chair Arthur Flemming criticized the NGA plan, saying it would "substitute an insurance program with a lottery." Justin Dart, Jr. warned, "The Medicaid plan proposed recently by some of the nation's governors will result in shorter lives and increased pain and sickness for millions of Americans with and without disabilities."[19]

"Shorter lives" appears to be the goal, as an editorial by that title in the *Weekly Standard*, the voice of the new majority, put it: "Sick people are expensive. The dead are a burden to no one. . . The only answer is some kind of rationing, Gingrich knows that."[20]

Former Surgeon General Everett Koop called the 104 Congress's attempt to cut Medicaid and Medicare "health care rationing." Looking at the figures one can see why. In 1995 the GOP proposed to cut Medicare $270 billion, Clinton proposed $124 billion. Congress wanted to cut $72 billion from Medicaid, Clinton, $59 billion. The Consumers Union estimated Congressional Medicaid cuts would force an additional 12 million low-income people into the ranks of the uninsured. The Long Term Care Campaign estimated that nearly three million Americans stood to lose Medicaid long- term care protection, since the plan would cut $88.5 billion from the 1995 funding level.[21] Because people with disabilities and those over 65 account for 27 percent of those on Medicaid but use 67 percent of the funds, they would be disproportionately impacted by the cuts.

The GOP, still pressing to block-grant Medicaid, has added Department of Education funds to their list. A block grant curtails citizen entitlement to services because federally guaranteed public services are converted to discretionary state expenditures; the entitlement or guarantee of assistance to the individual is lost. Generally, a grant caps the total federal expenditures so that programs can no longer expand to meet the need. Federal funding is etched in stone and as a result, there is no increase to accommodate state budget crunches. During recessions states would face hard choices like reducing benefit levels, instituting waiting lists, or decreasing the population served. A state could run low on funds and choose to turn away a citizen who now is eligible.

The *New York Times* described the Contract as "the greatest attempt in modern history to reward the wealthy at the expense of the poor" and in fact the results are in; the poor shouldered the burden of the 104th Congress's entitlement rollbacks. The Urban Institute reported that 93 percent of the cuts to entitlement programs—food stamps, welfare, SSI, subsidized housing—passed by the "revolutionaries" of the 104th Congress and signed by Clinton affect poor people.

The 1997 bipartisan budget agreement, although heralded as a balancing of social programs with tax cuts, is in fact a measure that provides for the decline or expiration of social program initiatives after a few years. The Center on Budget and Policy Alternatives points out that all but one of the social program initiatives expire or decline significantly. For example:

- Funding to protect some low-income elderly and disabled people from the costs of increased Medicare premiums terminates after 2002;

- The child health block grant, purporting to provide expanded coverage to some of the children of the poor and working poor, will actually provide coverage for fewer each year because the funding either freezes or declines for a number of years;

- The $3 billion annual funding to states and cities to help move those on welfare to work ends in 1999. (Do they think there will be enough jobs available by then?)

- The restoration of SSI to legal immigrants only applies to those who were in the U.S. before August 22, 1996 (all others can never rely on assistance no matter how disabled or old they may become).

John Kenneth Galbraith noted, "Government expenditures only become a burden when they are for the anonymous underclass. Medical care for the poor, urban education, public housing for the otherwise homeless and, above all, the welfare safety net, including for young mothers and their children, are heavy burdens."[22] Under the guise of flexibility and efficiency, the real intent of the devolutionaries is to unload the costs of providing public services. For the one out of every seven Americans, six million of whom are disabled adults and children, who depend on public support, "devolution" becomes a code word for de-funding. Funding for all social programs—which already falls short—declines from $46.7 billion in the next five years (2002) to $39 billion in the second five years (2007). We face a hocked future, a zero sum game, where one oppressed group gets pitted against another in competition over a greatly reduced public pie.

What can we garner from this? The GOP and neoliberal preoccupation with efficiency has not only led to a deterioration of the nation's collective concern for all but to an adeptness on the part of lawmakers at deceiving the public.

STATES RACE TO THE BOTTOM: WHOEVER CREATES THE MOST POVERTY AND THE LEAST HEALTH CARE "WINS"

Lowell Weicker, former Senator and former governor of Connecticut, commented on the dangers of devolution: "Many of us, in many states, see this as regression into the darker times of institutionalization, or worse." Weicker recalled the early 1980s, when federal judges admonished governors for inhuman and discriminatory civil rights violations of people with disabilities in institutions, and warned, "The potential exists in many states for this to happen again."[23]

There are harbingers of how the states will use their new authority. Twenty-six states have initiated welfare reform plans through federal waivers or changes to state law. The state plans exhibit a trend toward "race to the bottom" social service spending.

Republican Governor John Engler of Michigan, GOP poster boy for welfare "reform," severed 83,000 people from the General Assistance (GA) rolls, forty percent of whom were disabled. His state flexed its muscle and simply eliminated GA, the government program of last resort for the displaced surplus population.

There has always existed a federal/state tension on entitlements because when the federal government denies benefits, the financial burden falls on states or counties. Engler found a way around this. By eliminating GR, Michigan does not pick up any discards from the federal denials, cruelly practicing a hardnosed policy game and hoping the needy will just leave the state. Governors who once may have been willing to criticize Social Security for cutting disabled people off the rolls now have a model for avoiding the pitfall of being the aid of last resort: just callously eliminate general relief.

The mentally ill were particularly hard hit by Engler's terminating local aid, since GA is often the only resort to public assistance they may have. They need community-based alternatives to institutionalization and assistance with applying for SSI; those mentally disabled Michigan residents terminated in the CDR process will be left to the streets.

Dumping the physically disabled off PAS (attendant services) and into nursing homes seems to be a popular state reform. Governor Tommy Thompson of Wisconsin, heralded by Clinton as one governor whose reforms went "in the right direction," decided to cap Medicaid funding for community-based services, including PAS. People who need more attendant hours than Thompson would grant face institutionalization. Thompson has since tried to eliminate Medicaid PAS entirely by refusing to admit new clients into Wisconsin's Home Services Program. Activists, who don't think this is going in "the right direction" are suing to stop this regressive move. Republican Governor George Pataki of New York cut $1.2 billion from his Medicaid budget, then proposed to limit home attendant hours to 100 per month to compensate for these cuts.

The race-to-the-bottom movement is thriving in California. Governor Wilson targeted California welfare programs—which combine AFDC with SSI—for six consecutive years. Wilson's efforts are so multi-faceted and relentless that it is worth going into detail to discover where the devils reside in that golden state paradise.

During the recession in 1990, Wilson asked all Californians to "sacrifice" until times were better. For the taxpayers the sacrifice was a slight tax increase, but for those on welfare sacrifices began with the elimination of the cost-of-living adjustment (COLA) and continued with six years of cuts to benefit levels. In 1990, the federal share of SSI was $386 and the state share was $244 (total $630). In 1997, the federal share was $484, state share $156.40 (total $640.40). If the state had not reduced its share, benefits would now be $728. If the state had adjusted for cost-of-living, benefits would now be $789.76. Instead recipients lost 25 percent of their purchasing power, and disability organizations reported that people were having to choose between eating and paying their utilities and rent.

In 1996 Wilson attempted unsuccessfully to reduce SSI and AFDC benefits another 4.9 percent ($30) for those living in high-rent areas and a whopping 9.6 percent ($60) for rural Californians, to levels illegal under federal law. But the California Republicans were not going to give up. At the request of Governor Wilson, Wally Herger (R-CA) included a provision in the 1995 Personal Responsibility Act to repeal the despised federal protection that kept Wilson from dropping SSI below 1983 levels. When that bill died, the national GOP attempted to slip the same clauses into the Personal Responsibility and Work Opportunity Act of 1996, even though disabled people's SSI benefit level had nothing to do with "work opportunity" or "personal responsibility."

In 1996 California showed a substantial budget surplus ($676 million) and taxes were reduced for those Californians who had seen an increase in 1990. But instead of returning SSI benefits to the promised full level, state legislators, led by quadriplegic Republican assemblyman Tom Bordonaro, proposed to make the "temporary" Wilson cuts permanent for the aged, blind, disabled, and AFDC recipients. In addition, Wilson and these representatives attempted to stop the promised reinstatement of the $12.50 COLA increase. They wanted to put an end to state COLAs once and for all.[24]

Bordonaro claimed that this was necessary to prevent "blowing a hole in the budget of approximately $1.2 billion,"[25] the administration's estimate of the cost of restoring the cuts. But Wilson's budget included a 15 percent personal, banking and business tax cut over three years that would cost the state $10.2 billion, blowing a hole in Bordonaro's rationale. Columnist George Skelton exposed the fact that "the COLA theft would have pocketed the state $75 million and paid for the first-year installment on a business tax cut."

Assembly Democrats who had allowed the six-year plunder of SSI woke up on the COLA issue and fought the GOP-controlled legislature, threatening to block the budget if Wilson and the Republicans did not restore the COLA. "I'll do everything I can short of shooting people to make sure this rip-off is rectified," said John Burton (D-SF).[26]

But Wilson may win yet. As of this writing the 105th Congress has found another route to cut the SSI benefit—amend the Social Security Act to permit states to reduce or eliminate state SSI payments entirely. According to the Center on Budget and Policy Priorities, if passed, this will push nearly 2.7 million poor elderly and disabled people across the nation into deeper poverty.

Governors seek other ways to divert money that do not bode well for the disabled population. The National Governors Association supported a Medicaid proposal that would allow states the "flexibility" to redistribute up to 30 percent of federal grants to other programs without penalty. For instance, Pataki of New York introduced a budget that tapped into a $1.3 billion Medicaid "windfall" and Michigan's Engler earmarked $320 million in Medicaid "savings" to finance a 5 percent increase in funds for Michigan's state universities.[27] *Dollars and Sense* reported, "Overall Medicaid spending could be reduced by as much as 16.3 percent under the NGA plan."[28] This is the route that increased flexibility will probably take; states will spend federal funds on activities that have little to do with the intent of the original appropriation.

These state decisions are often based on how much power a special interest has to divert public money in their direction. For instance, in the same year Wilson proposed the illegal cut to SSI, prisons saw an increase in their budget of 17 percent, or $3.6 billion.[29] Is it any coincidence that the prison guard union contributed $1.5 million (1989-1995) to Wilson's campaign? Or that some guards make $100,000 per year? Disabled people on SSI have comparatively little money to line politicians' pockets.

On a similar note, state governments are rushing to move public health care into corporate-managed care as a cost-saving measure. Dr. Alieta Eck's medical group was approached by one managed care corporation, and offered $2.50 a month for each person signed on. At that rate, she explains, doctors will lose money on patients who become very ill. The state promises $568 per welfare family, but Dr. Eck warns, "Make no mistake—the caregivers will see a tiny fraction of that money, and the poor will get substandard care." The Medicaid HMOs intend to reap huge profits for their stockholders, but "it will happen by the poorest and the most helpless being told that 'nothing else can be done for you,' " Dr. Eck explains.[30]

Laura Mitchell, a policy analyst for the Multiple Sclerosis Society (MS-CAN), points out that the managed care pitfalls are enormous. "People with disabilities are to the health care system what canaries used to be to miners. Since our population is the most vulnerable, we are the first to see dangers that ultimately will affect everyone," says Mitchell.

For example, since managed care corporations refer patients to physicians within their provider networks, there will be little chance to go to an outside specialist for a particular disability. The World Institute on Disability points out, "There are some states in which there is only one urologist qualified and willing to treat people with spinal cord injuries on Medicaid. It is therefore imperative that people in managed care plans be able to go outside the plan for specialty care when necessary."[31]

Disabled people are witnessing a race to the bottom in after-injury care in the form of shortened rehabilitation, inadequate rehabilitation, or no rehabilitation. Quads are being released from managed care networks without the education to prevent bedsores or use catheters. Shortened hospital stays with penny-pinching incompetent follow-up care is resulting in unnecessary suffering. One young man was sent home after surgery and received such poor care from visiting nurses that a bedsore became an infection that resulted in the amputation of both legs.

Republican Governor Pataki and Republican Mayor Guliani of New York complained that Medicaid was creating a "burden" on the state and applied for a state waiver to allow them to mandate enrollment of all Medicaid recipients into managed care. In response, seniors, disability groups, and AIDS activists formed the Coalition for Health Care Choice and Accountability and joined with Bronx Legal Services to fight back by taking their case to federal authorities. Managed care recipients related horror stories about deceitful enrollment practices and substandard care. Elizabeth Benjamin of Bronx Legal Services exposed the HMO practice of separating Medicaid enrollees from commercial enrollees, creating a two-tiered system in which Medicaid patients were allocated fewer funds for care, and more for overhead and expenses, than were the commercial patients.[32]

According to coalition member Ellen Shaffer, when the feds learned from citizens just how the managed care corporations were "managing" care, the feds said that "they had never heard anything like this before" and told Governer Pataki that if he wanted to mandate enrollment, the state would have to agree to consumer protections and meet certain standards. The state of New York decided that it would not be willing to meet those requirements and dropped its waiver request.[33]

The New York City community effort was a great success by any standard. Citizens acting in unison revealed that the governor was looking at managed care as a way to cut costs without ensuring quality. Managed care enrollment before the meeting with the feds topped 480,000. After community advocacy got the word out, enrollment dropped to 390,000.

However, the 105th Congress has dealt with the federal regulators. According to Public Citizen's Congress Watch, the top dozen national managed health care companies and two industry trade groups spent at least $2,023,041 on lobbying expenses and campaign contributions to key lawmakers during the 15 months leading to passage of the 1997

Budget Resolution and it paid off. The Resolution gives states the authority—without going through a waiver process—to mandate the Medicaid population into managed care plans.[34] Corporations can operate Medicaid-only plans, and although the resolution contains some protections for enrollees, like a choice of plans requirement, rules on disenrollment procedures, internal grievance procedures, and marketing protections, many advocates believe them to be inadequate. The concern is that mandated enrollment will result in a further deterioration of the quality of care.

Two-tiered care is the general rule for those on Medicaid. When California Governor Wilson had his second throat surgery, disability advocate Maggie Dee of northern California, who relies on MediCal for health care, wrote to Wilson, "You can count yourself as lucky. If you were on MediCal you would not have had that second surgery."[35] Her point: Wilson would have had one hell of a time getting MediCal to pay for the first surgery much less a second one. Wilson, Pataki, Giuliani, Engler, Thompson, and state legislators like Bordonaro who have a job with adequate civil service health insurance paid for by the taxpayers will be untouched by their race-to-the- bottom policies for citizens who depend on public benefits.

DEVOLUTION: DESTROYING THE LAST VESTIGES OF POWER TO THE PEOPLE

"We want to give the power to the people," claimed a freshmen devolutionary on CNN. The rhetoric insists that more state control will promote democracy. Devolution, however, is not intended to result in democratic control.

The rights and programs of disabled people often get put at the bottom of local priorities and in many cases, the existence of national standards and policies have been crucial to ensuring that local governments meet their responsibilities. If state and local governments could be entrusted to do what is right, then social justice matters would never have gone to the federal level in the first place. The Civil Rights Act of 1964 was passed because the states were not interested in eliminating discrimination against African Americans. The Family Assistance Act of 1972 (SSI) was enacted because many poor elderly, blind, and disabled were going hungry and homeless in their home states. The Rehabilitation Act of 1973 and later the ADA were necessary to acknowledge the widespread discrimination against disabled people across the nation and to pressure states into implementing access laws. The Individuals with Disabilities Educational Act was necessary for federal intercession on behalf of disabled children, to tell school boards that they must provide access to an equal education.

With no national standards, devolution could cause wide variation from state to state. States that provide exemplary services could find themselves penalized for doing the right thing. For instance, if one state were to provide generous health coverage with all the options available—PAS, dental care, eye care, wheelchairs—and most others provide nominal care, people could choose to move to the state that would deliver the best care. But if that state became overrun with citizens needing assistance, its taxpayers would most likely vote to lower their state standards to withstand the migration, devolving all states to the lowest common denominator. Nationwide standards are essential to ensure access to all regardless of the state, county, or city of residence.

Most importantly, there is outright danger in turning Medicaid over to the states. Hard-won consumer protections that now exist in Medicaid law stand to be wiped out by block grants. For example, state governments have ignored consumer protections to such a degree that protective agencies have been compelled to sue states to force them to fulfill their obligations to citizens over very basic issues, such as nondiscriminatory access to services and due process, the right to a fair hearing, and uniformity of standards of service. Yet devolution would abolish the watchdog agencies' right to appeal adverse actions, and Medicaid "reform" would eliminate all rights to sue states over benefits claims. Since block granting would erase all Medicaid case law built up over the years, consumer protections would have to be re-established state by state.

"Revolutionary" bellows of "power to the people" ring hollow when devolution is a means of reducing expenditures, diverting public money from its intended use, and adversely impacting the people's welfare. The positive role that national standards play depends upon those standards staying in place.

Taking us to the Cleaners with "Personal Responsibility"

In the spring of 1995 Newt Gingrich said on *This Week with David Brinkley* that he would "cast a cold eye" on the ADA and other "compassionate excesses." True to his word, the Contract with America emulated in policy the spirit of his rhetoric. The 104th Congress spearheaded a demand to weaken, reduce, or extinguish the ADA, the Individuals with Disabilities Education Act (IDEA), SSI, job training, Medicare, and Medicaid, threatening 30 years of disability civil rights advances.

Because each of these programs contributes to making it possible for persons with disabilities to participate in the majority society, none are "excesses" to disabled people. For example: without SSI and public health care there is not the support to acquire an education; without access laws there would be no ramps or elevators to get into the classroom or job site. Each building block makes it a bit more possible for disabled people to "boldly go where everyone else has gone before."

Gingrich writes in *To Renew America*, "Our new-found sense of entitlement and victimization is exactly wrong." He calls for a return to "personal responsibility," citing John Smith's statement, "if you don't work, you won't eat," as an example of real Americanism.[36] His answer—gut the programs that "foster" dependency, ratchet down supportive programs, and ignore that there aren't enough jobs to go around.

Newtspeak perpetuates the myth that the individual, separate from social policy, separate from the structure of capitalism, separate from Federal Reserve policies, separate from a lack of employment opportunities, can conquer any adversity by lifting him or herself up by the proverbial bootstraps. The focus on personal responsibility belies the way that industrial capitalism works (as determined by current policy). Even though the Humphrey-Hawkins Act mandates the Federal Reserve Bank to promote full employment, the Fed actively works to keep unemployment high because it is good for Wall Street and the bond market. When the unemployment rate drops, the Fed will adjust interest rates to discourage more employment, which it connects to higher inflation. High unemployment is good for business because having more people desperate for work keeps workers' wages down, pleasing corporate America and investors.

In this light, welfare recipients are the unsung heroes of the capitalist system. The unemployed and abandoned at the bottom—the welfare recipients and those on disability benefits living in abject poverty—keep the rest "in the money." While Newtspeak puts the spin on the unemployed as bums who just need to take "personal responsibility" for their plight, the real culprits—the Federal Reserve, bankers, financiers, and Wall Street—are let off the hook.

Whining that the welfare state is undermining our society, Gingrich preaches that "we must replace the welfare state with an opportunity society." But Gingrich is publicly opposed to the idea of full employment and wants the Humphrey Hawkins Act—even though it has never been implemented—written out of the Federal Reserve Bank's charter. When David Frost asked Gingrich the naughty question, "What about people who aren't able to find a job?" Gingrich replied, "One of our goals, candidly, is to increase the total volume of private charity."[37]

Neither party has any intention of mounting a campaign to realize full employment in America, and they keep this brutal fact from the public by shifting the debate onto chiselers and cheats and the pathology of the poor. The Democrats joined in the GOP call for "personal responsibility" and signed a welfare "reform" bill without addressing childcare and without a jobs program to assure that women forced off welfare could find a job. Instead, from his presidential pulpit, Clinton told business leaders that the welfare they disliked was ended and it was up to them to hire the former welfare recipients.

Clinton has positioned poor women and disabled people in competition with the millions already searching for jobs and with those who have minimum wage jobs. Those forced off disability benefits by Continuing Reviews will have to take any job (if they can work) at any wage. Since welfare recipients will be a cheaper source of labor, with government footing part of the bill, they will be pitted against those workers who already have a minimum wage job. The neoliberal president has given business another winning round; the poorest will be pitted against the poorest ensuring that wages remain low. Gingrich says his number one priority is to repeal the minimum wage, OSHA standards, and other minimum workplace standards for any welfare recipient participating in a welfare-to-work program.

Americans are being taken to the cleaners. The reality is that Wall Street reform is much more vital to promoting an "opportunity society" than welfare reform. But neither political party will act against the interests of the speculators, bond holders, and corporations that feed their political coffers, to tell the American people that Wall Street and Federal Reserve policies promote unemployment.

LET THEM EAT SOCKS

The "revolutionary" Newt Gingrich is an old social Darwinist. Gingrich is a fan of Gertrude Himmelfarb, who wrote in *The De-Moralization of Society* that the "deserving poor" should receive goods like socks in place of welfare aid. Gingrich praised Gertrude's book, which is based on a Spencerian survival-of-the-fittest logic that blames those on the bottom for their poverty, for being off the "right track."[38] Himmelfarb's socks are certainly no substitute for cash to pay rent and buy food, but Gingrich's plan to undo entitlements and replace them with charity—not jobs—requires just such a distortion of reality.

Gingrich preached in the *New York Times*, "We must replace the welfare state" with a "strategy of dramatically increasing private charities," but just how does he propose to do this when reality bites? According to *Time*, "human services" donations dropped 6 percent from 1993 to 1994 and volunteerism, which staffs charities, dropped 5 percent from 1991 to 1993.[39] When families require two paychecks to support their children, just who is wealthy enough to have the spare time to do this "volunteerism"? It requires a breach of logic to think that it is possible for private charities to expand to the magnitude necessary to replace government aid. In addition, organizations that help people get back on their feet in times of crisis depend mainly on the federal government. For instance, Catholic Charities gets 63 percent of its $1.9 billion budget from federal, state, and local government grants. *Time* reported that while need is increasing for these services, funding is dwindling. One expert estimates that Congressional cuts could cost the charities as much as $70 billion during the next seven years.[40]

The virtue spin doctors weave the illusion that charity and volunteerism are solutions to the "welfare problem" while they cut much-needed social programs and shift the money to corporate and military welfare.

GINGRICH NANNY-STATE AT THE GOVERNMENT TIT

Gingrich gives a bad rap to "big bad government," and complains about the "nanny state," but he doesn't let on that Pentagon spending in his home county is 69 times the national average.[41] Nor does he announce that his home state of Georgia is also home to Lockheed Corporation, one of the biggest recipients of federal subsidies in the nation.

Gingrich calls for welfare "reform" to save people from "dependency" while his own district harbors corporations dependent on the "nanny state." Other corporate cash cows benefitting from handouts in Newt Gingrich's Cobb County pastures include insurance companies and technological firms. Citizens must ask, as does Rep. Bernie Sanders (I-VT) in an editorial appearing in the *LA Times*, why a proponent of the "free market" like Gingrich would be pumping public dollars into private business bank accounts. Can't these companies make it on their own in capitalism's "free market"?[42]

DEVOLVING DEMOCRACY WHILE BOOSTING CORPORATE RULE

If the corporate state and its henchmen are working to create a socialism for the rich and capitalism for the poor, they are also hard at work making sure the system stays in place by gutting what little political power remains in the hands of the poor and their advocates. In short, the GOP wants to make sure that the politically weak become weaker.

Several pieces of House legislation attempted to prohibit nonprofit agencies and restrict other organizations from engaging in "political advocacy" while receiving federal funds. Political advocacy was defined as making political endorsements; participation in political campaigns, judicial litigation, or agency proceedings—even as amicus curiae; or any attempt to influence any legislation or agency action through an attempt to affect the opinions of the general public.[43]

The rule would prevent citizens' groups from advocating at the federal, state, and local level. Disability nonprofits, for example, would be barred from affecting public opinion regarding disability issues. However, no similar restrictions on businesses that receive federal dollars have been proposed. General Electric, which received more than $6 million in federal grants in 1994, can continue to lobby in its interests.

Simultaneously, the GOP proposed to eliminate the Legal Services network across the country. It did successfully cut Legal Service Corp.'s funding and prohibited Legal Aid lawyers from filing class action lawsuits and challenging welfare "reform." Traditionally, Legal Aid attorneys have been advocates for the rights of the poor and often the last resort for a disabled person who has been wrongly denied Social Security, yet one proposal sought to end Legal Aid assistance for Social Security claims. Is it any coincidence that the Legal Services budget is cut and its activities restricted when federal benefit programs are being "rengineered" or dismantled?

Protection and Advocacy, which serves severely disabled clients, has lost funding to such a degree that attorneys find themselves in an ethical bind, unable to fulfill their responsibilities as advocates for their clients. Curt Decker, executive director of the National Association of Protection and Advocacy Systems, asks, "What will happen in institutions like the one we investigated last week where a guy was restrained for five days, over medicated, and beaten, if we don't go out there this week?"[44]

What will happen is that the ordinary citizen, who does not have thousands of dollars to pay an attorney, will have no means to counter the denial of services, no ability to protest the infringement of rights, and less standing to challenge the laws of the land that may be grotesquely skewed towards business. The average citizen will lose the power of redress while the capitalists, many of whom make their profits from egregious violations of humane standards, will go unchallenged.

A Cleansed Future: The Not-So-Grateful Dead

What is the implication of these trends and just where is the U.S. headed?

Population control has been a high priority since Henry Kissinger published the National Security Memorandum 200, which called for population reduction in Third World countries. Dr. Leonard Horowitz writes:

> Population control was deemed a high priority for foreign policy and national security objectives during the late 1960s and early 1970s by then the Honorable George Bush of Texas. More recently, groups active in the Council on Foreign Relations have urged policy makers and industrialists to reduce even the size of the U.S. population to between 125 and 150 million people, "or about its size in the 1940s."[45]

Disabled people were the first hit when 1930s Germany sought to cut government costs in the name of "efficiency" by reducing its population.

Larry Buckhalter, who was born with cerebral palsy and relies on SSI and Medicaid, wrote to Senator Dianne Feinstein (D-CA), "I can not and must not return to the concentration-like camp called 'institutions' to certain spiritual and psychological death . . . where I am forgotten and die! I do not want . . .to have to choose to take a lethal injection because I cannot get my health care needs met."

"You talk about Nazi Germany and you talk about extermination, this is a pretty damn good example of modern extermination," says Maggie Dee.[46]

The 1990s version of the 1930s horror will be the result of pernicious social policy, an indirect "civilized" way of cost-saving accomplished by neglect rather than by lethal gas. In a nation where the market rules, U.S. managed care corporations will reap their profits while disabled people die from lack of treatment, not even knowing what hit them. But make no mistake, "what hit them" will be unfettered capitalism coupled with a disintegrating society. It will be uncurbed "free" market individualism lacking any sense of common good or responsibility for others, and it will be deregulation that allows unconscionable businessmen (and women) to put bottom lines before protecting human life.

Think that it can't happen here? The American psyche is malleable. There are those who scapegoat the poor, single mothers on welfare, immigrants, and the disabled as the source of the nation's ills and spur on pernicious neglect in the name of the "American way." It is the American way to feel passionately about our freedoms—the rights to life and liberty—which are threatened now by corporate rapacity as surely as minority populations were threatened by Nazi Germany.

THE REAL PROBLEM: PATHOLOGY OF THE RICH

Multimillionaire Leona Helmsley honestly admitted, "We [the rich] don't pay taxes, only the little people pay taxes."[47] The standard elite practice is to get out of paying taxes by shifting the tax burden onto the less well-off. The rate of taxation on the richest one-fifth of Americans fell by 5 percent in the 1980s, while the poorest one-fifth saw a tax increase of 15 percent. Of course, the wealthy can go too far and get caught, as did Helmsley. The preferred method of keeping taxes down is to support politicians, like Reagan, who will legalize tax inequities by changing the tax code. Reagan reduced the richest one percent's income tax rate by 39 percent, which caused an annual revenue loss of $70 billion. Meanwhile, the holdings of America's richest 500,000 jumped from $2.5 trillion in 1980 to $5 trillion in 1989.[48]

Fortunes are amassed by manipulating the law to result in backdoor giveaways. For example, while the GOP attempted to kill the Earned Income Tax Credit, benefitting the poorest, GOP lawmakers proposed a $7 billion break to investors by cutting taxes on profits from the sale of stocks and other property. The GOP made the dubious claim that a capital gains tax cut would encourage investors to sell current holdings and use the profits to create new jobs, but Lars-Erik Nelson revealed that the GOP planned to raid the Treasury. By making the law retroactive, the GOP would deliver to investors that $7 billion in Treasury handouts for past transactions. Nelson wrote in the *Los Angeles Times*, "That's not a tax incentive to encourage growth. It is a pure giveaway to some of the wealthiest people in the land, at a time when we are all supposed to be tightening our belts to help balance the federal budget."[49]

There appears to be no limit to what the corporate state will do to satisfy pathological greed and corporate directives. Just take this one outstanding fact: in 1950 corporations had a 46 percent income tax rate but by 1990 it had dwindled to 9.2 percent. Federal income taxes have declined from 30.1 percent of total tax revenues during the 1940s to 12.2 percent in 1996. Harper's estimates that if the annual federal revenues of corporations were taxed at the 1953 rate the Treasury would gain $53 billion per year.[50] On top of that, the Internal Revenue

Service fails each year to collect some $200 billion in taxes due, most of it from the rich. The *Washington Spectator* declares that is "enough to balance the budget."[51] We can rightly conclude that if rich individuals and corporations paid a graduated tax with no loopholes, shelters, or major deductions, hundreds of billions of dollars would be collected yearly and there would be no federal deficit.

AID TO DEPENDENT CORPORATIONS

When government money goes to poor people it is derisively labeled "welfare," but when government money goes to corporations or to agricultural interests it is elevated to a "subsidy." State-driven socialism has long existed for the military and corporate America; increasing entitlements for corporations and their owners and decreasing expenditures for the poor and disabled is the 1990s reality.

The average taxpayer contributes about $415 each year for social welfare (food stamps, Aid to Families with Dependent Children, child nutrition, disability, and other entitlements) while s/he contributes $1,388 for corporate subsidies and tax breaks.[52] Narrowing that figure to traditional welfare or AFDC, the average American taxpayer spent $26 in 1994.[53] What the pundits don't tell us is that the government pays out billions of taxpayer dollars to corporations every year. According to Ralph Nader's Essential Information project, there were $167 billion in corporate subsidies in the 1995 budget—and that was not unusual. Typically, over $125 billion goes to corporations every year. Some of this Aid to Dependent Corporations, as Nader calls it, is worth listing here to illustrate the hypocrisy of the rollback forces' attack on the welfare state:

- In 1996 the Department of Agriculture gave corporations about $110 million in hard cash for "market promotion" abroad, $25 million more than in 1995. Typical recipients include M&M/Mars, Campbell's Soup Co., Uncle Ben's, McDonald's, and Sunkist Growers. Over the years Gallo Wines has received $46 million in taxpayer dollars for promoting their product, while mink breeders receive $1.9 million a year to advertise their fur coats overseas.[54]

- The Export/Import Bank, a federal agency that provides U.S. corporations with hundreds of millions of dollars to propel global transactions, gave corporations $744 million in taxpayer subsidies in 1996 alone. The money went to finance below-market loans and loan guarantees to assist with sales of aircraft, telecommunications equipment, electric power turbines, and other products to foreign markets. (Now Boeing, General Electric, AT&T, IBM, and Caterpillar want to extend these below-rate loans to assist in establishing the manufacture of their products in other countries. Those tax dollars would create jobs—but the jobs won't be on American soil and won't feed American families.)[55]

- As much as one billion dollars over a five-year period could be added to the Treasury if Congress repealed the General Mining Law, which allows corporations to extract minerals from public lands without paying royalties (the mining industry's PAC contributions to Congressional candidates totaled more than $3 million during the last decade).[56]

- Another $20-$70 billion could be raised by auctioning public airspace frequencies that broadcast corporations get for free. This giveaway could benefit the people instead of big business, which profits from use of the airwaves ($100 billion per year) but pays nothing to use our public property.

- $2 billion per year could be realized by eliminating the tax loophole for mutual life insurance companies.[57]

- $3.5 billion per year goes to tax breaks for companies doing business in U.S. territories like Puerto Rico and the U.S. Virgin Islands. Again, these are not small, borderline companies trying to make it, these are giant corporations like Johnson & Johnson and Bristol-Myers Squibb, Pepsi, and Coca-Cola.[58]

- The foreign tax credit and tax deferral on foreign income cost the treasury about $24 billion per year. [59]

- $150 million in tax dollars could be regained by the Treasury if below-market fee deals with Getty Oil, Pacific Power, and others were halted.[60]

- Citizens for Tax Justice has identified $412 billion in savings over five years just from closing corporate tax loopholes that provide tax advantages for business mergers and acquisitions.

Corporate give-aways also include those sums businesses manage to "externalize" or shift onto taxpayers. For example:

- The drug Taxol for ovarian cancer was developed at the expense of $31 million to the taxpayer through the National Institute of Health, yet Bristol-Myers-Squibb Company "owns" the drug and does not pay any royalties back to the Treasury. In addition, the drug costs $10,000 to $15,000 per patient, which the taxpayer again pays through Medicaid.[61]

- $3.3 billion in tax dollars is spent annually to build forest roads, provide forestry services below cost, and provide enormous tax breaks for timber and forest companies like Weyerhauser and Georgia Pacific.[62]

- Mining companies pay an insignificant $2.40 per surface acre for the rights to strip federal lands of gold, iron, coal, and other minerals, leaving extensive environmental cleanup to taxpayer expense.

Ralph Estes, author of "The Public Cost of Private Corporations," shows how socializing costs onto the public amounts to a hidden taxation. Since corporate accounting does not include the costs business imposes on society—on consumers, workers, the community, the nation—Estes adds in these external costs for one year and comes up with a horrifying reality: the total public cost of corporate activities is estimated at approximately $2,622 billion per year (1994 dollars).[63] This means taxpayers spend about $2,622 billion a year allowing companies to deplete commonly owned natural resources, pollute our air and water, generate toxic sewage and trash, manufacture dangerous products, destabilize communities, and repair the damage they cause (to the extent the damage can be corrected). If one multiplies this yearly estimate over the years corporations have been in business, the cost to taxpayers reaches the trillions.

CORPORATE LOBBYISTS, A "NATURAL" FIT

How do these corporations manage to get such special treatment when it's obvious that these subsidies do not benefit the average American citizen? In an article called "The Thursday Regulars: How

Republican legislators gather a key group of lobbyists every week to help pass the Contract with America," *Time* reports, "[Gingrich's] lieutenants. . .were not so natural a fit. They were not fellow lawmakers or even Congressional staff members. They were lobbyists representing some of the richest special interests in the country."[64]

Time portrays the political reality incorrectly; the lobbyists are the power behind the legislation—the "natural fit"—whether invited to sit at a table or not. Gingrich collected $424,299 from corporate PACs between 1993 and 1994 for his re-election, and another $10-20 million went into GOPAC, which served to fund candidates of his choice, those "revolutionaries" who designed the Contract on America. Daniel Franklin, writing for *The Nation* makes the connection clear:

> No one has mastered the campaign contribution game nearly as well as Archer-Daniels-Midland chairman Dwayne Andreas. From 1991 to 1994, Andreas and A.D.M. doled out $2.6 million in campaign contributions and "soft money" gifts to the two major political parties (two-thirds went to the G.O.P.). He knows a good investment when he sees it. His generosity, combined with persistent lobbying by A.D.M. and other ethanol producers, has maintained a tax break that last year alone saved the industry $700 million. A.D.M., which produces more than half the ethanol in the country, took home the lion's share of that benefit. Representative Archer tried to kill the subsidy earlier this year but was stared down by Bob Dole and Newt Gingrich, longtime friends and beneficiaries of Andreas.[65]

The *New York Times* reports that top corporate lobbyists have unusual access to the National Governors Association and its policy makers. For a tax-deductible donation of up to $12,000, the Association allows a firm to designate a "corporate fellow" to work on social and economic policies at its Center for Best Practices. Membership in the nine-year-old program is restricted to no more than 100 large companies, while unions and advocacy groups are not invited. Fellows often play significant roles in meetings that formulate the governors' recommendations. Among participating corporations are AT&T, Exxon, Dow Chemical, and Philip Morris.[66]

According to Public Citizen, an estimated half billion dollars was spent in the last election cycle by corporate interests and lobbyists anxious to preserve their favorite corporate tax breaks and loopholes.

MILITARY MADNESS: THE COLD WAR IS OVER

President Eisenhower warned, "We must guard against the acquisition of unwarranted influence, whether sought or unsought, by the military-industrial complex."[67] That was during the Cold War, which is most decidedly over, but the U.S. military still consumes over 50 percent of the nation's discretionary budget (more than $250 billion per year). That is five times more than any other nation. The War Resisters League estimates that 80 percent of the national debt is military debt, yet the military has been promised a 40 percent increase in procurement over the next five years—while entitlements are being cut.[68]

The Soviet "threat" is gone but the Pentagon budget goes on and on like the Energizer Bunny. For instance, in 1994 $18,247,100,000 was spent on major weapons programs initiated before 1989.[69] Taxpayers have wasted $40 billion since 1983 on Star Wars—the Strategic Defense Initiative—and the Congressional Budget Office estimated that taxpayers would have to provide an additional $60 billion to defense contractors by 2010 for Dole and Gingrich's "Defend America Act," a Star Wars sequel that calls for a nation-wide missile defense system.[70]

If Americans think that military money is spent wisely and "efficiently," the Center for Defense Information (CDI) will burst that illusion. The editors of CDI's *The Defense Monitor* (August 1995) write, "The Pentagon remains the largest source of wasteful spending in the federal government. The institution that gave us the $400 hammer, $600 toilet seat, and $7,600 coffee pot can also lay claim to [other] examples of tax dollar waste." A small sample of questionable spending could include the $14.7 billion in Pentagon expenditures unaccounted for by invoice during the last decade, $450 million spent to partially construct two Navy oil tankers now rusting on the James River, and the $380 million required annually to maintain a 600-plane fleet for the single purpose of flying military and civilian VIPs to their destinations.

While the deficit hawks asked citizens to tighten belts in 1995, the Congress (and president) awarded the military $7 billion more than it asked for, and $11 billion more in 1996. Although the Pentagon said it did not need more B-2 bombers, more were funded in the Congressional budget. Why? Because the U.S. military continues to be one of the biggest cash cows for defense contractors in the world, corporate lobbying for military contracts matches, if not tops, lobbying in the civilian sector. Defense contractors building the B-2 "Stealth" bomber (Northrop-Grumman) and the Seawolf (General Dynamics) spent nearly $900,000 in campaign contributions in 1994. The next year Congress voted to give the military $11 billion more than requested for the purchase of jet fighters made by Northrop-Grumman.[71] While programs for health care, housing, nutrition, and welfare are being mercilessly cut, government subsidies to defense companies increased to more than $7.5 billion in 1995.[72]

There is another reason to be concerned about the business side of our military. This excerpt from an editorial in the *New York Times* makes it clear why:

> The United States is the world's premier arms dealer. According to some estimates, 85 percent of the arms Washington sells to developing nations go to nondemocratic countries. These sales strengthen repressive and corrupt militaries and rob the poor of money better spent on health or education. In countries such as Turkey and Colombia, American weapons have been used against civilians and villages.[73]

The U.S. robs its citizens in a similar fashion. CDI suggests that military money could be better spent in other ways. For instance, for the cost of a single B-2 bomber ($2.2 billion) the country could pay for health care for 1.3 million Americans. Disability activists could propose that for the projected cost of the ballistic missile defense program ($91 billion), Congress would not "have" to rob $13 billion from Medicaid and would have $79 billion left over— more than enough to reinstate the estimated 300,000 disabled children they will sever from SSI. In fact, CDI estimates that national security could be fully assured with a seven-year Pentagon budget cut of $510 billion, which would still leave a $175 billion military expenditure in 2002.

DEVOLUTION AND UNIVERSAL HEALTH CARE:
THE RENEWED CHALLENGE

What are the chances of realizing disability-sensitive universal health care for all Americans in a downsized public sector? It is probable that devolution, the co-opting of public health by HMO corporations, and deficit reduction will lower the value and quality of Medicare/Medicaid and will end the chance, once and for all, for humane medicine in the USA—just when it is needed the most.

The paradoxes are glaring. No industrialized nation has a weaker public sector than the U.S.; 24 percent of our nation's children live in poverty. The elderly in France can live on government benefits, but who can live on Social Security in the U.S.? Public welfare programs that do exist are demeaning and dehumanizing. Is it justifiable that a disabled person who needs assistance is meted out so little that they must choose between eating and staying warm?

America is a country where private health care corporations exist at the expense of the have-nots. A 1993 Harris Poll found that 53 million Americans had no health insurance during the previous two years. Experts document that the numbers of the uninsured are growing. According to the American College of Physicians, 12.5 million people lost their employer-sponsored coverage between 1988 and 1993. Employers are abandoning responsibility for providing health care for working Americans.

According to a survey published in the *Journal of the American Medical Association*, one in four Americans had difficulty obtaining medical care due either to no health insurance or inadequate coverage, and three-fourths of the uninsured adults in poor health had trouble getting medical help. Yet the 1993 Harris poll revealed that Americans pay more out-of-pocket for health care than do citizens of other countries. A study by the Urban Institute concluded that lack of health insurance is associated with a 25 percent higher risk of death.[75] More Americans will, if the current path remains unaltered, face this risk. Is it plausible that the private industry will lower premiums so that the uninsured can afford coverage? Not likely.

U.S. public health care is succumbing to the "free" market—the industrialization of medicine—where corporate bottom lines drive the course of health services. Both Medicare and Medicaid are on the fast track to managed care corporatization. This is how HMO corporate math works. Private insurance administrative costs are about 14 percent compared to Medicare at 4 percent; when profits are added in, insurance corporations' "costs" go up to 25 percent-30 percent. HMOs' overhead, advertising, and profits consume between 18 percent and 25 percent of total HMO revenues, even higher that the traditional 14 percent for private insurers.[76] The government pays these HMOs about $400 monthly per Medicare enrollee, but it has been alleged that in some instances as little as 67 percent of Medicare dollars now going to HMOs are spent on patient care. Simply put, the government-HMO corporate partnership is one big cash cow—a few shareholders gain monetarily while patients lose out on "care."

The U.S. and South Africa are the only two industrialized nations that do not provide universal health care to their citizens. (States of the former Soviet Union have recently joined the U.S. and South Africa.) According to the Congressional Budget Office, under a single-payer plan, a publicly administered, not-for-profit plan that eliminates out-of-pocket costs for covered services, the country could save $100 billion per year by eliminating insurance companies, enough to extend quality coverage—including long-term care and most prescription drugs—to all Americans. The single-payer approach would sharply cut the $50 billion spent annually on insurance overhead by eliminating marketing costs, efforts at selective enrollment, stockholders' profits, executives' exorbitant salaries, and lobbying expenses.[77]

Other factors are at work keeping universal health care for Americans at bay. Medicaid is lousy health care because it was designed for "the poor;" the physician reimbursement rate is low, it has been narrowing coverage, and fewer physicians will take it at all. It is the last resort for people with disabilities, those who cannot obtain or afford private coverage, cannot qualify for Medicare, or have lost their private coverage and become poor enough for Medicaid.

Medicare is a better public program and more doctors will take it, but it omits coverage for very important things, like prescriptions. Already Medicare is underfunded, yet both political parties are in agreement to cut billions from the program. As Congress curtails treatments and undercuts payments to providers, it increases providers' costs for rehabilitation and services, which will affect access to and quality of care. For example, states can now pay the Medicaid (lower) rate for those people on both Medicare and Medicaid, which is likely to hinder access because many providers will be reluctant to see these patients for lower fees. Other proposals like placing a lifetime cap on what can be spent on any one individual or raising the Medicare eligibility age to 67 mean less health security for all citizens.

The 105th Congress cut $115 billion from Medicare (over the next five years). Meanwhile, Associated Press reports that 14 cents of every dollar spent by Medicare in 1996 was lost to fraud, abuse, or simple errors—about $23 billion. That is exactly the amount that Congress cut from providers and increased citizen premiums. If the government recouped these losses due to white collar crime it would not need to cut provider fees or raise our premiums. In effect, the honest providers and the public are being punished for ineffectual oversight of hospital, doctor, and home health care corporate billing practices.

Polls during the 1992-93 health care reform debate revealed that a majority of people favored the idea of universal health care such as a single-payer system. But corporate state "reform" is moving public health care in the direction of the private mode. Managed care is devolving towards undertreatment, not evolving towards better, adequate, or even competent care. Americans may soon face the inevitability that the idea of public health care will become unpopular, because quality will deteriorate drastically with less Medicaid and Medicare funding and people will suffer under corporate-controlled "public" medicine. That is enough to undercut public confidence and result in less appeal for government-administered universal health care. This is what Gingrich's "wither on the vine" strategy is all about.

This is not to say that there would not be difficulties in designing a good universal system, but single-payer starts at a moral juncture; everyone, rich and poor, is included in the same system, making it more likely that a quality system would be the outcome.

FAILURE OF GRADUALISM

The liberal belief that a pluralistic balance of power, equilibrium of class interests, and ethic of opportunity could be maintained under capitalist-dominated society has simply been blown apart in the past 20 years. "Reform" by way of gradualism has not produced equality of results or social justice.

It appears that our political lesson is a hard one; at democratic socialism's highest challenge to U.S. capitalism, during FDR's presidency, economic equality through redistribution of the wealth downwards never materialized. The liberal New Deal paid for itself by creating a new base of taxpayers;[78] Keynesian policy was supported by more people paying taxes, not by an uncompromised demand that the wealthiest pay an equitable portion out of their pockets. Democracy in America has never posed a real threat to those concentrating the wealth in fewer and fewer hands; instead, the wealthy have found ways to load their own pockets by becoming the beneficiaries of our public tax dollars.

Americans are just experiencing the preview of "ending the social contract as we know it," with global capital in charge of producing the show. The question is, will Americans allow the dismantling of our stingy social system, or meet the challenge by not only resisting the devolution of the New Deal but by demanding worldwide socio-economic policy that will offer dignity and justice for all? Will we demand the government we were promised in the Constitution that will "promote the general welfare," or will we settle for pernicious neglect, the excessive accumulation of capital at the expense of human life?

The Republican/Democrat equation is clear: the rich get unimaginable wealth and power, and we get Mother Teresa.

CHAPTER 13

DEMOCRACY UNDER SIEGE

The Democratic Party is the second most capitalist party in the world.

—Kevin Phillips

The business of politics *"consists of a series of unsentimental transactions between those who need votes and those who have money…a world where every quid has its quo."*

—Don Tyson, Senior Chair of the Board,
Tyson Foods, Inc.

The cornerstone social contract is that of the promise of democracy itself, but world citizens stand at a crossroads of immense magnitude. The ethos of the capitalist market-driven society—increased concentration of wealth and power—is dismantling hopes for democracy where "the people" rule. The corporate state has all but wiped out any chance to realize the promise of democracy made in Philadelphia. A "democracy" controlled by the money of the few is contradictory to majority rule and to minority representation; it is no democracy at all.

Why should corporate dominance of government be of concern? What is the connection between disability rights and the threat to the social contract? How are capitalism and democracy, or more accurately, lack of democracy, intertwined?

GLOBAL TOOLS AND TYRANTS:
RATCHETING DOWN DEMOCRACY

Prophetically, Thomas Jefferson warned that capitalism would create a greater tyranny than the one the English king inflicted upon the colonists. Jefferson called for a representative government to counter "the excesses of the monied interests." By philosophical contrast, President Madison held that the role of government was "to protect the minority of opulent against the majority." As a member of the conservative elite, Madison believed that if given constitutional power, the democratic masses would interfere with his class's amassed property and wealth. But Madison eventually joined Jefferson in distrust of the developing business class, which he called "tools and tyrants" that forced their will upon government and reaped special favors from it.[1]

Today tobacco industry lobbyists hand out checks on the floor of Congress but there is no Madison to call them "tyrants" for such practices. Instead, tools of business like Representative Dan Schaefer (R-Colorado) unabashedly admit, "We go to industry and we ask industry, 'What is it we can do to make your job easier and to help you in this competitive world we have,' rather than writing legislation and having industry comment on what we write."[2]

Washington analyst William Greider in *Who Will Tell the People?* explains:

[Corporations have] tremendous financial resources, the diversity of their interests, the squads of talented professionals—all these assets and some others are now relentlessly focused on the politics of governing.[3]

Corporations make huge contributions to politicians' coffers via soft money political action committees (PACs). In 1974 there were 608 PACs lobbying the U.S. government; by 1995 that had grown to 3,954.[4] Contributions to political parties from PACs in the 1996 election cycle were $193 million. Total soft money contributions hit a staggering $263.5 million, or three times higher than in 1992.

One *Los Angeles Times* headline—"Major GOPAC Donors Got Special Access, Files Show"—and the subheading, "Gingrich group offered personal attention from the Republican representative to those giving $10,000," make the connection between representation and money crystal clear. For $10,000 a corporation could "enjoy extraordinary access to the Republican congressman from Georgia."[5]

The contemporary business class tools include former government officeholders and elected representatives converted into corporate lobbyists, influence peddling for $350 per hour on "Gucci Gulch," as K Street is now called. The business class tools include those in Congress making public policy who have links to corporate interests. For example, California Senator Feinstein acted on behalf of

Eidetics, which makes spare parts for F-5E fighter planes, when she pressured Congress to allow sales of the F-5E to murderous Indonesian generals of the Suharto regime (in 1965 it executed an estimated one million citizens) because Eidetics stood to lose $1 million in sales when Clinton blocked the deal.[6]

Jefferson's fears have been realized; the political power of amassed capital has usurped the "voice of people"—the government. "Democracy" is an illusion when less than one percent of the public provides 77 percent of the money to national elections, 70 percent of all political contributions come from corporations, and that money buys results. Political entrepreneurialism has turned the democratic process into a revolving cash register where, as Charles Lewis of the Center for Public Integrity described the 1996 GOP convention, an endless stream of "corporate representatives buy legislative favors with a wink and a nod."

Since the business of making more money knows no ideology, corporate lobbyists pour coin into both political slot machines. Goldman Sachs, AT&T, Archer Daniels Midland, Lockheed/Marietta, to name a few, give to both Democrats and Republicans to hedge their bets. Fred Wertheimer calls the "alternative" to corporate lobbyists, the nonprofit organizations, a mail-order democracy where "you send the money to Washington, they spend it to lobby politicians that are already bought."

When former Majority Leader George Mitchell (D-ME) left the Senate and it was safe to tell the truth, he earnestly told Congress, "Every Senator who participates in it knows this system stinks. And the American people are right when they mistrust this system. . . money dominates this system. Money infuses this system. Money is the system."[7] Then Mitchell went on to lobby on behalf of the tobacco industry.

When in 1996 Congress made a meager attempt to reform campaign laws, and failed, columnist Russell Baker wrote:

> If I had a Senate seat bought for me at great expense to a lot of gigantic corporations, I too would vote to kill such a bill. I can hear me now: "What is wrong, Senators, with letting the corporations who run not only America but also the world . . . what is wrong with letting these great corporations choose the Senate which not only

makes laws they must obey, but provides, protects and preserves the Federal subsidies on which they thrive."[8]

The political dominance of the multinational corporations and banks is no "conspiracy" theory. The decision-making class's interests are similar all over the world and they simply *act in their own interests.* They have formed organizations like the Business Roundtable, the Bilbertberg group which met on Lake Lanier near Atlanta in 1997, and the Council on Foreign Relations to promote those mutual interests (the Business Roundtable gave $25 million in contributions to the Republicans in 1996, $11 million to Democrats). Holly Sklar has exposed the Trilateral Commission founded by David Rockefeller of Chase Manhattan Bank, in her well-documented book *Trilateralism:*

> To put it simply, trilateralists are saying: (1) the people, governments and economies of all nations must serve the needs of multinational banks and corporations; (2) control over economic resources spells power in modern politics (of course, good citizens are supposed to believe as they are taught; namely, that political equality exists in Western democracies whatever the degree of economic inequality); and (3) the leaders of capitalist democracies—systems where economic control and profit, and thus political power, rest with the few —must resist movement towards a truly popular democracy. In short, trilateralism is the current attempt by ruling elites to manage both dependence and democracy—at home and abroad.[9]

Corporations do not act on the basis of what is good for society, but on what will maximize profits. Most dangerously, corporations, acting in their own interests, lull citizens into a false sense of reality. David Korten writes in *When Corporations Rule the World:*

> An active propaganda machinery controlled by the world's largest corporations constantly reassures us that consumerism is the path to happiness, governmental restraint of market excess is the cause of our distress, and economic globalization is both a historical inevitability and a boon to the human species. In fact, these are all myths propagated to justify profligate greed and mask the extent to which the global transformation of human institutions is a consequence of the sophisticated, well-funded, and intentional interventions of a small

elite whose money enables them to live in a world of illusion apart
from the rest of humanity.[10]

THE VENAL CENTER

In former times, the Democrats offered some ideological alternative to the corporate state. That is not the case in the 1990s.
Democrat Bill Clinton's Presidency exemplifies the power business
wields in Washington. Author Kevin Phillips explains it this way:

> Clinton abandoned yesteryear's "interest-group liberalism" for an
> "interest-group centrism" of collaboration with the capital's new busi-
> ness-financial-international power axis.[11]

Take Clinton's 1992 campaign pledge to "Put People First" by
assisting "people who drive pickup trucks" (the ordinary worker)
rather than rewarding people "who speculate in paper" (investors).
What happened to the "people's party" promises?

Columnist Paul Gigot observed that the Clinton Democratic
administration "has done best by the same people Mr. Clinton
accused Reaganomics of benefiting most—the wealthy. And it has
done least for those he pledged to help most—working stiffs." Ethan
Kapstein, writing in Foreign Affairs, says that Clinton has shifted
"Hoover-like" to the very positions that are undoing the welfare of
the country. Kapstein writes, "Restrictive economic policies—
reduced deficits, reduced spending, reduced taxes, and, the most
exalted deity, low inflation—have favored financial interests at the
expense of workers and have created an international rentier class."[12]

The Wall Street Journal remarks, "On issue after issue, Mr. Clinton
and his administration came down on the same side as corporate
America."[13] For example, the North Atlantic Free Trade Agreement
(NAFTA), originally Republican policy that Clinton pushed through
Congress, has cost the U.S. 120,000-600,000 jobs. A study by
Cornell University shows that NAFTA has empowered corporations
to break the back of U.S. labor organizing, to cut worker benefits,
lower wages, expand hours workers must put in on the job, and relax
health and safety regulations. Cornell found that 62 percent of U.S.
employers have threatened workers with moving corporations to
countries where they can get cheap labor, like Mexico at $.70 an

hour. Contrary, to the corporate public relations rhetoric, NAFTA is leveling workers' standard of living downwards towards the Mexican level, it is not raising the Mexican worker's standard upwards.

Bob Dole was dead right when he said, "The only thing he [Clinton] hasn't done is joined the Republican Party." Clintonite policies do favor the owning class of investors, bondholders, shareholders above the working class, unemployed, and underemployed, but the Democrats' claim to be "the party of the people" was sullied years earlier when former Congressman Tony Coehlo and his ilk placed the Democrats into competition with the Republicans for corporate money, destroying political representation for the "working stiff."

Now that the "Big Tent" party is owned by corporate money, politicians feel free to move away from democratic principles. The Republicrat party of money is busily narrowing the debate to conform to the corporate agenda: both parties call for austerity to balance the budget; the GOP calls for rollbacks in the safety net with deep cuts to entitlements and social programs, Clinton only a little less. Both parties follow the same Federal Reserve Bank high unemployment directives that permit the "natural" rate to go unchallenged, and both parties—knowing that there aren't enough jobs—push "free enterprise" as the solution to welfare by supporting "reform" that leaves the fate of millions of mothers and children to private business to "do the right thing." Neither party is concerned about universal health care and both espouse the Victorian volunteerism hoax. This atmosphere made right-winger Dick Armey (R-Texas) so confident that he forecast that when the 105th Congress reconvened, "the two" parties won't discuss whether to implement conservative ideas, but how.[14]

CORPORATE HACKS ON THE INTERNATIONAL BENCH

Walden Bello concludes, in *Dark Victory*, that multinational corporations viewed the social contract as a "key constraint on corporate America's ability to compete" on a global scale.[15] On the international front, the global corporations are using market "competition" to derail the social safety net, to devolve protective regulations that stand in the way of unlimited worldwide profiteering at the expense of our environment, national resources, and democracy itself.

NAFTA and GATT (the General Agreement on Tariffs and Trade), a couple of examples of multinational, bipartisan, corporate-friendly legislation, contain clauses that can negate the sovereignty of the polity of any country, via overriding powers granted to the World Trade Organization (WTO). Once the WTO is ratified, any member country can challenge any law of another member country that it believes deprives it of benefits it expected to receive from the new trade rules, including any law that requires imported goods to meet local or national health, safety, labor, or environmental standards that exceed WTO standards.

To illustrate how the WTO could interfere with disability access, let's take the New York City toilet battle as a point of departure. A few years back, Paris-based JCDecaux Company contracted with the city of New York to provide the city with street-side toilets. The contract became controversial when the company insisted on building separate toilets for the disabled, claiming that it could not make a "universal" accessible toilet that was "safe." Instead, the company proposed to design two different toilets, one for the nondisabled that would be enterable at any time without a key, and one for the disabled that would require a magnetic card key to be obtained from the local police station or some other designated place. To make a long story short, quite legitimately the disability community said this would be setting up a "separate but equal" standard, questioned the viability of the key concept, and called for universal design to be applied to all the company's installed toilets in the city.

The WTO agreement allows a transnational corporation that believes itself to be disadvantaged by a particular law to look for a government to bring a challenge against it. Now, had the WTO agreement been in effect during the toilet episode, JCDecaux could simply have pressured the French government—or any other nation—to challenge the ADA universal access standard as obstructing trade. The objecting nation could bring a complaint against the U.S., calling for it to bring its national law into line with the lower international standard or be subjected to perpetual fines or trade sanctions.

As it was, disabled citizens brought their grievance to bear on the city of New York and the national government. Shortly thereafter, another company, Bel & Tom of Israel, said it could design a universal accessible unit that was "safe" and wanted to bid for the contract. But had the GATT-WTO judicial body been in place and had JCDecaux pursued their interest in the WTO court, there would have been a panel of three "experts" composed of trade lawyers (most likely corporate interest careerists) making the decision on the worthiness of universal access. Since these secretive WTO "courts" have no mandate to gather alternative perspectives, such as amicus briefs, public comment could be omitted from the hearings. Further, since all documents going to the panels are kept secret, it would be unknown to interested parties who might be asked to present a brief or comment. For instance, corporations could be asked to submit papers on the trade merit of universal design from the point of view of their interests and citizens would not know that had been a part of the decision-making process. And, since open public hearings are not a part of the WTO court process, citizens would have no voice in the determination. Under WTO rules disabled people would have had no means of redress to insist upon universal design for the New York toilets. The ADA could be rendered internationally moot by a three-member panel of corporate hacks.

In the name of what is good for business, the global CEOs pledge allegiance to their stockholders and seek to dissolve "barriers" to free trade. In the process they gut our environmental laws, construction standards, and health and safety regulations and destroy our national sovereignty. While sovereignty (a government that deems itself superior to all others) is not a political ideal to which humanity needs to aspire in an age when humane policies need structuring on a global scale, a world governed by corporate CEOs is in prime opposition to citizens realizing a world where the people have the political and economic power to design their own destiny. Corporate control is carting us back to the 19th century.

DWINDLING POWER OF THE VOTE

Conventional wisdom would have it that America is a full-fledged democracy, but retracing the history of the vote challenges that assumption. At best, America has practiced incremental "democracy" that has blood on the trail of its partial realization throughout our political history.

As Howard Zinn documented from the point of view of the disenfranchised masses, in A People's History of the United States, Madisonian philosophy won out in the U.S. Constitution over Jeffersonian democratic principles. Jefferson's "All men are created equal" only went so far in ruling class reality. The Declaration of Independence written by Jefferson, with its high-minded ideals of broad equality, was not implemented in solid socio/economic policy that would secure his democratic ideals. Instead, the Constitution was drafted to reflect the Madisonian/Hamiltonian vision of America; it entrenched the white monied male hierarchy as the locus of political power by establishing that only propertied white males could vote or hold government office. Nothing was done to equalize who owned property. Of course, democracy—meaning rule by the majority of the people—is negated under such a system, for the simple reason that the larger numbers of disadvantaged people and women had no vote, no legitimate representation, no voice.

> The Constitution, then, illustrates the complexity of the American system: that it serves the interests of a wealthy elite, but also does enough for small property owners, for middle-income mechanics and farmers, to build a broad base of support. The slightly prosperous people who make up this base of support are buffers against the blacks, the Indians, the very poor whites. They enable the elite to keep control with a minimum of coercion, a maximum of the law—all made palatable by the fanfare of patriotism and unity.[16]

American popular history is the story of rebellion against this "democracy" for the few. Much political effort went towards widening the democratic voting base to include people of color and women, against tremendous hostility from the ruling class. For example, it took a bloody struggle for African Americans to get the vote, and still they had to fight off intimidation at the polls and risk their lives to exercise that right. Southern blacks remained disfranchised until 1965. Women suffered the humiliation of public ridicule in their struggle for enfranchisement, obtaining the vote in 1918, but did not see it fully granted until 1928. Native Americans did not get the vote until 1934, and its granting was problematic in that it weakened their struggle for sovereignty.

Mortimer Adler in his *Philosophical Dictionary* concludes that the U.S. began as a "constitutional oligarchy" and did not become a "constitutional democracy" until 1964, when the 24th Amendment abolished the poll tax and created universal suffrage.[17] But consider that the Madisonian oligarchy is alive and well in our times. For instance, to retain political power today the decision-making class does not need to control national affairs by making it necessary to own property to vote, or to collect poll taxes or literacy fees. It can graciously allow motor-voter registration laws that make it easier to register to vote (despite California Governor Wilson fighting their legality in court), and not fear a loss of control over governance. Why? Because the democratic vote has been greatly diluted by politicians' need for an excess of private money: money to build a campaign, money to sustain office, money to ensure the next election, which is on average $12,000 a week. For the most part, elected officials have become irrelevant; they are either the tools of the corporate tyranny or they have been rendered ineffective if they opt to rally against it. The vote can be rendered moot when the political process gives the dollar the power to dominate elections, politicians, and policy-making.

The party line is that we have a "representative" government, but when General Electric, Time/Warner, and wealthy individuals like Rupert Murdoch are the ones actualizing their representation by buying their way, the resulting concentration of political power in a few hands must be seen as a reversion to oligarchical rule. The country may have extended the franchise to more Americans since the Constitution was written, but the power of money to buy policy—no matter who gets elected—demonstrates that the ruling class has simply gotten around the democratic vote.

Such governance means that when the people ask for meaningful health care reform, even a modest reform like the Clinton plan, it will be defeated by the wealthy special interests who can spend over $100 million to stop it. It means that we will continue to get Kennedy-Kassebaum band-aids that preserve the American profiteering health care system at the expense of the uninsured (the 1996 Democratic platform did not even include universal health care). It means that when 80-90 percent of the public says it wants the campaign finance process cleaned up,[18] we get a token handshake between Gingrich and Clinton that does not result in thorough action, because neither fox wants to be shut out of the corporate donor hen house. Public pressure may produce a mock campaign "reform" that, like the health care band-aid, gives an illusion of "doing" something but does not get the job done.

It is apparent that public government "of and for the people" has been replaced with corporate government of and for the bottom line. Money has long interfered with democracy, but the past 20 years are indicative of the cumulative power that the elite, via financial institutions and corporations, have amassed over the judicial, executive, and Congressional branches of our government. We now have a "public" government of "checks and balances" largely controlled by the private multinationals and wealthy elite. America is what Jefferson warned against, a plutocracy: government by and for the wealthy.

PROMISE OF DEMOCRACY:
THE FUNDAMENTAL SOCIAL CONTRACT

Thwarted democracy is the largest single problem now facing the country—indeed the world—because without citizen control of government there is no means to address the rights of the citizenry nor "to promote the general welfare" of the people. Without democratic control of our institutions, the self-serving elites will preserve their corporate welfare and the monied interests will see that the elected "representatives" do not step on corporate toes.

When the few accumulate the political power to perpetuate massive unemployment, level wages to the lowest global common denominator, devolve the welfare state, undermine social services, further redistribute the wealth upwards, engage in capital flight, practice destructive currency speculation and disinvestment, unload the costs of doing private business on the public, and destroy the environment upon which we all depend for life, then our "democratic" government has proven a failure for the majority.

Yet government is necessary for social order. Political theorist Max Weber warned, "In anarchy it's not just the king who loses his rights but the worker as well."[19] A government which acts in the public interest is necessary to solve social problems, to determine the common good, to act as protector of the people against the ravages of free market excess. In these times, both Clinton and the GOP free-marketeers call for a reduced role of government, when a more precise role is called for. Only the public representative, the government, can provide the security that the private sector seeks to unravel, such as environmental protection, Social Security, wage standards, the goal of full employment, protection against discrimination, and protection from corporate flight.

It is simply subterfuge on the part of those who would undo government to claim that government does not "work," because social policy has been consistently thwarted by monied interests. It is cowardly capitulation to those interests to label the welfare state obsolete when social welfare has never been fully implemented. One can argue whether Keynesian liberalism in the long run perpetuated economic evils that might have been overcome by a more humane system or whether liberalism postponed a bloody rectification of capitalism's misery-producing components. One can argue whether the decline of a socialist threat, and consequent lack of a countervailing force to curb capitalist excess, have made the Democrats and Republicans so cozily subservient to "free" market doctrine, but of immediate concern is that the globalization of capital has generated a crisis in which even the meager underpinnings of the Keynesian welfare state are threatened by the enormous growth of power of the multinationals. The welfare state with all its imperfections remains the moral apex of social consciousness in America. As long as capitalism is here to stay, the welfare state is imperative to cushion against its inherent inequities.

There is no justice without democracy but there can be no democracy without economic justice. We need economic as well as political democracy. The questions raised by the "left" are as legitimate as ever, maybe even more so now that "democracy" in America has been exposed to be blatantly auctioneered to the highest bidder. Can equality, democracy, social justice ever be met under capitalism? Can capitalism rid the world of inequality, poverty, or unemployment? Can the market forces worshipped in Washington stop the impending ecological disaster? Can the destruction of the environment be avoided under a system that glorifies profit, consumerism, and short-term gain over sustainability?

CHAPTER 14

MANIFESTO
OF AN UPPITY CRIP

PEOPLE, THE CENTER OF CIVILIZED SOCIETY

Economic justice can be measured by the screams of anguish from the very rich.

—John Kenneth Galbraith

The world's billionaires—all 358 of them—own more assets than the annual combined incomes of 45 percent or 2.5 billion of the world's people.[1] In 1994, the top 500 global corporations owned 25 percent of all private sector assets (worth $2.68 trillion), which include all manufacturing, retail, wholesale, construction, mining, health and business services, finance, insurance, and commercial real estate. The rest is divided among 3.8 million corporations.[2] By 1997 200 global corporations owned that quarter of the world's wealth.

FREE MARKET = FETTERED PEOPLE

Capitalism is a relatively recent event in world history. Only over the past couple of centuries have human beings been subjected to a market-controlled society, where competition, capital accumulation, and increased labor productivity dominate our economic and social lives. Preoccupied with productivity, efficiency, and making money, we are living an economic experiment the social consequences of which have not been fully fleshed out.

Karl Polanyi, author of *The Great Transformation: The Political and Economic Origins of Our Times*, warned in the 1940s that laissez-faire capitalism would result in what he called a "wilderness":

> Our thesis is that the idea of a self-adjusting market implied a stark utopia. Such an institution could not exist for any length of time without annihilating the human and natural substance of society; it

would have physically destroyed man and transformed his surroundings into a wilderness.[3]

Because this is true, Polyani said that capitalism must be regulated. But the regulations, which today are known paradoxically as "free trade," are geared to protect the powerful from market forces, usually at the expense of everybody else. Polanyi did not mean a natural "wilderness," rather he meant a society-eating-its-own nightmare. He forecast the self-destruction of civilization under an economic system that destroys human bonding by eliminating reciprocity and community. Consider that Polyani's warning was visionary.

At the end of the 20th century the corporate state is busily unloading everything perceived as of no use to building more wealth: private managed-care corporations are usurping public health care; "free" market happy-faced Orwellian "opportunity" is replacing public entitlements; and mutual fund privateers threaten Social Security, promising that they can deliver "security"(for a price, of course), while the poor may be wedged out of retirement security. The Social Security Administration is paring down disability while the government puts Medicare and Medicaid on the road to rationing. As the government devolves national standards, a citizen's right to redress social wrongs is curtailed. Job security disappears as corporate profits soar. The prison business booms while the social contract...contracts.

When banks control monetary policy and global corporations control government policies, the "economy" is raised to highest esteem, "efficiency" the goal. Under corporate governance a person's "worth" is measured by his/her dollar value to the Gross Domestic Product (as previously noted, disabled people are "worth" more to the GDP as a slot in a nursing home bringing in $50,000 a year than we are living in our own homes). The horrible end result is a society that reduces personhood to a commodity, diminishing human dignity and eroding the human substance of the culture.

The peril of an economy-inspired system is that it automatically sheds through its "efficient" workings all of no use to generating capital. In our discard society the irrelevant "surplus" population (which is an immoral nomenclature) for whom there are no jobs, the disabled who cannot work or cannot get jobs, the sick and the elderly who dare to live too long, the poor children who cannot vote are increasingly abandoned by the corporate state. Assisted suicide becomes the hot social issue, while correcting grossly inadequate socio/economic policy—such as the lack of universal health care—remains back-burnered, off the agenda. Medical costs skyrocket, placing adequate care out of financial reach for millions, but the health corporations' stockholders' dividends rally upwards. Congress targets the ban on Medicaid assisted-suicide for reversal, while Medicaid is on the chopping block for cuts. Corporate-controlled medicine makes people "worth" more dead from assisted suicide, because treatment siphons off profit dollars from the HMOs.

What effect does this have on the citizenry? This surge of monied power is about more than building excessive wealth for the few, it is also about building more social control over the many. When collective security is threatened, individual fear increases. The reduction of the social safety net breeds an increasingly desperate population that retreats into individualistic concerns, because the message people get is that to survive they must be ever focused on acquiring money. Desperately poor people can be forced into below-living- wage jobs and made to feel "lucky" to have any kind of job, intimidated into silence, and manipulated into political submission, when they have families they can barely feed. Middle class people can be politically neutralized by having to work longer hours to keep their standard of living, narrowing the time for policy education much less for civic and political participation. The contrived threat that Social Security won't be there for the younger generation instills a fear that fosters a no-holes-barred individualism to get-what-you-can-when-you-can, at any cost and by any means.

"Free" market ideologues like William Buckley, Ronald Reagan, Newt Gingrich, and converted presidential candidate Bob Dole hold that competition rises above cooperation, rugged individualism above shared responsibility. Margaret Thatcher goes so far as to say that society does not exist, only individuals do. Win or lose, eat or be eaten, they reject the notion that society has a responsibility to evenly spread its resources—unless that spreading is to Lockheed, Chrysler Corporation, or British Petroleum.

The marketeers point to the "free" market as the solution to our social problems, but a free market is not synonymous with human freedom. The market is based on where money finds its highest return and has only mathematical results (individual), not human results (collective). As the architects of capitalism, the banks, the corporations, and the wealthy wield power over government to act in their own interests; the result is an economy disconnected from the common good.

It is unrealistic for the disability movement to expect resolutions to social injustices from "free" market principles, because left to individualist values, the free-marketeers would do away with government-supported mutual responsibility. Carried to the nth degree, an "unfettered" market would mean no civil rights, Medicaid, Medicare, Social Security nothing for individuals who cannot pay their own way, except, of course, the rich, who transcend these "natural" laws with inheritance money in the bank. Since disabled people are interdependent with government—as with our assistants and the fact that many must rely on government support—it is contradictory for us, if we have any solidarity with our own kind and with other oppressed people, to follow market ideologues because the very remedy to disabled people's historical exclusion is a strong government that acts on behalf of social justice inclusion principles. It takes a strong government to remove the barriers that the skewed market system erects. Our interests are far more in alignment with values of cooperation and community than with the "free" market, fettered competition, and individualism.

In countries where there are counter-ideologies to market doctrine—such as Socialist, Green, Labor, and other political theories—citizens know that the market is not "free," but largely subject to corporate manipulation. In social democratic countries success or failure is connected with social organization, not attributed to a single individual's ability to sink or swim in an inherently unjust laissez-faire economy where corporations and banks have power to manipulate public policy.

Collective security is vital to maintaining the peace and promoting a healthy community. Several years ago a fire erupted in a canyon in Alta Dena, California. Homes were destroyed, quite unintentionally, by a homeless man who lit a fire to keep warm on a cold night. The fire caught some bushes and spread into the hills, burning everything in its path for miles. The homeowners' loss was a social issue for the entire city, for if this man had had shelter and warmth there would have been no brush fire to burn out of control. The unheeded lesson of the Alta Dena fire was that we are all linked and until everyone is safe, no one is safe; until everyone has a home, no one's home is safe.

Yet the notion is growing that individuals with enough money can protect themselves from the ravages of the "wilderness" by living in gated communities and hiring enough security guards. For example, Disney promises consumers in "A Disney you Can Go Home To" a corporate-built and maintained security-driven town where the rabble is kept out of the city limits by private guards.[4] Do we want a Disney "community" of armed guards as the model society for our children—even if it could "work"? The Disney walled-off approach will only result in a vain attempt to acquire the security we all want, but can only get by acting collectively, democratically, and responsibly out of concern for all of humanity.

Polyani explores the possibility that the primary human motive is not private gain, what he calls "gain or truck," but rather cooperative reciprocity—where social relations dominate material acquisition and redistribution.[5] He eloquently makes the case (basing his conclusions on studies of successful precapitalist societies) that humans need to foster genuine and healthy socialization. He says that people would rather be friends with their neighbors than be placed in competition with them, would rather live in an economic system where they are not forced to profit from exploiting others' labor. When social relations dominate material exchange, a more equitable redistribution is the natural result, because social standing in the community is directly connected to social responsibility.

Should we dare to envision such a reciprocal society today, it would be necessary to revive local community. It would call for a conscious effort to develop interexchange where people mutually give and take, a reworking of cultural values so that we create rewarding work that has meaning beyond making money. The captain of the *Enterprise* in the movie "Star Trek: First Contact" envisioned such a future—a society where money does not exist. He said, "The acquisition of wealth no longer is the driving force of our lives. We want to better ourselves." The challenge is to get beyond our current social adolescence and build an inclusive, more equitable and creative community where the economy serves people rather than enslaving them.

PEOPLE AT THE CENTER

Jefferson was far more adept at digging out the radical—getting to the root of things—in his day than the homogenized U.S. pundits of the 1990s. Forty years after the Declaration of Independence, Jefferson wrote, "Each generation has a right to choose for itself the form of government it believes most promotes its own happiness. . . A solemn opportunity of doing this every 19 or 20 years should be provided by the Constitution." The framers did not amend the Constitution to include Jefferson's suggestion, but Jefferson believed that rebellion, even revolution, is "as necessary in the political world as storms in the physical." He asked in 1787, "What country can preserve its liberties, if its rulers are not warned from time to time, that this people preserve the spirit of resistance?"[6]

As a relative of one signer of the Declaration of Independence, Charles Carroll, who risked his life by signing a document that could have landed him on the gallows for treason, I see that tyranny remains amongst us; corporate practices are destroying the bonds of community, Business Roundtable economics are not working for the majority, inequities are endemic and growing. The unfulfilled democratic promise rings as the greatest tragedy of this dubious Republic. In the spirit of Jeffersonian dissent, the basis for social reorganization must be predicated upon the understanding that the major decision a cooperative society makes is about how it distributes goods and the means of production.

❦

When, later in the course of human events, it becomes known that 86 percent of the people believe the wealthy have too much influence in government, 84 percent believe that large corporations have too much influence, 83 percent that the media do, and 64 percent that special interest groups do,[7] then it becomes necessary for the PEOPLE to demand the fulfillment of the unrealized democracy.

When a long train of abuses and usurpations in pursuit of global capitalist profits evinces a design to reduce citizens under the absolute despotism of the banks and corporations, it is the People's right, it is their duty to throw off such tyrants, and to provide new principles for their future security.

In proof of this tyranny, the grievances of the people, the following facts, are submitted:

The corporate-driven government does not promote the "general welfare" as its goal, and large portions of the population continue to live in poverty; too many are not able to find jobs; too many are not paid a living wage; too many are discriminated against; too many go without health care; too many receive substandard health care; too many are trapped in profiteering nursing homes; too many live on below-poverty benefits; too many are subjected to environmental pollutants; too many cannot obtain a decent education; too many are injured in the workplace; too many are homeless, too many hungry, too many have been cast out as the "surplus" population by the magnates of global capital.

Be it resolved that if even one person is lacking in shelter, food, clothing, a decent income, or a living wage job, capitalism has failed. Be it resolved that the capital/worker paradigm that judges human worth in relation to work or defines human worth in terms of how one is of use to the capitalist economy is simply wrong.

Remedies are called for. A world-wide democracy—not a "democracy" that acts as a front for capitalist exploitation, but one that places people's welfare above corporate profits and dissolves economic inequities—is of the first order. Economic democracy means no one is too rich or need be too poor.

PRESCRIPTION FOR REORGANIZATION:

- *Democratic Control.* The people must have democratic control over all business: industry, banking, finance, land, commerce—the works—because without that, there can be no genuine democracy. Business must be reeled in to the public domain.

- *Corporate Accountability.* It is not a matter of converting corporations into "good corporate citizens." As Richard Grossman and Frank Adams make the case in "Taking Care of Business: Citizenship and the Charter of Incorporation," corporations are not individuals and should not be allowed status equal to a citizen. Citizens need control over corporations (including worker-owned) to conduct yearly reviews to determine whether a business's practices are for the good of the community. Corporations must pay the costs they socialize onto the community. Citizens need the power to revoke corporate charters when reviews are not satisfactory.

- *Campaign Finance Reform.* It is clear that PAC and corporate money controls public policy. During the last election cycle soft money contributions topped $263 million, and PACs gave another $193 million. The people can thwart such anti-democratic practices by legislating the public financing of political campaigns,[8] placing a cap on what can be spent by campaigners, placing a cap on what can be donated, and mandating that all media grant free time to candidates on an equal basis during the campaign season. Business must be barred from making any contributions or gifts to public officials. Corporations must not be allowed to sponsor initiatives on any state or federal ballot to level the playing field.[9] It will be necessary for citizens to initiate campaign finance reform through a national initiative to override the bought-out elected officials, otherwise the Beltway politicians will serve up a half-measure "reform" that will not do the job.

- *Corporate Subsidies.* Subsidies and tax breaks to business cost the average taxpayer three times what goes towards social spending. Corporate tax rates need to be returned to 1950 levels, loopholes need to be closed and corporate subsidies ended.

- *Electoral Reform.* "One person-one vote" is not meaningful under our current system. Winner take all does not give a true accounting of an election. Americans must break up the "two party" system which has become one party of money. Aside from making politics boring and predictable, the current system has a monopolized political thought. Proportional representation would make it easier for new parties to get on the ballot and acquire representation in the legislature. Citizens need to hear from socialists, Greens, the New Party, Labor, as well as from parties that have not yet been conceived, because new ideas are the hope for the future.

- *Participatory Democracy.* Voting every four years is not sufficient to hold government accountable to the people. More issues need to be put before the public via national referenda and initiatives.

Democratization needs to be practiced at every level. Government entities (like the National Organization on Disability) that hold "public" meetings by invitation only, where citizens must "apply" and be "accepted" to participate in a public gathering, must be quelled, because democracy by-invitation-only is false democracy. Public entities that use hierarchical procedures like Roberts' Rules of Order to deny equal access to all citizens must be opened in a manner that equalizes participation.

- *Capital Accumulation.* Excessive wealth in the hands of one, a few, or the global corporations is destructive to the well-being of all. Wealth that only creates more wealth rather than contributing to the well-being of the community acts against the goal of sustainable community. Short-term profit incentives destroy the biodiversity necessary to sustain life by polluting and raping the planet's natural resources. Environmentalists conclude that we cannot have infinite growth on a finite planet, yet capitalism is an economic system built on infinite growth: growth in productivity, in quantities of commodities, in usage of the world's resources, and in expanding consumption. The paradigm needs to be shifted so that we produce for use.

- *Government Accountability.* Government is corrupted, removed, and not directly responsible to the people it serves. Yet people, including disabled people, need government services. Community and citizen boards composed of people who are directly served by a program and answerable to their peers need to oversee public programs, both to enhance program outcome and to keep officials focused on the people they are meant to serve. Regular citizen review and oversight of agencies, such as Social Security and departments like Health and Human Services, can work to hold bureaucrats, who have so much power over our lives, accountable.

- *Environmentally Sustainable Development.* Business practices that threaten the survival of the planet's biodiversity must be banned. Free market systems that bring health and environmental standards down to the lowest common denominator must be regulated and laws strongly enforced. Our society must replace excessive consumption with values that support human dignity and cooperation.

- *Decorporatizing the Media.* When the public's knowledge is limited by media empires' ever-increasing ownership of information (and control of it), tyranny over and corruption of the flow of information is the outcome; the public is kept ignorant and democracy suffers. The media is one of the first businesses that needs to be held to democratic principles and made independent of corporate and government influence.

- *Universal Access.* Universal design principles need to be applied to all public and private spaces, to ensure easy access for all. Further, technology can be used to promote democracy. For instance, making speaker phones standard practice at public meetings would help stop the social Darwinist survival of the fittest politics where those most able to physically attend meetings have the advantage and power over those who cannot get there.

- *Disability-Sensitive Universal Health Care.* Health care must be an entitlement, a right, not a luxury, and not tied to a job. The national health care system in Canada is an excellent model. All insurance and HMO corporations (profit and nonprofit) must be removed from controlling health care policy.

- *Income Gap.* Inequality of income breeds poverty. Excessive wealth in the hands of the elite few causes deprivation for those at the bottom of the economic ladder. The income gap must be radically altered to end this vicious reality. European solutions like adding a wealth tax need to be considered.

- *Fair Taxation.* America does not redistribute its wealth equitably. It falls behind France, Sweden, and Germany in what the rich are expected to contribute. Loopholes that subsidize special business interests and the elite must be eliminated to develop a truly progressive tax system, where the rich pay their fair share. The corporate tax could be based on what a corporation pays its shareholders. Off-shore multinationals evading taxes must be taxed.

- *Full Employment and Income Maintenance.* A sustainable living must be a right, not happenstance. The current "opportunity" society is a cruel hoax that promotes high unemployment. If Federal Reserve policy and corporate practices create unemployment, then the "surplus" population—the byproduct of the financial magnates—

must be provided with a guaranteed income adjusted to reflect the actual cost of living. This could be accomplished through legislating profit taxes that would go to expand Social Security to minister to all the nonworking "surplus" population, or by initiating a tax on all speculative financial transactions.

- *Social and Ecological Use-Values of New Jobs.* Use-value must be a part of a full employment strategy. Jobs that destroy the environment and promote an unsustainable lifestyle obviously do not need to be created, they need weeding out.

- *Living Wage.* The vast majority of the poor work but remain in poverty because they do not earn enough to live on. The taxpayer subsidizes business once again when low wages make it necessary for the worker to use food stamps to make ends meet. All work must pay a living wage, at least $9 per hour.

- *Disability Benefits.* Benefits must be modernized to accommodate disabled people who wish to work. The current punitive structure must be replaced with a supportive one. For those who cannot work due to disability, a benefit level must be maintained at which one can live free from want.

- *PAS Programs.* Institutional profiteering needs to be replaced with home-based community services with disabled people in charge of designing those programs. Assistants must be configured into the workplace.

- *30/20 Hour Work Week and Job Sharing.* Many people cannot work a full 40-hour week. A part-time job threatens disability benefits, but often does not pay enough to replace those benefits or provide enough to live on. No one should lose their Social Security if they are working at a job that does not completely sustain them. Altering the rigid 40-hour week to accommodate populations with different needs and provide adequate income and benefits is imperative.

- *Government Conduct.* The rollback meisters' attempt to dismantle the social contract must be counteracted with a citizen call for increased government responsibility. Government has a role to play in equalizing society; standards must be set and enforced unilaterally to stop the "race to the bottom" from degrading our society.

- *Social Security.* Originally Social Security was a separate fund, but in 1968 President Johnson rolled the Social Security trust fund (which was in surplus) into the general budget to obscure the Vietnam war deficit. The commingling of funds in the budget has meant that Social Security dollars are vulnerable to politicians using the funds for other purposes, but also leaves the funds open to budget balancers who blame entitlements for the deficit. Removing Social Security from the budget would unmask the huge amounts the nation expends on military and corporate welfare.

  Social Security must be adequately funded. The attempt by Wall Street, right-wing think tanks, and mutual fund corporations to privatize Social Security must be stopped in its tracks. Social Security is our most important anti-poverty program because it pools wealth to provide some security to everyone. Again, the rich who have more can pay more. Instead of stopping payroll contributions at $62,700 of annual income, the cap needs to be raised so that those making $100,000, $500,000, or $millions continue to add to the fund.

  Social Security must be made more equitable for all groups served. Seniors can earn up to $30,000 (by the year 2002) without being disqualified from their retirement benefits, while disabled people, who often have not worked as many years to build up much savings but have greater expenses, are severed from their SSDI benefits once they earn over $500 for nine months (for the blind the figure is $960).[10] It must be questioned why rich seniors can earn $2,500 a month and not lose their Social Security when disabled people are forced into abject poverty to keep theirs. The formula must be leveled to reflect hardship.

- *Right to Equal Education.* Quality education that does not perpetuate corporate values (but does teach people to think) must be accessible to all.

- *Quality Child Care.* Policies need to be implemented to ensure that every family has access to childcare and no parent need go to work worried about a child's safety or well-being.

- *Clean Air and Water.* Environmental laws that protect all life must be enforced with jail terms and large fines. Many disabled people are very susceptible to toxic substances in the environment.

- *Occupational Safety.* Government must legislate strong safety regulations and enforce them with jail terms and heavy fines.

- *The Deficit.* Both political parties say that the budget needs to be balanced, but only 5 percent of the people agree if that means gutting entitlements. Deficit-servicing is a boon to financial markets. The wealthy and the very financial institutions who created the debt profit from holding the paper that finances the deficit. If the balanced budget meisters prevail while corporate subsidies remain untouched, then the people need to simply call for the abolition of the debt, not pay it off.

- *Acting Globally.* Integrating these concepts into international policy and making them binding globally is imperative to prevent corporations from evading social responsibilities or getting around environmental, health and safety, or civil rights law by moving operations overseas.

Be it resolved that the sleight of hand in Washington is to give the illusion of change while actually preserving the "status quo;"

And be it resolved that the elites have never pursued social or economic justice, that in fact the decision-making class—the Business Roundtable (whose membership is composed of white males over 50 years of age whose annual income averages more than 170 times the U.S. per capita),[11] the Free Congress Foundation, the Bilterberg Group, the Council for National Policy, the Hoover Institution, and the American Defense Institute—has unremittingly practiced what Adam Smith called "the vile maxim of the masters; all for ourselves and nothing for other people" and cannot be entrusted as guardians of equality;

Be it resolved that for these reasons, the PEOPLE have a duty to demand change, or, as the Dead Kennedys predicted, "Bedtime for Democracy" will be our common fate;

Therefore the PEOPLE must take it upon ourselves to turn the longstanding tide of economic inequality, not only for the common good but for the very survival of the earth itself.

CHAPTER 15

BEYOND RAMPS?

IDENTITY POLITICS, FDR, AND THE PROBLEM OF POWER

*...we have to learn to live now the future we are fighting for,
rather than compromising in vain hope of a future that is
always deferred, always unreal. This creative leap implies a
kind of recklessness born out of the death of false hope.*

—Mary Daly

*When good people in any country cease their vigilance and
struggle, then evil men prevail.*

—Pearl Buck

Can any one identity-specific group affect the broader universal
social justice questions raised in this book? It is important to take
note that while identity groups have been transforming the culture,
infiltrating university curriculums, reframing history to include non-
elite perspectives, the global capitalists have gained worldwide political domination, soon to be world governance.

The challenge for those still sane enough to be concerned with
the shrinking social contract immediately comes down to acquiring
political power to end monied and corporate dominion over our
political, economic, and cultural lives. How can we put out this very
big fire in our collective barn when we are divided into so many
identity subgroups—women, people of color, disabled, gay, workers,
seniors—competing over the shrinking crumbs the powerful choose
to throw our way?

"CRIPPLES AT THE GATE"

The positive is that there are signs of mass resistance in France,
where *tens of thousands* turned out in the streets when the corporate
state attempted to cut back civil service benefits. In Belgium students
rioted when the government attempted to gut education benefits,

and in Canada 250,000 demonstrators marched through the streets of Toronto when the Conservative government proposed public program cutbacks there. Similar demonstrations have occurred in Italy and Spain. The left won a major victory in France, where the socialists, radical leftists, communists, and ecologists easily took control of the National Assembly in protest over Chirac's conservative austerity government. From Luxembourg to Finland there have been marches against unemployment, job insecurity, and marginalization.

In America, when the entire social welfare system is attacked by a meanspirited GOP to provide tax cuts for the wealthy, comparatively little happens. Where are our European counterparts, the liberals? Following the global transnationals, the neoliberal Clinton has delivered American citizens into the hands of managed care corporations, sells Medicare HMOs as providing more "choice," and justifies the billions of dollars to be slashed as "strengthening Medicare and Medicaid." When welfare "reform" places over one million children into deeper poverty and dumps 300,000 disabled children off SSI, Clinton agrees to sign it and what happens? The protectors of the children and Marian Wright Edelman, after briefly rallying the troops, cancelled a planned demonstration, according to investigative reporter Alex Cockburn, because Edelman did not want to be "Sister Soulijahed."[1]

Shari Rowlands, the hooker who listened in on and then blabbed on Dick Morris's (Clinton's advisor and campaign strategist) conversations with the president, quoted Clinton on proposed Medicare cuts: "Ah, hell, I don't want to wake up and see a whole bunch of cripples in wheelchairs chained to my front gate."[2] It seems that the disabled have Clinton more worried than the liberal establishment in Washington. While Clinton may recoil at the momentary inconvenience of "cripples" chained to his gate, let us not think that 2,000 or even 5,000 disabled people—nor any other identity group alone—offers a countervailing force strong enough to mount a successful challenge to the rollback forces intent upon gutting entitlements and devolving the social contract in the U.S.A.

No "Cripples" on the Memorial Lawn: The FDR Social Lie

In these government-slashing times it seems appropriate to turn our attention to the godfather of the social safety net, Franklin Delano Roosevelt, who was recently honored with a new memorial in Washington, D.C. on seven and a half acres off Capitol Mall. It seems a patriotic duty to expose how the unsuspecting visitor to the Memorial will be misled on several fronts.

In an editorial, columnist Charles Krauthammer comments that the FDR Memorial twists FDR's words and actions to fit today's "politically correct touchstones of liberalism."[3] Krauthammer makes hay with several boo-boos. For example, he points out that the monument quotes FDR, the "environmentalist," to say, "The throwing out of balance of the resources of nature throws out of balance also the lives of men." Krauthammer counters that FDR's public works projects "moved more water than anyone since Moses," some of which was doubtful as to its ecological value. The memorial quotes FDR, the "anti-war activist," to have said "I hate war" but Krauthammer reminds us that FDR was the greatest warrior president, naming himself "Dr. Win the War." The memorial also makes FDR out to be a modern-day civil rights supporter, by quoting him, "We must scrupulously guard the civil rights and civil liberties of all our citizens, whatever their background." The reality? The speech was actually written about the rights of immigrants, not blacks. In fact, FDR was so politically codependent upon Southern segregationists that he would not endorse a federal anti-lynching bill.

Krauthammer asks, weren't FDR's great achievements, the New Deal, the creation of a social safety net, and the defeat of Hitler enough to make him worthy of memorializing? Perhaps we also need to ask why it is that when the nation goes through the process of memorialization it reverts to propaganda that places the "hero" in what is considered to be the best light, but doesn't attempt to even-handedly report history. What is omitted is often as telling as what is included. What about the fact that it was FDR who established the military-industrial complex and the national security state? Is that not worthy of mention for the sake of greater clarity on our current predicament? And we might take note that the leader who was celebrated for going against his class interests was one of that class's greatest benefactors. Whatever "the people" got in the New Deal, business got more. Doris Kearns Goodwin writes, "It [private business] was exempted from antitrust laws, allowed to write off the full cost of investment, given the financial and material resources to fulfill contracts and guaranteed a substantial profit."[4]

The FDR Memorial omits another historical reality. It does not depict our disabled four-term president sitting in his wheelchair. Many Americans are probably unaware that FDR was severely disabled from polio and that from 1921 on he did not walk without assistance. They are probably unaware that when FDR was president, the White House was ramped so that he could get around in his custom-built wheelchair. True, FDR chose to not be seen or photographed in his wheelchair, but he made this decision based on his accurate political conclusion that the people would assume that he was a less "able" a leader if they knew he could not walk. So, as Hugh Gallagher makes the case in his book, *FDR's Splendid Deception*, FDR hid his disability from the public; the people thought he had been "cured" of his polio and he, fearing physicalist political repercussions, chose not to disrupt their illusion.[5]

In 1996, a similar set of concerns drove the members of the FDR Memorial Commission, co-chaired by Senators Mark Hatfield and Daniel Inouye. The committee proposed to construct three statues of FDR to preserve this monumental man in the memory of the thousands visiting the capital every year. In dispute was the question whether to depict FDR as having a disability. Commission members objected to *any* of the statues showing FDR sitting in his wheelchair, choosing instead to perpetrate the deception.

The reasoning against portraying FDR in his wheelchair is antiquated by today's standards—or so we thought. Commission member and grandson of FDR Curtis Roosevelt Dahl held that FDR would have preferred his disability to remain private and not public. But this is not entirely clear, since FDR's prior concerns about the public knowing about his disability seemed to be for political expediency. FDR spent much of his time away from Washington in the company of other disabled people at a rehabilitation facility in Warm Springs, Georgia, with no concern about who saw him in his wheelchair there. Gallagher points out that FDR felt more at home in Warm Springs, where he was accepted completely without having to hide his disability. It is probable that if FDR could have his say, he would vote with the disability pride point of view in the 1990s.

Co-chair Senator Inouye says, "I for one, would not want to re-do history. FDR was commander-in-chief of the greatest fighting force in the world and he wanted to be viewed as a strong leader."[6] Inouye's statement needs examining in light of physicalism. Does not being able to walk negate FDR's ability to be a strong leader? FDR, who spent his entire four terms as a disabled man, never walking without assistance, proved that not being able to walk does not equate with inability or lack of strength. It is Senator Inouye who would "re-do history" by falsely portraying FDR as a walking person.

For many in the disability rights movement, the FDR monument became a litmus test for disability acceptance and equality. Would the world embrace the famous FDR as a severely disabled man? The Commission's resistance spoke the oppressors' language, a biased dialect that says disabled people are victims "confined" to wheelchairs. In their view, wheelchairs symbolize tragedy, so how could they honor FDR if they portrayed him as a "tragic victim"? Showing FDR as "crippled" would lessen his heroic stature and make him appear "less than a man." Besides, goes this logic, it would be too shocking to the public to see an American hero sitting in a wheelchair.

The FDR wheelchair controversy is revealing as to the nature of identity politics born from the mother of invention, necessity. That there is any FDR Memorial controversy is evidence that disabled people have not been brought fully into the human race. If, for instance, the Commission originally agreed to depict FDR as disabled, then we might conclude that disabled people are at least on the road to being accepted as social equals. Instead, what we have is a reality check; the monument is a *social lie*.

The horrible irony is that while the disability rights movement promotes the employment of persons with disabilities under our national civil rights act, our own government refuses to depict the most famous and capable employed wheelchair user in history as disabled. The Commission's concerns about "political correctness" (however inappropriately applied to the FDR Memorial) did not extend to disability rights. The Commission's decision makes it perfectly clear that there is a continued need for narrowly focusing on disability identity politics to realize social and economic empowerment. Our movement is most certainly testimony to the validity of the saying, "If we don't do it, no one else will."[7]

THE "MORAL MAINSTREAM:" DAZED AND CONFUSED

Identity-group politics configures around pluralism, a view of society which holds that all political life involves a competition for group influence within a mainstream political framework. The identity-group approach, like the disability rights movement, assumes that mainstream electoral politics is on the moral course and seeks to gain power within it. So identity groups use their group power in a bipartisan foray to call for equality, directing attention to "their" issues within the Democratic and Republican parties. But *what the pluralists do not seem to grasp is that the dominating elite has placed them in the position of having to compete for their equality by creating the inequality, exclusion, and "scarcity" of funds in the first place.*

At the FDR Memorial dedication ceremony, President Clinton quoted FDR, "The test of our progress is not whether we add more to the abundance of those who have much; it is whether we provide for those who have too little." Yet, the Clinton "economic boom" has benefited the top third of the population, leaving the majority two-thirds of Americans with less economic security.[8] The United Nations reports that American poverty is on the rise.[9] President Clinton did not mention at the ceremony that he had signed a bill that severed disabled immigrants from entitlements that FDR wanted to protect and cut thousands of disabled children off SSI and Medicaid.

Few seem to ask, why hasn't social and economic inequality already been eradicated? Rather our political "mainstream" condones the reality that two in five American children live in poverty (largely due to the fact that the median income for hard-working young two-parent families has dropped by 33 percent for a total decline of $10,000 per year since 1973), that millions are homeless, and that 27 million are unemployed or underemployed, by accepting that that is "the way it is."

The country has had several hundred years to accomplish equality of results, having sent men to the moon in the meantime. If the "moral" mainstream wanted to solve the problem of inequity, wouldn't it already have done so? The lack of results points to the reality that both political parties represent what is basically a corrupted system, the goal of which is to protect and serve the status quo. For example, if we all had a living wage job as a Constitutional right, then capitalists would have to share the wealth to make that happen; businesses could not reap profits by paying below living wages and operating sweatshops. If we all had disability-sensitive health care, including mental health care, then the insurance industry would not be making record profits.

The very reason identity groups are not "equal" is because we *are* marginalized, we are kept from political and economic power. Do we want to clamor to the "mainstream," into a system of unholy alliances that does not work for all but works very well for the wealthy few?

Todd Gitlin has pointed out, in "The Rise of Identity Politics," that "the thickening of identity politics is inseparable from a fragmentation of commonality politics."[10] By "commonality politics" (Robert Jay Lifton's phrase) Gitlin means those issues which centered on commonality, what was shared rather than what was "different." As Gitlin makes the case, the development of identity politics has splintered the "universalist" forces that managed to obtain the meager social contract in America, dissolving this center into smaller interest group fragments which by exclusively focusing on "their" issues are no longer watching out for universal justice, the common good of the whole of humanity.

When group competition, individualism, and dog-eat-dog capitalism are unchallenged dominant values, cooperation, interdependence, and social justice suffer. How just is it if disabled people have Medicaid but children go hungry because their food stamps are cut? How just is it if Medicaid is expanded to cover more people but disabled people's care is rationed? Yet that is symbolically what identity politics, exclusive of universal social justice principles, produces in an inequitable system. Identity groups are competing for "our" piece of a reduced pie, when what we need to do is demand a transformation that delivers a different pie—one big enough for all of us.

Most dangerously, identity groups seem to have accepted that the mainstream system of poverty, unemployment, rationed health care is inevitable, and limit their activities to playing the competitive pluralist game with little vision or hope for universal justice. When groups agree to compete instead of placing the onus on the corporations and military, political energies become split and options narrowed.

Disabled people should be proud we have garnered a voice. But our disability identity has become so rigid a political construct that to venture beyond "our" issues is to risk criticism from within our own ranks. The unspoken consensus, that disabled people can be activists as long as activism is disability-centric, not only produces a tunnel vision that can limit one's understanding of overall reality, but can dangerously isolate our cause, to be chopped off by greater powers.

What the identity politics game is likely to birth is a white people's identity politics—the Timothy McVeigh stranded-whites-without-an-economic-future identity movement. The Patriots, for instance, correctly assess the harm of globalization to their individual lives, understanding the danger of losing national sovereignty to the monied global forces, but they uphold that the New World Order is a Zionist banker conspiracy. Another identity group, the Christian Coalition, has monopolized the moral and family values corner of the political game, while yet another, the Promise Keepers, composed of males of all varieties, touts that women must promise to honor, love, and obey the "wronged" and rightful head the household—the male, be he white, black, red, or yellow. The sheer numbers of these people (the majority of the population are Christian Caucasians) could challenge and win this identity politics game.

The liberal tradition of the Enlightenment coupled with the radical left kept the focus on liberatory issues like equality, economic justice, peace, and democracy—underlying ideals that affect all of humanity. Let us not be dazed and confused about the fact that once the countervailing philosophy of universalist politics is buried by the individualist "free" marketeers, capitalism will run unbridled and rampant, producing more human misery than most Americans could imagine possible.

BEYOND RAMPS?

Yet identity-based politics have come from non-addressed or unsatisfactorily addressed questions of equality within the larger universalist base. We must ask, then, how do we deal with the problem of respecting one another's issues and building much-needed common power? How do we build an interdependent politics that does not leave one group dangling in the wind? Is it possible?

Human beings need some form of ideal to which to aspire. Universalism represented the possibility of a common humanity; it found resonance with the thought that we could put an end to inequality and misery. Universalists viewed human emancipation as a worthy goal; it still is.

We must recognize that identity-based movements *have* transformed the culture by expanding the dominant society's consciousness. Identity movements have provided an opportunity to gain a deeper understanding of oppression and progression. Radical feminists, gay, black, and disabled writers have provided ample material to glean what "difference" means and what the issues are. The challenge for reviving social solidarity is to build upon mutual respect and support *without dismissing or diluting difference*. For instance, *to move beyond ramps, we must first agree that ramps are indisputably necessary*. That would be making a common political "home," blending difference into commonality.

For instance, universal single-payer health care will remove disabled people from the tyranny of insurance company profiteering by providing all with health care security not tied to a job or to one's physical condition. Full employment goals will help disabled people get a job because more jobs will be available. A guaranteed livable income for all will sustain disabled people who can work but are unable to get a job, and that would elevate our humanity. A sustainable economy with environmental safeguards would contribute to our health and well-being. Restoring our democracy will insure that we have a public voice without having to buy one. An equitable distribution of wealth would mean more opportunities for disabled people to live to their full potential because more public money would be available for such purposes. (This is not to say that government is to be trusted. We all must be vigilant watchdogs of government; all forms of government are prone to abuses of power.)

Not to be Pollyanna-ish; *the complexities are immense*. Sampling a few disabled people about building common ground brought these immediate responses: "We will get swallowed up by such alliances because these groups are ignorant on our issues;" "the liberal left doesn't give a damn about disability;" "the progressives don't include universal access on their platforms;" and "we can't afford to spend the time to find out if they will accept us as equals."

As to the suggestion that the failings of democracy can be cured by more democracy, one person remarked, "If we have more democracy that democracy may not include us." Another asked, "Would that be like the democracy in Oregon, where they voted to ration health care at disabled people's expense?"

Indeed there are risks to genuine democracy. Our technology has not produced a more educated society. The "information society" has left millions in the dark on underload. Too many of our citizens do not know about the Bill of Rights and cannot name their elected representative. Forty-one percent of Americans believe that every holder of a Ph.D. has attended medical school. Thirty-five percent of Americans do not know that Hiroshima was the site of the first atomic bomb attack and ninety-eight percent of Americans do not know who is the president of Mexico. In October 1994, forty-two percent of Americans said they had "never heard of" Newt Gingrich.[11] And the information society has produced another phenomenon—overload—where the truth is obscured by so much information, disinformation, and holes in our information that it is difficult to make sense of it all, so many just tune out. That effectively thwarts meaningful political action.

In addition, we are precariously positioned in a "society" of consumers, lulled by their products and technology into the drug of entertainment, where meaningful public discourse is not even a topic of interest. Neil Postman posits in *Amusing Ourselves to Death* that it is not Orwell's propaganda ministries that are the greatest threat to our society, but Huxley's *Brave New World*, where the people "come to love their oppression, to adore the technologies that undo their capacities to think."[12] Postman makes the convincing case that people have willingly submerged themselves in the show business era where entertainment and trivia rule and genuine public discourse has little place or value.

This is to say that increased democracy does not guarantee enlightened rule. A democracy is only as just as the people who live in it. "The people" gaining more control could result in almost anything, from the growing Christian Coalition to the Promise Keepers to Jesse Helms-type bigots running the nation. For example, what if we get a democracy that aligns itself with the spirit of a Pat Buchanan in a Father Coughlin-type populism that is homophobic, anti-Semitic, and racist and pans disability rights? What if greater democracy results in a Dick Lamm "democracy," where it is counterproductive to educate disabled people and old people have the duty to die? How about the possibility of a libertarian-type "democracy" that believes government can't work, so it abolishes taxes, eroding the base for promoting the general welfare and Social Security? What if we get a Ross Perot "democracy" that thinks that FDR could not solve the problems of the nation today because "he was a man in a wheelchair, for him it would be an uphill climb"?

Taking heart, political theorist Antonio Gramsci would call for an "optimism of the will" to overcome the "pessimism of the mind." All transformation must start at home and spread into the larger society. We must retain enough optimism to believe that we can revive the meaningful public discourse so vital to ensuring a just society, that we can consciousness-raise, educate ourselves and others, and join in public debate through town hall meetings, the internet, and local and national referendums that can result in more participation and justice worldwide.

Otherwise we just give up, and none of us can afford the consequences of that. We are already dangerously close to a Jerry Lewis "democracy," where middlemen beggars and corporate CEOs earning $384,000 a year may replace entitlements with charity. We are already on the verge of a Dr. Kevorkian-style "democracy," which believes that if one is in a wheelchair one would be better off dead. We've not had a real democracy. It's time to give it a chance.

NOTES

CHAPTER 1: WHY BE "NORMAL?"

1. Speech at the Disability Summit, Anaheim, CA, 1994.
2. "Including All of Our Lives," in Encounters with Strangers: Feminism and Disability, Jenny Morris, ed. (The Women's Press, 1996) p. 211.
3. Carol Gill, Disability Rag & ReSource, Sept./Oct. 1992, p. 5.

CHAPTER 2: AMERICAN AND NAZI EUGENICS, EUTHANASIA AND ECONOMICS

1. Alfred Hoche and Rudolf Binding, Die Freigabe der Vernichtung lebensunwerten Lebens (Leipzig, 1920) in Robert Proctor, Racial Hygiene: Medicine Under the Nazis (Cambridge: Harvard University Press, 1988) p. 178.
2. Herbert Spencer, Principles of Biology (D. Appleton and Co, 1914), Vol.1, p. 530.
3. Charles Darwin, The Descent of Man and Selection in Relation to Sex (New York: Appleton, 1922), p. 136.
4. Proctor, pp. 29, 98; and Robert Jay Lifton, The Nazi Doctors: Medical Killing and the Psychology of Genocide (Harper Collins, 1986), p. 24.
5. Darwin, p. 632.
8. Lifton, p. 30.
9. Proctor, p. 96.
10. R.C. Elmslie, The Care of Invalid and Crippled Children in School (1911); Lifton, p. 23.
11. Lifton, p. 30.

12. Proctor, p. 117.
13. Friedrich Nietzsche, Twilight of the Idols, "Morals for Doctors."
14. Proctor, p. 185.
15. Proctor, pp. 183-184.
16. Proctor, p. 66.
17. Lifton, pp. 65-66.
18. Procter, p. 186.
19. Proctor, p. 187.
20. Description by Reich chemist August Becker, quoted in Proctor, p. 190.
21. Hugh Gregory Gallagher, By Trust Betrayed: Patients, Physicians, and the License to Kill in the Third Reich (New York: Henry Holt, 1990) pp. 146-147.
22. Gallagher, p. 243.
23. Alexander Mitscherlich, The Death Doctors (Eleck Books, 1962), p. 239.
24. Gallagher, p. 259.

CHAPTER 3: BACKHANDED SOCIAL DARWINISM

1. Dave Anderson, "The Guilty Bystander," Colorado Daily, Nov. 19, 1996.
2. Floyd Cockran on KPFK radio, Oct. 1995; Ingo Hasselbach, "How Nazis are Made," New Yorker, Jan. 8, 1996, p. 41; "Disabled Germans feeling echoes of Nazism," Disability Rag, March/April 1993, p. 13.
3. U.S. News & World Report, July 15, 1996, p. 17.
4. Jack Kevorkian, Written Statement to Court, Aug. 17, 1990, p. 11 (emphasis in original).
5. Washington v. Glucksberg, 95-110, U.S. 9th Circuit Court of Appeals; Vacco v. Quill, 95-1858, U.S. 2nd Court of Appeals.
6. Figure from Joseph Shapiro, "A Life Worse Than Death,"

Washington Post, April 15, 1990.
7. Calculated at California maximum benefit of 283 hours at minimum wage (admittedly inadequate).
8. Joseph Shapiro, "Larry McAfee, Invisible Man," U.S. News & World Report, Feb. 18, 1990, p. 59.
9. Eleanor Smith, press release, "Suicide?" Sept. 1989.
10. Paul Longmore, "The Shameful Treatment of Larry McAfee," Atlanta Constitution, Sept. 10, 1989.
11. McAfee quoted by Joseph Shapiro, "A Life Worse Than Death."
12. Longmore.
13. Shapiro, "A Life Worse Than Death."
14. Longmore.
15. ACLU attorneys arguing for Elizabeth Bouvia's right to die also incorrectly connected disability (cerebral palsy) with terminal illness, claiming Bouvia, who was then in her twenties, had 15 years to live when her life span was actually 80 years.
16. Eleanor Smith.
17. "Unanswered Questions," Disability Rag, Sept./Oct. 1990, p. 26.
18. Carol Gill, "Letting Go or Giving Up, How Disabled Is Too Disabled for Life?" Mainstream Magazine, May 1993, pp. 21- 27.
19. Wesley J. Smith, "Creating a Disposable Caste," San Francisco Chronicle, Dec. 6, 1995.
20. Dr. Burke quoted by Wesley Smith, ibid.
21. Lucy Gwin, "Putting Us Out of Our Misery," Mouth, the voice of disability rights, March/April 1996, p. 12.

22. Vacco quoted in *Mouth*, July/Aug. 1996, p. 17.

23. "In Royal Oak: the Death Machine," *Detroit Free Press Magazine*, March 18, 1990, p. 24.

24. Jack Kevorkian, *Prescription Medicide* (New York: Prometheus Books, 1991), p. 215.

25. Jack Kevorkian, "A Comprehensive Bioethical Code for Medical Exploitation of Humans Facing Imminent and Unavoidable Death," *Medicine and Law*, Vol. 5 (1986), p. 195.

26. Jack Kevorkian, in a speech to the National Press Club, "Dr. Death: No law is needed on euthanasia," *USA Today*, Oct. 28, 1992, p. 6A.

27. "2 Surveys Find Doctors Back Physician-Assisted Suicide," *Los Angeles Times*, Feb. 1, 1996.

28. *Washington Times*, March 13, 1987. Battin also wrote a treatise, *Ethical Issues in Suicide*, where she discusses "Suicide as the Removal of Social Burdens."

29. March/April 1996, p. 16.

30. "Survey of ICU Nurses Finds 20% Have Aided in Deaths," *Los Angeles Times*, April 26, 1996.

31. Editorial, *The Weekly Standard*, Sept. 18, 1995, italics mine.

32. Ellis quoted by *Disability Reports*, Dec. 21, 1995, p. 212.

33. *Medical Decisions About the End of Life: Report of the Committee to Study the Medical Practice Concerning Euthanasia* (2 vols.), The Hague, Sept. 10, 1991.

34. *Medical Decisions*, Report I,

p. 15.

35. *Euthanasia: Report of the Working Party to Review the British Medical Association's Guidance on Euthanasia*, British Medical Association, May 5, 1988, p. 49, no. 195.

36. *Los Angeles Times*, April 26, 1996.

37. Vacco quoted in *Mouth*, July/Aug. 1996, p. 17.

CHAPTER 4: THE POLITICS OF "PERFECT" BABIES

1. Reuters, "Sterilization Effort in Sweden for Racial Purposes is Revealed" Aug. 25, 1997.

2. *The Nation*, citing the *New York Times*, April 18, 1995.

3. Jane Norris on KFI radio, July 22, 1991.

4. "Aesthetic anxiety" coined by Harlan Hahn in the *Journal of Social Issues* edited by Adrienne Asch and Michele Fine (New York: Plenum Publishing Corp for the Society for the Psychological Study of Social Issues).

5. Adrienne Asch, "Real Moral Dilemmas," *Christianity and Crisis*, July 14, 1986, p. 239.

6. Larry Thompson, "The Price of Knowledge: Genetic Tests that Predict Conditions Became a Two-Edged Sword," *Washington Post*, Oct. 10, 1989.

7. Robert Cook-Degan, *The Gene Wars* (New York: W.W. Norton & Company, 1994), p. 253.

8. "Insurance Falls Prey to Genetic Bias," *Los Angeles Times*, March 27, 1994.

9. Study conducted by Virginia Lapham of Georgetown University and Joan Weiss, Director of the Alliance of Genetic Support Groups,

Journal of Science, Oct. 25, 1996.

10. CNN Presents, "Perfect People."

11. "The New Eugenics," *Dollars and Sense*, March/April 1996, p. 4.

12. "The New Discrimination," *Los Angeles Times*, July 20, 1997.

13. Anton Chaitkin research quoted by Lenoard G. Horowitz, *Emerging Viruses, AIDS & Ebola: Nature, Accident or Intentional?* (Maine: Tetrahedron Publishing Group, 1996), p. 344.

14. D.J. Kevles, "Out of Eugenics: The Historical Politics of the Human Genome," *The Code of Codes: Scientific and Social Issues in the Human Genome Project*, pp. 3-36.

15. The term "diability sensitive" was coined by MS-CAN policy analyst Laura Mitchell.

CHAPTER 5: A MISSING LINK

1. Michael Parenti, *Demoracy for the Few* (New York: St. Martin's Press, 1995), p. 10.

2. Adolph Hitler, *Der Fuehrer*, 1926, U.S. edition, p. 287.

3. Walter Russell Mead, "Long After War, Taint of Nazis Remains in Europe," *Los Angeles Times*, Nov. 3, 1996; Howard Zinn, *A People's History of the United States* (New York: Harper & Row, 1980), p. 401.

4. Michael Harrington, *Socialism Past and Future* (New York: Penguin Books, 1989), p. 4.

5. Harrington, p. 10.

6. Baker quoted by Alex Cockburn, "Eugenics Nuts would have Loved Norplant,"

Los Angeles Times, June 30, 1994.

7. Proctor, p. 180.

8. Proctor, p. 16.

9. Rockefeller and Carnegie quoted in Richard Hofstadter, *Social Darwinism in American Thought* (Boston: Beacon Press, 1971).

10. Ward quoted in Hofstader, p. 82.

11. Charles A. Murray, *Losing Ground* (New York: Basic Books, 1984).

12. Gallagher, p. 78.

13. Proctor, p. 22.

14. Proctor, p. 259.

15. Proctor, p. 265.

16. Carl N. Degler, *In Search of Human Nature: the Decline and Revival of Darwinism in American Social Thought* (New York: Oxford University Press,1991), p. 11.

17. Figures reported by the *Los Angeles Times*, April 17, 1996.

18. United Nations 1996 Human Development Report.

19. Karl Polyani, *The Great Transformation: The Political and Economic Origins of Our Time* (Boston: Beacon Hill Press, 1944), p. 57.

CHAPTER 6: THE ECONOMIC STRAITJACKET

1. Adam Smith, An Inquiry into the Nature and Causes of the Wealth of Nations (Encyclopaedia Britannica, 1952), p. 309, 311.

2. Adam Smith quoted in George Seldes, *The Great Quotations*, p. 641

3. Edward D. Berkowitz, *Disabled Policy, America's Programs for the Handicapped* (Cambridge University Press, 1987), p. 52.

4. Berkowitz, p. 53.

5. Berkowitz, p. 77.

6. Berkowitz, p. 69.

7. The blind get about $30 more per month.

8. Harris quoted in Berkowitz, ibid, p. 118.

9. Berkowitz, p. 117.

10. *Left Business Observer* #61, "Who's Poor?" Dec. 13, 1993, p. 5.

11. Ibid, p. 5

12. *The Nation*, "In Fact," (Feb. 12, 1996), p. 7.

13. *Report on Disability Programs*, Nov. 23, 1995, p. 195.

14. Deborah A. Stone, *The Disabled State* (Philadelphia: Temple University Press 1984), p. 7.

15. *Left Business Observer*, p. 5; figures from John Coder of the U.S. Census using data from the Luxembourg Income Study, a 1989 national effort to compare income distribution and poverty in about a dozen countries.

16. *60 Minutes*, "Help Wanted," CBS, Oct. 1, 1978; "Suicide Blamed on Threat to Cut Off Disabled Woman's Aid," *Los Angeles Times*, March 3, 1978.

17. *Associated Press*, Oct. 3, 1997.

18. *Washington Post*, April 16, 1995.

19. Esther Fein, "What Is Disabled?" *New York Times*, Aug. 12, 1997.

20. An exception: the blind do not have to prove that they can't work to qualify. Lobbying efforts brought them a higher benefit amount and tax breaks. Also, the definition of disability under the ADA is significantly broader.

CHAPTER 7: FROM TINY TIM TO JERRY LEWIS

1. Sept. 2, 1990.

2. Op-ed, Sept. 3, 1981.

3. *Los Angeles Times*, Sept. 1991.

4. *Report on Disability Programs*, Aug. 17, 1995, p. 135.

5. Leslie Bennetts, "Letter From Las Vegas: Jerry vs. the Kids," *Vanity Fair*, Sept. 1993, pp. 87, 82.

6. *Los Angeles Times*, Sept. 8, 1992.

7. Bill Bolte, "Jerry's Kidding and the Joke's on Millions of Disabled People," *In These Times*, Sept. 1992, p. 24.

8. *Moving Forward*, Sept./Oct. 1992, p. 35.

9. *Disability Rag*, Sept./Oct. 1992, p. 12.

10. Dianne Piastro, "The MDA Story That's Not Being Told," *Newspaper Enterprise Association Wire Service*, Aug. 26, 1991.

11. Gary Sifra, *The Daily News*, Sept. 14, 1995.

12. Gina Graham, "Foundation Culture," *Left Business Observer* No. 70, Nov. 4, 1995, p. 4.

13. Doug Henwood, "The Business End," *Left Business Observer* No. 70, p. 5.

14. Gregory Colvin, "Keep Charity Clear of Politics," *Los Angeles Times*, Jan. 8, 1997.

15. National Press Club, Nov. 20, 1995.

16. Lewis letter printed in *Disability Rag*, Sept./Oct. 1992, p. 23.

17. Oct. 28, 1991.

18. *Disability Rag*, Sept./Oct. 1992, p. 7.

CHAPTER 8: THE FINAL (PROFITABLE) SOLUTION

1. Wolf Wolfensberger, *The Origin and Nature of our Institutional Models* (New York: Human Policy Press, 1975), p. 55.

2. Paul Longmore, speech delivered to the 1994 Disability Summit, Anaheim, CA.

3. Laura Hershey, "Wade Blank's Liberated Community," *Disability Rag*, July/Aug. 1993, p. 16.

4. Mike Collins, "Is There a Nursing Home in Your Future," *New Mobility*, Fall 1992, p. 45.

5. Victoria Medgyesi, "Fear & Retribution," *The Disability Rag*, July/Aug. 1991, p. 18.

6. Trudy Leiberman, *Consumer Reports*, Aug. 1995.

7. California Advocates for Nursing Home Reform 1993 Report Card.

8. Robert Rosenblatt and George Skelton, "U.S. Inspectors Sent to State's Nursing Homes," *Los Angeles Times*, March 7, 1991.

9. California Advocates for Nursing Home Reform 1995 Report Card.

10. Figures from *Mouth: the voice of disability rights*, Nov./Dec. 1995. Because insufficient community-based services for people with mental illness are funded by taxpayers, no reliable number is available for comparison. Florida, one state where some such supports are available, is cited here. In Florida, in 1994 ,260,000 people received community support services at a cost of $440.2 million dollars. National average tax dollar expenditures for mental institutions are higher—$83,573 per person served.

11. *Disability Rag & Resource*, July/Aug. 94, pp. 4-6.

12. *Denver Post*, June 2, 1996.

13. Stephen Monroe, "*Provider Surveys Top Chains*," Jan. 1994, p. 37.

14. ADAPT, Denver, Colorado.

15. *Business First* quoted in *Mouth, the voice of disability rights*, Sept./Oct. 1996, p. 5.

16. Source: In Fact, 256 Hanover Street, Boston, MA

17. Alex Cockburn, "Beat the Devil," *The Nation*, March 14, 1994, p. 332.

18. Judge Needles quoted by Cockburn, p. 332.

19. Cockburn, p. 333.

20. Figure source: *Mouth: the voice of disability rights*, Sept./Oct. 1996, p. 5.

21. *Consumer Reports*, Aug. 1995.

22. Center for Responsive Politics as available from the FEC.

23. *Consumer Reports*; *Los Angeles Times*, "U.S. Inspectors Sent to State's Nursing Homes," California Advocates for Nursing Home Reform 1995 Report Card, p. 10.

24. Correspondence from Maggie Dee Dowling, July 17, 1997.

CHAPTER 9: THE ADA IN THE NEW WORLD ORDER

1. Figures from Michael Parenti, *Democracy for the Few* (New York: St. Martin's Press, 1995), p. 81.

2. *New York Times*, March 14, 1985.

3. Parenti, p. 209.

4. Parenti, p. 10.

5. Lincoln quoted in Howard Zinn, *A People's History of the United States* (New York: Harper Collins, 1980), p. 186.

6. Berkowitz, *Disabled Policy*, p. 209.

7. Harris quoted in a National Organization on Disability press release, April 29, 1996.

8. "Louis Harris refuses blind applicant," *Disability Rag,*, May/June 1992, p. 26; The blind applicant, Jay Levanthol, brought discrimation charges against Harris which were upheld by the New York Commission on Human Rights. But even then, Humphrey's company appealed to the New York Supreme Court to have the decison overturned, rather than hire him.

9. Joseph P. Shapiro, *No Pity*, (New York: Random House, 1993), p. 121.

10. Shapiro, p. 123.

11. Shapiro, p. 9.

12. *Disability Rag*, Jan./Feb. 1991, p. 17.

13. *Wall Street Journal*, June 30, 1996.

14. *Disability Rag*, July/Aug. 1992, p. 38.

15. Evan Kemp Jr., letter to the editor, *Disability Rag*, May/June 1992.

16. *One Step Ahead*, Vol. 3 No. 3, March 1996.

17. *Business Publishers Special Report*, June 8, 1995, p. 99.

18. David Burnham, *Above the Law* (New York: Scribner, 1996), p. 37.

19. Patrick McGreevy, *Daily News*, Jan. 9, 1995.

20. April 2, 1995.

21. Turner quoted by *Washington Post*, Sept. 3, 1995.

22. Marta Russell, "Tracking the ADA," *Graduating Engineer* magazine, Dec. 1994, p. 19.

23. Russell, p 19.

24. Dec. 1995 figures from *New Mobility*, p. 30.

25. *Washington Post*, Feb. 11, 1996.

26. Howard Zinn, *A People's History*, p. 499.

27. Justin Dart, Jr., "Fallacies,

Attack on ADA," Justice for All Mailing list

28. Reich quoted by *Business Week*, "N.O.D. Survey of Americans with Disabilities," May 30, 1994.

29. *San Francisco Chronicle*, July 3, 1995.

30. *San Diego Union Tribune*, Aug. 6, 1995.

31. Coelho, from California, has a disability. He was accused of financial misdoings but resigned before Ethics Committee hearings were conducted.

32. Jay Matthews, "Disabilities Act Failing to Achieve Workplace Goals: Landmark Law Rarely Helps Disabled People Seeking Jobs," *Washington Post*, April 16, 1995.

33. Leslie Kaufman-Rosen, "Who are the Disabled?" *Newsweek*, Nov. 7, 1994, p. 80.

CHAPTER 10: LET THEM EAT UNENFORCEABLE CIVIL RIGHTS

1. "Full Participation: A Dream Deferred," Special Advertising Section, *Business Week*, May 30, 1994.

2. "Willing and Able: Americans with Disabilities in the New Workforce," Special Section, *Business Week*, Oct. 1991.

3. "Full Participation," Part 1.

4. Zinn, *A People's History*, p. 448.

5. Malcolm X, *Malcolm X Speaks* (New York: Meret, 1965).

6. Schlesinger quoted by Zinn, p. 449.

7. Shapiro, *No Pity*, p. 129.

8. Zinn, p. 440.

9. Richard Rodriguez, *Los Angeles Times*, July 20, 1995.

10. bell hooks quoted in "Thinking About Capitalism," *Z Magazine*, April 1996, p. 39.

11. *Report on Disability Programs*, Sept. 28, 1995, p. 165.

12. Survey by Henry J. Kaiser Family Foundation, Harvard School of Public Health and the University of Chicago's National Opinion Research Center, published in the *Journal of the American Medical Association*, Oct. 23, 1996.

13. Figures from David Dembo and Ward Morehouse, *Too Much*, Council on International and Public Affairs, Summer 1996, p. 7.

14. The figure is adjusted for the official definition of "employed." David Dembo and Ward Morehouse, *The Underbelly of the U.S. Economy: Joblessness and the Pauperization of Work in America*, Council on International and Public Affairs, 1995, p. 13.

15. OECD study by Institute for Global Communications, Dec. 1995, in Robert Wright,"Who's Really to Blame?" *Time*, Nov. 6, 1995, p. 36.

16. Ben A. Franklin, editor, *Washington Spectator*, The Public Concern Foundation, March 15, 1996, p. 2.

17. Figures from Jeremy Rifkin, *Los Angeles Times*, Dec. 7, 1995; Ken Silverstein and Alexander Cockburn, *CounterPunch*, Vol. 3, No. 8, April 15, 1996, p. 3; *Los Angeles Times*, Feb. 3, 1995.

18. Figures from *Mother Jones* in *The Nation*, March 18, 1996; *CounterPunch*, April 15, 1996.

19. Dembo and Morehouse, *The Underbelly of the U.S. Economy*, p. 35; Reich quoted by *Washington Spectator*, p. 3.

20. *Los Angeles Times*, Sept. 4, 1995; Peter Kilborn, "Factories That Never Close Are Scrapping 5-Day Week," *New York Times*, June 4, 1996.

21. *Harper's*, Aug. 1994, p. 11.

22. Bureau of Labor Statistics Report, June 3, 1996.

23. Richard K. Scotch, *From Good Will to Civil Rights: Transforming Federal Disability Policy* (Philadelphia: Temple University Press, 1984), p. 102.

24. *Sunday Newsday*, Feb. 5, 1995; John M. McNeil, "Americans with Disabilities: 1991-92," Bureau of the Census.

25. At the time of this writing the legislation failed to be brought to the floor.

26. *Disability Funding News*, (May 20, 1996), p. 11.

27. Ken Silverstein and Alexander Cockburn, *CounterPunch*, Vol. 3, No. 9, May 1, 1996, p. 3.

28. Vickery address to the American Economics Association in 1993, Sheila D. Collins, Helen Lachs Ginsburg, Gertrude Schaffner Goldberg, *Jobs for All, A Plan for the Revitalization of America* (New York: Apex Press, 1994), p. 10.

29. *Wall Street Journal* "Credit Markets" article quoted in Bureau of Labor Statistics, June 5,1995.

30. Noam Chomsky and David Barsamian, *Class Warfare* (Monroe, ME: Common Courage Press 1996), p. 103.

31. Chomsky, p. 103.

32. Chomsky, p. 104.

32. *Too Much*, Council on International and Public Affairs, Winter 1997, p. 2.

CHAPTER 11: ENDING THE SOCIAL CONTRACT

1. *McNeil-Lehrer News Hour*, June 10, 1996.

2. Chomsky and Barsamian, *Class Warfare*, p. 17.

3. Noam Chomsky, "From Containment to Rollback," *Z Magazine*, June 1996, p. 22.

4. *Christian Science Monitor*, "World's Politicians Grope For Ways to Cut Safety Net," Oct. 11, 1995; *Left Business Observer* No. 67, Dec. 22, 1994, p. 3.

5. Mitchell quoted by Ken Silverstein and Alexander Cockburn, *CounterPunch*, Vol. 3, No. 11, June 1996, p. 2.

6. Silverstein and Cockburn, p. 1.

7. David C. Korten, *When Corporations Rule the World* (Hartford, CT: Kumarian Press, 1995), p. 12.

8. Nov. 2, 1995.

9. Figure from *Report on Disability Programs*, Feb. 29, 1996, p. 36.

10. Conversation with Gale Swenson, Los Angeles County Department of Public Services.

11. *Disability Rag & Resource*, July/Aug. 1994, p. 43.

12. *Report on Disability Programs*, Feb. 1, 1996, p. 18; *Report on Disability Programs*, Mar. 28, 1996, p. 56.

13. Ibid, p 29; *Report on Disability Programs*, May 25, 1995, p. 87.

14. "Fairness of Reagan's Cutoff of Disability Aid Questioned," May 9, 1982.

15. *Los Angeles Times*, Sept. 1981.

16. *Baltimore Sun*, May 28, 1983.

17. Berkowitz, pp. 122, 124, 127.

18. Bunning quoted in *Report on Disability Programs*, May 25, 1995, p. 18; *Report on Disability Programs*, May 25, 1995, p. 87; *Washington Watch*, published by United Cerebral Palsy, June 11, 1996, p. 2; *Report on Disability Programs*, Feb. 1, 1996, p. 18.

19. SSA employee quoted by Berkowitz, p. 126.

20. State office worker quoted by Berkowitz, p. 133.

21. Interview with Rob Peters, April 1996.

22. *Disability Funding News*, May 20, 1996, p. 11.

23. "Social Security Plans New Tests of Disability Pay," *Los Angeles Times*, March 17, 1996.

24. Interview with Peters, April 1996.

25. Interview with Leidner, July 1996.

26. Interview with Peters, April 1996.

27. SSA memo quoted in *New Mobility*, June 1997, p. 16.

28. Interview with Leidner, July 1996.

29. *Disability Funding News*, Oct. 20, 1995, p. 3.

30. *Report on Disability Programs*, sample issue, p. 3.

31. *Report on Disability Programs*, sample issue, p. 3.

32. Ken Silvertein and Alexander Cockburn, *CounterPunch*, July 15, 1995, p. 1.

33. Interview with Marilyn Holle, May 1995.

34. Report on Disability Programs, July 6, 1995, p. 112.

35. Interview with Holle, May 1995.

36. Interview with Holle, May 1995.

37. Interview with Stein, April 1995.

38. Interview with Stein, April 1995.

39. *Disability Funding News*, June 3, 1996, p. 3; *Report on Disability Programs*, Sept. 28, 1995, p. 163.

40. Berkowitz, p. 112.

41. Families USA, "Comparision of Current Law with the Personal Responsibility and Work Opportunity Reconciliation Act of 1996," Nov. 6, 1996.

42. *Justice for All*, "Senate Cover 'Disabled' as Defined by States!" Oct. 18, 1995.

43. Interview with Rock Burks, Feb. 1997.

44. *Report on Disability Programs*, Feb. 15, 1996, p. 26.

45. *Disability Funding News*, June 3, 1996, p. 3.

46. Frank Bowe, "Deficits," *Disability Rag*, Jan./Feb. 1993, p. 14.

47. *Report on Disability Programs*, May 25, 1995, p. 88; *Disability Funding News*, May 20, 1996, p. 11.

48. *Los Angeles Times*, "Social Security Plans New Tests of Disability Pay," March 17, 1996.

49. *Report on Disability Programs*, Aug. 3, 1995, p. 129; *Disability Funding News*, June 17, 1996, p. 4; *Disability Funding News*, May 20, 1996, p. 11; interview with George Waters, June 1995.

50. *Report on Disability Programs*, Aug. 3, 1995, p. 129.

51. GAO quoted by *Report on Disability Programs*, June 6, 1996, p. 94.

52. Interview with Peters, April 1996.

53. Letter printed in *Washington Watch*, a publication of UCPA, July 1996.

54. *The Nation*, June 16, 1997, p. 7.

55. *The Washington Spectator*, April 1, 1997, p. 3.

56. Clinton quoted by *Washington Watch*, Vol. 2, Issue 24, Aug. 6, 1996, p. 1.

CHAPTER 12: BURSTING GRAND ILLUSIONS

1. Mary Johnson, "There's Always a But," Disability Rag, March/April 1992, p. 11.

2. Christopher Hitchens, *The Missionary Position* (London: Verso Press, 1995), p. 70.

3. Hitchens, p. 47.

4. Hitchens, p. 11.

5. David A. Stockman, The Triumph of Politics: Why the Reagan Revolution Failed (Boston, MA: G.K. Hall, 1987), pp. 409-410.

6. Walden Bello, *Dark Victory: The United States, Structural Adjustment, and Global Poverty* (Oakland: Institute for Food and Development, 1994), p. 3.

7. Von Hayk quoted by Scott McLemee, "Theater of the Absurd," *In These Times*, Dec. 11, 1995, p. 15.

8. *Harper's*, Harper's Index, Oct. 1994, p. 13.

9. Parenti, p. 85.

10. Bruce Clayton, *Forgotten Prophet, The Life of Randolf Bourne* (Baton Rouge: Louisiana State University Press, 1984).

11. Robert McElvaine, *What's Left? A New Democratic Vision for America* (MA: Adams Media Corporation,

1996), p. 155.

12. *Washington Spectator*, The Public Concern Foundation, Nov. 1, 1995, p. 2.

13. Letter to Senator Dole from the GOP Governors, Oct. 6, 1995.

14. Becky Ogle, *Justice For All on Internet*, Oct. 10, 1995.

15. Markey quoted in *Report on Disability Programs*, Feb. 29, 1996, p. 37.

16. ARC quoted in *Report on Disability Programs*, Feb. 29, 1996. p. 38.

17. *Washington Post*, Oct. 14, 1995.

18. Families USA New Analysis-Gov's Proposal, Feb. 20, 1996.

19. Flemming quoted in *Report on Disability Programs*, Feb. 29, 1996, p. 37; Dart statement to the National Press Club, Feb. 12, 1996.

20. *The Weekly Standard*, Sept. 18, 1995.

21. Families USA press release, Dec. 7, 1995.

22. Galbraith quoted in the *Washington Spectator*, April 15, 1996, p. 1.

23. Report on Disability Programs, Nov. 9, 1995, p. 189.

24. *Los Angeles Times*, "Wilson, Allies Seek to Make Cuts in Welfare Benefits Permanent," March 3, 1996.

25. *Los Angeles Times*, March 3, 1996.

26. *Los Angeles Times*, April 12, 1996; George Skelton, "Governor's Learning Curve for the Elderly," *Los Angeles Times*, July 4, 1996; Burton quoted in *LA Times*, April 12, 1996.

27. *Report on Disability Programs*, Feb. 29, 1996, p. 37; *Washington Post*, Feb. 26,

1996.

28. *Dollars and Sense*, "Defunding the Poor," May/June 1996, p. 43.

29. *Los Angeles Times*, "Budget," July 30, 1995.

30. Dr. Alieta Eck, "Poor Get Poor Treatment from Managed Care," from *Managed Care List on Internet*.

31. World Institute on Disability, Medicaid Policy Statement, Sept. 25, 1995.

32. "Democracy Now," KPFK Los Angeles, May 30, 1996.

33. Shaffer on "Democracy Now."

34. Exceptions: without a waiver states cannot mandate enrollment for disabled children who meet the SSI definition of disability, children in foster care, persons who are eligible for both Medicaid and Medicare, and Native Americans.

35. Letter from Maggie Dee to Governor Wilson, May 1996.

36. Newt Gingrich, *To Renew America* (New York: Harper Collins, 1995), p. 37.

37. David Frost Show, March 1995.

38. Gingrich, p. 77.

39. *New York Times*, Feb. 1994; David Van Biema, *Time*, "Can Charity Fill the Gap?" Dec. 4, 1995, p. 44.

40. Van Biema, p. 44.

41. *Harper's*, May 1995, p. 11 (ratio for 1994).

42. July, 11, 1996.

43. See Continuing Resolution House bills 1995 with Ishtook (R-OK) and McIntosh (R-IN) amendments.

44. *Disability Funding News*, Jan. 22, 1996, p. 2.

45. Leonard G. Horowitz, *Emerging Viruses AIDS and Ebola: Nature, Accident or*

Intentional? (Maine: Tetrahedron, 1996), p. 496. Negative Population Growth, Inc., "Why we need a small U.S. population and how we can achieve it," *Foreign Affairs Magazine*, Council on Foreign Relations, March/April 1996.

46. Interview with Maggie Dee, May 1996.

47. *New York Times*, July 12, 1989.

48. *Washington Post*, June 3, 1991; House Democratic Policy Committee.

49. Nov. 16, 1995.

50. Harper's, Harper's Index, Aug. 1995, p. 13.

51. May 15, 1997, p. 4.

52. Source, 1996 General Accounting Office, figures quoted by Kjerten Jeppesen for the Alliance for Democracy, "Can We Save the Government Services that People with Disabilities Need?"

53. *Harper's*, March 1995, p. 9.

54. "Corporate Welfare: Why Subsidies Survive," *Time*, March 25, 1996, p. 46; James P. Donahue, "The Fat Cat Freeloaders," *Washington Post*, March 6, 1994; Common Cause and Ralph Nader, Corporate Welfare Project and Taxwatch.

55. William Greider, "The Ex-Im Files," *Rolling Stone*, Aug. 8, 1996, pp. 51-52.

56. Source: *Public Citizen*

57. Daniel Franklin, "Ten Not So Little Piggies," *The Nation*, Nov. 27, 1995, p. 670.

58. Franklin, p. 671.

59. *CounterPunch*, May 1, 1997, p. 4.

60. Common Cause.

61. Ralph Nader, "Free Enterprise Runs Too Free," *Washington Spectator*, Aug. 1, 1996, p. 2.

62. Common Cause and Wilderness Society.

63. See Ralph Estes, "The Public Cost of Private Corporations," *Advances in Public Interest Accounting*, Vol. 6, pp. 329-351, JAI Press Inc.

64. Jeffrey H. Birnbaum, "The Thursday Regulars," *Time*, March 27, 1995, p. 30.

65. Franklin, p. 670.

66. New York (Associated Press) May 17, 1997.

67. Eisenhower quote in Carruth and Ehrlich, American Quotations (New York: Wings Books , 1992), p. 181.

68. War Resisters League, US Federal Budget for 1998.

69. *Harper's*, Aug. 1994, p. 11.

70. Figures from Women Strike for Peace, Legislative Alert, June/July 1996.

71. Franklin, p. 671; *Los Angeles Times*, July 11, 1996.

72. Women Strike for Peace, *Legislative Alert*, March/April 1997, p. 3.

73. April 22, 1997.

74. Edwin Chen, "Number without Health Insurance Rises," *Los Angeles Times*, April 27, 1996.

75. David Himmelstein and Steffie Woolhandler, *The National Health Program Book* (Monroe, ME.: Common Courage Press 1994), p. 223.

76. Himmelstein and Woolhandler, p. 219.

77. Parenti, p. 73.

CHAPTER 13: DEMOCRACY UNDER SIEGE

1. Noam Chomsky, *Class Warfare*, p. 123.

2. *Energy Daily*, March 31, 1995.

3. William Greider, *Who Will Tell the People? The Betrayal of American Democracy* (New York: Simon & Schuster, 1992), p. 331.

4. *New York Times*, June, 29, 1996.

5. Dec. 17, 1995.

6. Alexander Cockburn and Ken Silverstein, *Washington Babylon* (New York: Verso, 1996), p. 183.

7. *Washington Spectator*, Nov. 1994.

8. *New York Times*, June 29, 1996.

9. Holly Sklar, *Trilateralism* (Boston: South End Press, 1980), p. 4.

10. Korten, *When Corporations Rule the World*, p. 12.

11. Kevin Phillips, *Arrogant Capital* (New York: Little, Brown & Company, 1994), p. xv.

12. "Workers and the World Economy," *Foreign Affairs*, Vol. 75 No. 3, May/June 1996, p. 29.

13. Aug. 15, 1996.

14. GOP Weekly Radio Address, as reported by the *Los Angeles Times*, Nov. 24, 1996.

15. Bello, p. 3.

16. Zinn, pp. 98-99.

17. Mortimer J. Adler, *Adler's Philosophical Dictionary* (New York: Touchstone, 1995) pp. 78, 79.

18. Percentage from Charles Lewis, Center for Public Integrity, KPFK, Aug. 15, 1996.

19. Max Weber, "Politik als Beruf," 1918-19, quoted by Daniel B. Baker, *Power Quotes* (Detroit: Visible Ink Press, 1992), p. 135.

CHAPTER 14: MANIFESTO OF AN UPPITY CRIP

1. United Nations 1996 Human Development Report.
2. *Corporate Power and the American Dream*, The Labor Institute (New York: Apex Press) p. 5, from U.S. Dept. of Commerce, Bureau of the Census, *US Statistical Abstract* and "The Fortune 500: The Largest U.S. Industrial Corporations," *Fortune*, April 18, 1994.
3. Karl Polanyi, *The Great Transformation: The Political and Economic Origins of Our Time* (Boston: Beacon Press,1944), p. 3.
4. Title of an article in the *Los Angeles Times*, Sept. 27, 1996.
5. Polyani, pp. 46-49.
6. Thomas Jefferson quotes in Letter to Colonel William S. Smith, Jan. 30, 1787, *Bartlett's Familiar Quotations* (New York: Little Brown & Co, 1992).
7. CNN/*Time* poll, Aug. 1994.
8. Voters in Maine approved public financing for state elections in 1996, a precedent for meaningful reform.
9. Voters in Montana in 1996 approved a measure that bans direct corporate contributions to ballot measures.
10. This disparity between blind and disabled which was based on the blind having more adverse economic consequences than other disabled people has recently been determined by the GAO to be unfounded (National Senior Citizens Law Center Memo, March 29, 1996).
11. Based on 1992 average of $3.84 million for the CEOs of major coporations. *Business Week*, April 16. 1993.

CHAPTER 15: BEYOND RAMPS?

1. Alexander Cockburn, "Bill: He Stood by His Principles," *The Nation*, Aug. 1996.
2. Rowlands quoting Clinton in *The Star* was read on "Dateline" NBC News, Sept. 1, 1996.
3. "A Monument to History Rewritten," *Los Angeles Times*, May 11, 1997.
4. *No Ordinary Time* (New York: Simon & Schuster, 1994), pp. 607-608.
5. Hugh Gregory Gallagher, *FDR's Splendid Deception* (New York: Dodd, Mead,1985).
6. Inouye quoted by P.I. Maltbie, "The FDR Memorial: Will the Real FDR Please Sit Down," *New Mobility*, Aug. 1996, p. 19.
7. As of this writing activists have been pressuring President Clinton to introduce legislation that a statue of FDR in a wheelchair be added to the Memorial.
8. Worldwide figures indicate that one third of the population prospers while two thirds experience hardship. See Richard J. Barnet and John Cavanagh, *Global Dreams: Imperial Corporations and the New World Order* (New York: Touchstone, 1995).
9. Reuters, "United Nations Human Development Index," June 13, 1997.
10. Todd Gitlin, "The Rise of Identity Politics," Nicholaus Mills, editon, *Legacy of Dissent* (New York: Touchstone, Simon & Schuster, 1994), p. 144.
11. *Harper's*, March 1995, p. 9; *Harper's*, Aug. 1995, p. 13; *Harper's*, Jan. 1995, p. 11.
12. Neil Postman, *Amusing Ourselves to Death: Public Discourse in the Age of Show Business* (New York: Penguin Books, 1985), p. vii.

INDEX